WITHDRAWN

CHARLES LAMB AND HIS FRIENDS

CHARLES LAMB AT FIFTY-ONE
From the painting by Henry Meyer, now in India Office

CHARLES LAMB
and His Friends

BY

WILL D. HOWE

THE BOBBS-MERRILL COMPANY

INDIANAPOLIS   *Publishers*   NEW YORK

COPYRIGHT, 1944, BY WILL D. HOWE

PRINTED IN THE UNITED STATES

Second Edition

PR
4863
H6

To
NED AND LOUISE
*who have helped more than
they know*

71910

PREFACE

"Memory is the power to gather roses in Winter," runs an old English saying. In the life of Charles Lamb memory gave warmth and sunshine and humour and happiness that radiated from him to all who knew him. His were the qualities that were not affected by time nor tarnished by use. His life was not "like a star that dwelt apart"; rather his was the life in a great city where he loved the people and the streets with their silent meanings, where nothing was too small or too common to be interesting, where lay the daily task he did not allow to dim his brave spirit. To catch that enduring spirit in words, in old literature, in friends, howsoever ill-appearing, was a lasting possession to Lamb, for the world was good to him. It was no easy place but it could be sweet and courageous. "Every heart that has beat strong and cheerfully has left a hopeful impulse behind it in the world," wrote R. L. S. in his brave "Æs Triplex." So it was with Charles Lamb.

Fortunate is the reader who comes upon this lovable character in early years and can go with him along the road of life's experiences. That way leads to a happy land where bloom the choicest qualities of human nature.

To see Charles Lamb as he was to himself and to those who knew him has been the purpose of this book. It seemed best to present him in his different relationships and in reference to his favourite interests, rather than to follow the years of his life in a strict order that possessed less significance. And to understand him the reader, it was thought, would appreciate generous quotation from an author whose writing was so intimately a part of himself.

Anyone who aspires to write about Charles Lamb must acknowledge the debt to those who have made possible the research and the collections which are priceless: Thomas Noon Talfourd, Barry Cornwall, Percy FitzGerald, R. H. Shepherd, William Macdonald, Canon Alfred Ainger and above all others, E. V. Lucas.

The authorities of the Bodleian Library at Oxford, the British Museum, Dr. Williams's Library in London, where I was graciously accorded the exciting privilege of reading the manuscript of the diary of Henry Crabb Robinson, the New York Public Library, the Widener Library at Harvard and the Henry E. Huntington Library at San Marino, California, to these I am under special indebtedness for many favours not in the routine of daily service.

My special gratitude I desire to convey to the publisher, D. Laurance Chambers, who so promptly and heartily gave me encouragement in the writing of the book and so ably contributed valuable suggestions for the revision of the manuscript. To Ethel M. Thackray I desire to express my acknowledgment for continuing encouragement and for definite criticism in the reading of the proof, to Helen E. Tarbox for much more than the preparation of the manuscript and to Patricia Jones of the editorial staff of the Bobbs-Merrill Company for most careful attention to the editing of the manuscript and for checking the proof.

At the end of each of the thousands of bills of lading which passed through Lamb's hands were the words:
"God send the good ship safe to harbour."

—W. D. H.

TABLE OF CONTENTS

LIST OF ILLUSTRATIONS

CHARLES LAMB AND HIS FRIENDS

I

London in the Eighteenth Century

IN THE spring of 1940, bombs that fell on London did more than carry death and destruction to stone and men and women and children. They awoke in the minds and hearts of millions of Englishmen and Americans throughout the world a horror and a courage to stand firm against the unbelievable atrocities of a vicious and determined enemy. For London was a sacred shrine, rich in traditions, in moving pageantry, in social and literary associations and in personal experiences. Not merely was London a great city; it held within its confines St. Clements, the British Museum, Hyde Park, Piccadilly, Covent Garden, Westminster Abbey, the Houses of Parliament, St. Paul's and the Temple. It held in safe keeping memories of men and women who had made London great and beloved—Chaucer, Shakespeare, Ben Jonson, Milton, Defoe, Addison, Pope, Samuel Johnson, Garrick, Thackeray, Dickens and Charles Lamb.

Of all the centuries of London history none is more alluring than the Eighteenth. There was the enormous growth in trade, the power of England was being welded more firmly into the great Empire, there were signs of a prosperity which had never been known on the island. For those who had money or position there were new comforts, a new philosophy of life, a new knowledge of the world, new means of communication and still more important, a new English prose which would be the means of expression for an ever-increasing public of the accomplishments and ideals of the English race.

Whatever the scene—social, political, financial or literary—London was the centre. From London went forth men who controlled the trade of the world, men who directed the government of great countries. There was no other city comparable to London—especially to an Englishman. London did one-third of the business of the kingdom. To it came artists, actors, writers, men of finance, men of all business not only from the island but from all parts of the widely scattered Empire.

Many writers began to find their subjects in the life of the city, especially its low life—Tom Brown, Swift, John Gay in his *Trivia,* Defoe and the novelists, especially Fielding and Smollett, and perhaps best of all, the painter Hogarth; the names of great authors of Eighteenth-Century England—Pope, Addison, Steele, Burke, Johnson, Goldsmith, Sheridan—were so closely associated with the social, political and literary life of the city that to know them is to know London; and finally it was a golden age for the theatre and the profession of acting, represented by such popular actors as Garrick, Mrs. Siddons, the Kembles, Kean, Fanny Kelly, Elliston, Mathews, Munden and many others.

In 1775, the year of Lamb's birth, London contained about three-fourths of a million people in a community of almost fifty villages, loosely held together. It was a queer composition of old and new houses. After the Great Plague and Great Fire of the preceding century, many sections had been rebuilt but there were still innumerable old structures which were on the point of falling to pieces. Records of the time abound in references to buildings which of their own weight collapsed, often with tragic consequences. The fine old houses of which there were so many in the early years of the century were rapidly disappearing, for example, Craven, Clarendon, Bedford, Burlington, Buckingham, some of them torn down to be replaced by finer buildings. Along with the houses went the handsome gardens which had for so long a time been an attractive feature of most parts of the city.

London consisted first of the City, which retained its separate entity, nearly the whole of which had been built after the Great Fire, a quarter at Whitechapel where the workers lived, a quarter for lawyers, extending from Gravesend to the Temple, a section north of the Strand where were most of the coffee-houses, taverns, theatres and great markets, and the more aristocratic section, lying east of Hyde Park, and Westminster, which included the Houses of Parliament, the Abbey and the worst slums of the city.

In the first quarter of the century some of the streets had been straightened and paved and many of the old obstructions, such as tavern signs, penthouses and overhanging structures, were removed so that walking became less hazardous. But the noises remained, a continuing roar—one American visitor said it was like Niagara. And there was not a great improvement in the cleanness and smells of the streets. There was dust in summer, mud in winter, innumerable cries of things for sale and interminable street brawls at all seasons. There was not a great difference in the traffic in the streets from the days of Elizabeth until those of Victoria. There were changes, of course, but for long periods of time there was little variation in the crowding of the streets, the kind of vehicles and the manners of the people. Until late in the century a Hogarth picture would have been no great exaggeration of the London which Lamb knew as a boy. Duels were not uncommon in the streets but more often were held in certain special localities such as Lincoln Inn Fields, Hyde Park and the area behind Montague House. Thomas Burke, in his comments on London street manners, wrote: "Crude gestures, indeed, have always been a part of the London scene. In Tudor times the invitation to quarrel or combat was given by biting of the thumb; in the middle

Eighteenth Century, by cocking the hat; later by jerk of the thumb over the left shoulder, implying illegitimate birth; in the early Nineteenth Century, by the thumb to the nose, and within living memory, by two fingers jerked upwards."

The watch, a notorious feature of Eighteenth-Century London, was being supplanted by the capped Bow Street runners called familiarly "Robin Red Breasts," from their scarlet waistcoats, and these gave way to the blue-coated "peelers," more recently "bobbies," named after Robert Peel. There was the saloop-stall, to be found at all corners of the town in Lamb's early days, so affectionately described by him in his Elia essay, "The Praise of Chimney-Sweepers"—a small kitchen table with cupboards, on wheels, and fitted with an urn for the making of the saloop—an infusion of sassafras, sugar and milk, sold at "three half-pennies" a bowl. Its price made it a popular drink with many workers. There was never such a time for beggars, although Lamb with his usual sympathy for the underprivileged could even regret what he considered was the passing of "the parting Genius of Beggary."

Researches of recent years make it possible for us to describe with considerable detail the signs and shops of Fleet Street of that day. There were many taverns, such as the Mitre and the Rainbow, which were approached by long passages or courts leading from the street. Some were very old and some took the place of other taverns reaching back into the Sixteenth Century. Alongside of the Marigold, for example, a passage led to The Devil tavern which may have been there when Shakespeare was born. These were the signs: The Bear, The Cock, The Lamb, The Swan, The Red Lion, The Falcon, The Boar's Head, The Red Bull, The Dolphin. The Devil was pulled down when Charles Lamb was a boy of twelve, in 1787. There were signs for many trades, the most common being the bookseller, then, in order, the goldsmiths, printers and watchmakers.

There was a continually growing number of inns and taverns on the roads to London and in the city, due to the increase of stage-coaches and travelling. Books of the day reflect the inconveniences as well as the humour which characterized this kind of travel. Lamb knew many of these taverns and had association with the following: The Angel, The Bull-faced Stag, The Bell, The Bull and Mouth (a distortion of the words Boulogne Mouth), The Crown and Horseshoe, The Flower Pot, The Four Swans, The Golden Fleece, The Greyhound, The Horse and Groom, The Jolly Farmer, The Swan and Two Necks, a Rising Sun, of course, Goat and Compasses (a delightful misunderstanding of "God encompasseth us") and The Salutation and Cat in Newgate Street where Coleridge and Lamb spent many nights discussing pantisocracy and other universal themes which occur to young men in their early twenties and certainly occurred to them in the catastrophic years immediately following the French Revolution.

Perhaps the grandest sight of all was the setting out of the night mails, the blasts of their bugles, the bustle at the inn, the high colour of the drivers and coaches, the powerful horses and the excitement of going into a far country, York, perhaps, Bristol or even Edinburgh!

"Hark, hark the hour! The mail-guards are the soloists, and very pleasant music they discourse, not a few of them are first-rate performers. A long train of gaily got up coaches remarkable for their light weight, horsed by splendid-looking animals, impatient of the curb and eager to commence their journey. Stout gents in heavy coats, buttoned to the throat, ensconce themselves in reserved seats, commercial men contest the right of a seat with the guard or coachman. Some careful mother helps her pale and timid daughter up the step,—a fat old lady already occupies two-thirds of the seat—what will be done? Bags of epistles innumerable stuff the boots, formidable bales of the daily journals are trampled small by guard's heels. The clock will strike in less than five minutes, the clamour deepens, and the hubbub seems increasing; but ere the last sixty seconds expire, a sharp winding of warning bugles begins. Coachie flourishes his whip, greys and chestnuts prepare for a run, the reins move but very gently, there is a parting crack of the whip-cord and the brilliant cavalcade is gone."*

Walter Besant, whose *London in the Eighteenth Century* is an inexhaustible reservoir of information concerning the period, has described how it was indoors when London depended upon candles for its light before the introduction of gas in 1807.

"The poor man's evenings were spent around the fire without other light or else faintly illuminated by a single tallow candle. The rich man had to spend immense sums in lighting his house with wax candles. The churches were dimly lit with candles, the pulpit had four which the sexton snuffed from time to time; the long pews had a candle at each end which also wanted snuffing. The cook had to hold the candle in one hand while she cooked with the other. The best lighted street was provided with no more than a feeble glimmer at intervals; the shops showed one or two candles in the window and one or two on the counter; at the taverns they placed a candle on every table; at the clubs, two candles on every table. The real terror of the winter was not the cold so much as the long hours of darkness. All this was changed by the discovery of gas."

Pages from Percy's *London* in 1788 and in other contemporary writings reveal a sordid picture of the slums of the city—the filth of the streets, the poverty, the horrors of overcrowded lodging houses with avaricious landlords whose acts, confirmed by contemporary writers, seem well-nigh incredible now, prostitution, thieving, drunkenness, cruelty and murder.

The century closed upon London more dismally than can be

---

* Quoted in *Eighteenth-Century London Life,* by Rosamond Bayne-Powell.

well understood—long exhausting war, trade carried on by con-
voys, French privateers in the Channel, bankruptcies everywhere, failures of crops because of a series of cold and rainy
summers, riots, and for ten years a lack of brilliant success in
war. It has been called the most trying time in modern English
history. Then the news of peace came in 1801 and, after only
a little more than a year, war began again and extended for
twelve long years. The persisting fear of Napoleon and invasion of the island by the French lasted for a long time. Napoleon was so certain of success that he ordered the preparation of
a medal in 1804, falsely stating that it had been struck in London, as if the conquest had already been carried out! It would
seem that we were looking at a newspaper of yesterday when we
read the indictment of Napoleon in a contemporary broadsheet
in which he is charged with having destroyed the faith of
Christendom, having murdered women and children, murder-
ing his comrades, ignoring all the laws of civilized warfare and
betraying the Polish legion. "There is not I think," wrote
Walter Besant, "any story in the world's history more wonderful than that of Great Britain during this long war—now single-
handed, now with this combination of allies, now with that,
contending with the greatest conqueror of any time, and beating him in the end."

If we look into a copy of the *Examiner* for the year 1820 we
find some telling pictures of the age which a host of poets,
philosophers and satirists were setting forth to save. The absorbing topic of the year was the scandal of Queen Caroline and
the flunkey: finally, as a result of what the *Examiner* calls a
general "change of feeling respecting her Majesty's chastity,"
she was acquitted, and the whole country was ablaze with con-
gratulatory fireworks. Many pages of the volume are occupied
with a description of the hanging, before an immense crowd,
of the five Cato Street Conspirators, an operation so clumsily

carried out that it amounted to public torture. In another place
we read of the execution of six persons, some for forgery, one
for "sacrilege" in breaking open a church. This procession went
to their death headed by the Sheriff chanting, "I am the resur-
rection and the life."

Castlereagh, Eldon, Dismouth and the Prince Regent watched
the bed on which England lay so sick. And to these guardians
the enormous majority of educated men resigned themselves
without a protest, indeed with apparent servility. "The first
gentleman of Europe!" exclaimed Thackeray. "There is no
stronger satire on the proud English society of that day, than
that they admired George.

"An age such as was this one; an age of misshapen and dis-
credited revolution, of combined fear of the future and reaction against the past, which yet remained on its constructive side
apparently impotent; an age where the crudest atheism and
religious persecution dwelt side by side, was in sore need of
healing. Perhaps more in need of healing than any other in the
world's history—for the disintegration was world-wide, and
social institutions and religions, where they yet hung together,
were fastened with the rottenest threads."

Then came the hour of reckoning for the people, the price
which a country has to pay for war, the heavy burden of debt,
the collapse of trade, the fall in prices of agricultural products,
the swarms of discharged soldiers and sailors, riots, robberies,
recriminations which England endured after twenty-two years
of looking forward with hope for the return of peace and the
halcyon days when the "sword should be turned into the reap-
ing-hook."

It is difficult for the Twentieth-Century reader, familiar with
the beautiful visions of Keats and the elegant humour and
humanity of Jane Austen, the superb lyrics of Shelley and the
mediaeval splendour of Scott's novels, to realise what the actual

WILLIAM HOGARTH WITH HIS DOG TRUMP

Painted by himself

Courtesy New York Public Library Print Room

THE HUMOURS OF AN ELECTION ENTERTAINMENT BY WILLIAM HOGARTH

"a world of good natured English faces came up one by one to my recollection, and a glance at the

state of England was in the late years of the Eighteenth Century
and in the early years of the Nineteenth. One does not easily
conceive the sonnet "On Seeing the Elgin Marbles," the simple
realism of Elizabeth Bennet, the immortal romances of Walter
Scott, the Manchester Massacres, the Battle of Trafalgar, the
Cato Street Conspiracy, the orgies of the Regent, as all belonging
to the same decade. And yet in spite of great evils, ignorance,
vice and cruelty, we can discern the torch of faith and goodness,
of love of freedom and of mankind which was beginning to
glow with greater intensity.

Some of the streets and places which Lamb knew so well
were St. Bride's, where was the grave of Richardson and had
been the original print shop of Wynkyn de Worde; Bolt Court
where Johnson had lived; the Cheshire Cheese and Gough
Square where Johnson had written the Dictionary; St. Dunstan
in the West where Isaak Walton had been the Warden; Fetter
Lane, so named from "faitours" or beggars; the four great Inns
of Court and naturally all the crannies of the Temple and the
Temple gardens.

From any part of London it was possible to get into the
country in a walk of a quarter of an hour. North of Gray's Inn
and the Temple was open country with fields, so that the resi-
dents in Bloomsbury could enjoy the view of Highgate and
Hampstead. Perhaps the village which had the reputation of
being most beautiful was Islington, where Lamb spent a part
of his summers and in later life had a house in Colebrook Row.
A walk even in the centre of London would doubtless have impressed one that there was plenty of room. Back of Fetter Lane
and north of the Strand were the halls of the Temple and the
gardens reaching down to the river. And the river!

If the Thames which ran beside the Temple gardens led one's
imagination into the far corners of the world, to the ships which
brought the precious cargoes, to exploration and adventure

which had built a tiny island kingdom into the mighty British Empire, there was something overwhelming in the Temple itself. In former times this had been a lodge of the Knights Templars, a military and religious order founded at Jerusalem in the Twelfth Century for the purpose of protecting pilgrims on their way to the Holy Land and so-named from their original designation of "poor soldiers of the temple of Solomon."

The building had passed from the Templars into the possession of the crown, then to the Knights of St. John, who leased it to the students of the Common Law. In the time of Lamb and since, it has been occupied by the Inns of Court, called the Inner Middle Temple, where lawyers live. The Inner Temple was so called from its position within the precincts of the City; the Middle Temple was between the Inner and Outer, and the Outer Temple, which was not leased to the lawyers, lost its ancient name. As you enter the gloomy Inner Temple Lane through a low archway, on the east side is the church; on the west, a line of buildings occupying the site of former chambers, now destroyed; to the west an open court with a sun-dial and a fountain. Midway between the Inner Temple gate and the Thames there was a range of substantial chambers overlooking the gardens to the river, known as Crown Office Row.

In this building in the latter half of the Eighteenth Century lived Samuel Salt, the friend and benefactor of the Lamb family. A precious record of a "parliament," that is, one of the fixed meetings in each term of the Benchers of the Temple for the purpose of transacting business read:

"13th May, 1768. At this Parliament: it is ordered that Samuel Salt, Esq., a Barrister of this Society, aged about Fifty, be and is hereby admitted, for his own life, to the benefit of an Assignment in and to All that Ground Chamber, no. 2, opposite the Garden Walk in Crown Office Row: he, the said Samuel Salt having paid for the purchase thereof into the Treasury of the Society, the sum of One Hundred and Fifty Pounds."

Into this building, then, moved Samuel Salt. And a little later the Lambs came to serve in many ways a beneficent master. So it was in No. 2 of Crown Office Row in one of the rear rooms of the ground floor, which looked into Inner Temple Lane, that Charles Lamb was born on the tenth of February 1775.

2

Charles Lamb, the Brief Story of His Life

OF THE Lamb family not much is known aside from the incidents and descriptions included by Charles Lamb in his letters and Elia essays. The family came from Lincolnshire; there are few references to help us into more intimate knowledge of his ancestors. John Lamb, rather late in life, married Elizabeth Field, who was much younger than her husband, a native of Hertfordshire and a daughter of a certain dignified Mrs. Field. For more than fifty years Mrs. Field continued as housekeeper in the Plumer family's fine old mansion of Blakesware near the village of Widford, so that her grandchildren, as they came along, thought of the old place to be enjoyed as their own, especially on holidays. Mrs. Lamb was tall and handsome; friends used to say that she could well be taken for a sister of Mrs. Siddons, while her husband had "a face as gay as Garrick's, whom he was said to resemble."

We do not know when John Lamb came to London but soon thereafter he was successful in securing a position as clerk and confidential servant to the barrister named Samuel Salt. This was a stroke of good fortune, not merely for the clerk but for the world in general, as subsequent events showed that Salt was a rare character and rendered service of exceptional proportions to the Lamb family and to others.

At the time Charles was born, John Lamb was a lively little man about fifty-six years old, once a footman, an active member of a Friendly Society which met at the Devil Tavern at intervals.

For some of the annual meetings of this society John Lamb wrote addresses in verse. These addresses are the chief poetical pieces which John Lamb left to his son, by the world at large not highly regarded, although a copy of this volume, if discovered, would probably be worth its weight in gold.

For the first seven years there is no definite knowledge of any event in the life of Charles Lamb except that he developed a nervous stammer and almost died of smallpox when he was nearly five years old. The household was very poor. The father's income was meagre. To help out, there was a small income from his sister Sara, commonly known as "Aunt Hetty," but with seven children born in a dozen years, of whom four died in early childhood, it may be surmised that there was not much left to put by. From the first, son John, twelve years older than Charles, was seemingly inclined to go his own way and, as soon as he could afford it, moved from the family and was of no assistance during the rest of his life. Mary, ten years older than Charles, little favoured by the mother who seemed to have a great lack of sympathy, became both sister and brother to the boy. From letters and other sources it is evident that there soon grew a close relationship between the two. The interest Mary had in books and in walks through the London streets found growing support in her youthful companion. In the very year that the Lambs moved into the Salt lodgings in Crown Office Row, old Mrs. Plumer died, and for almost twenty-five years after her death Mrs. Field was housekeeper in the mansion back in Hertfordshire. In *Mrs. Leicester's School* Mary told of their joy of going into the country in the summertime to visit their grandmother and of the associations there which left a lasting impression upon both sister and brother.

Probably due to the generosity of Samuel Salt, Mary and Charles were able to attend the little school off Fetter Lane not far from the Temple, taught by a William Bird. The school building was on the edge of a discoloured, dingy garden in the passage leading into Fetter Lane from Bartlett's Buildings. The boys attended in the morning, the girls in the afternoon, and the result was successful if, when they left the school, the boys and girls could read, write and figure.

When he was a little past seven, in October 1782, Charles was presented to the foundation of Christ's Hospital, again through the influence of Samuel Salt, as "the son of John Lamb, scrivener, and Elizabeth, his wife." This famous institution, founded by Edward the Sixth in 1552 only ten days before his death, occupied the site of an old monastery of the Grey Friars, not far from the Temple, and inherited many of the privileges and customs of that holy order. Among its more interesting observances was the ceremony that took place on Easter Tuesday, when the entire school was presented to the Lord Mayor, who bestowed upon a representative of the school a coin fresh from the mint.

So this boy, none too strong, with the nervous stutter, was put into the dark blue gown, red leather belt, knee breeches and canary yellow stockings of the Blue-coat School. Here Charles spent many happy days and here he met boys who became friends for life. He was a good student but not of the best. He was not fitted for mathematics or science, but he did well in language and literature, better in Latin than Greek, especially Latin Composition, and certainly no one in school was more adept in turning nursery rhymes into Latin. For a boy of fourteen he probably had a fairly good knowledge of Latin when he left the school and certainly he had read a great deal from English authors.

Of the teachers we know not much. James Boyer, the headmaster, was apparently something of a tyrant. Lamb must have learned from his teachers, he certainly got a great deal from books, but more than anything else he learned from his schoolmates. Delicate and sensitive, shy and retiring, he was the sort of youngster who often finds it difficult to make friends. However, the talent for friendship was there and it was soon evident that he could make friends of a great variety. There were the two Le Grice boys, young Favell, Allen, and young Thomas Middleton, who afterwards became Bishop of Calcutta, and others, but the greatest of all was the "inspired Charity boy," Samuel Taylor Coleridge. When Lamb and Coleridge became acquainted we do not know. Coleridge was almost three years the older, a country lad from Devonshire; Lamb, in every sense a city boy, lived just round the corner from the school. But in some way the two boys began a friendship lasting throughout their lives, which had great results.

It was a bitter thing for Lamb to have to leave school, realising that this was the end of his school days, but he accepted his fate. The family needed real help and, though only fourteen, he must now find some work to do. Other boys were going to Oxford and to Cambridge. They had been Grecians, that is, of high rank at school. He had held the rank of Deputy Grecian. Evidently part of his work was of sufficient quality to give him Grecian standing, but his stammering would be a hindrance to his taking holy orders, the ultimate destiny for Grecians, according to the custom of the school. No reader should miss the pleasure of Lamb's descriptions of the school given in two essays, nor the equal delight of the chapters in Leigh Hunt's autobiography where he writes lovingly of the Blue-coat School and recalls times when he saw Lamb back on visits to his friends.

That Charles Lamb loved the school there can be no question. Even if there were memories of hardship, of harsh rules, of unsympathetic teachers, there were also happy holidays, a chance to learn and to read, to meet new friends, and perhaps a welcome change from what must have been a dreary home. It is pleasant to know that the school even today shows its pride in Lamb by awarding a medal in his honour for the best English essay. As a sign of the regard in which he was held, E. V. Lucas tells this story. "A blue-coat boy, walking through a residential street in London, was astonished to hear himself hailed by a strange, bare-headed, elderly gentleman standing on a doorstep. 'Come here, boy,' he cried, 'come here'; and when the boy reached him he pressed a five-shilling piece in his hand, with the words, 'In memory of Charles Lamb.'"

Mary showed rare wisdom in her guidance of her younger brother and from the time when he could not remember, he had been among books in the library of Samuel Salt, and in the old family mansion in the country. He had come into a liking for books. How much the teachers at Christ's helped we do not know, but we can surmise that the talks with other boys, if there were others like young Coleridge, must have borne fruit. Before he left the school, a little book of sonnets had appeared by one William Bowles. Simple and melancholy though these sonnets were, the young readers liked them and tried to imitate them. So poetry was not all in the classics, nor all the poets dead! In some way Lamb had come across the poems of Burns and Cowper. It was Bowles especially who interested Coleridge. Lamb was beginning to have a taste for books.

During one of those summer trips to Blakesware while he was still at Christ's Hospital, Charles came under the spell of the "fair-hair'd maid." "Then I told how for seven long years, in hope sometimes, sometimes in despair, yet persisting ever, I courted the fair Alice W——n." That was the way he described it in the delightful Elia fantasy, "Dream-Children." Not much is known of this Hertfordshire girl. Her real name was probably Ann Simmons, and she lived with her mother in a cottage in the village of Widford. The boy and the girl knew well "the winding wood-walks" and the "shady pathways sweet" and often came to:

SAMUEL SALT, MODELLED IN WAX

By John Lamb, brother of Charles

From *The Life of Charles Lamb* by E. V. Lucas, by permission
of G. P. Putnam's Sons

JOHN LAMB, FATHER OF CHARLES

From *The Life of Charles Lamb* by E. V. Lucas, by
permission of G. P. Putnam's Sons

"... the little cottage which she loved,
The cottage which did once my all contain."

It was a lovely dream, long cherished, but it was not to become a reality, except as "Anna" of the sonnets, "Rosamund" of *Rosamund Gray,* and "Alice W——n" of Elia.

In the fall of 1789, Charles Lamb left Christ's Hospital with his days of formal schooling behind him, and with a future probably never more uncertain to any fourteen-year-old son. As he was not fitted for any special work, and not good at penmanship or figures, evidently there was a bare chance that he could find anything to do. The most painstaking search has so far failed to reveal information about Lamb during the weeks immediately after he left Christ's Hospital in November 1789. According to one story, Thomas Coventry, whom Lamb afterwards described with affection in "The Old Benchers," is said to have remarked to his friend Joseph Paice, "There is a lad whom I placed some years since in the Blue-coat School, now on the point of leaving it, and I know not what on earth to do with him." Paice replied, "Let him have the run of my counting-house until something better offers."

On September 1, 1791, he began work as a clerk in the examiner's office at the South Sea House where his brother John held a superior position. After only six months and just a few days before he was seventeen, he left the service of the South Sea House and some weeks later, on April 5, 1792, entered the employment of the East India Company. The first Elia essay, though written thirty years afterwards, gives with the usual mixture of fact and fancy something of the life at the South Sea House, with descriptions of some of the people who worked there.

For the years 1792-1796 we have little information regarding the Lambs. Samuel Salt died in February and Grandmother

Field died in August 1792. Both events made, of course, a great difference in the conditions of the Lamb family. Salt had been almost like a good fairy of romance. His beneficence continued after death, for in his will he left £200 to Mrs. Lamb and annuities to John Lamb. As might be expected, the Lambs had to move from the Temple. They found quarters at 7 Little Queen Street, now Kingsway. When they moved we are not sure, but they were in their new quarters early in 1794. The family was in a pathetic condition. The father was more and more senile. The mother, evidently under great strain, almost an invalid, seemed to be very fond of John but had little sympathy for Mary and Charles. Mary, a mantua-maker, doing her work at home, in constant attendance upon her mother, was carrying a load too heavy for even a person much stronger than she was. From her childhood she had shown signs of mental disturbances and once or twice these had been serious and ominous. John had evidently looked after himself and gone elsewhere to live, and, although his fortunes were rising at the South Sea House, he showed no concern for the family on Little Queen Street. At home there was not much in the way of happiness for Charles.

The friendship between Charles and Coleridge continued. During the winter of 1794-1795 Coleridge lived in London, and he and Lamb spent probably the happiest evenings of their lives at the Salutation and Cat, where they smoked and drank and talked over school days and made plans for the world to come! In 1795 Coleridge brought Lamb and Southey together. The last six weeks of that year Lamb spent in the insane asylum at Hoxton, of which he writes in his first letter to Coleridge in 1796, and of which more will be said later in this book. In 1795 we have the first pieces of Lamb's writing in the form of the four sonnets which Coleridge included in his own first volume.

To his active imagination and alert interest Lamb's transfer to the East India Company in the old building on Leadenhall Street must have been like a voyage over strange seas. Certainly he could not be very sure of himself in the new place, he had no special qualities to recommend him, and the clerkship did not look too promising. During the three years' probation he was to receive no pay. After that he would earn £40 annually and with good work there would be increases. Going every morning to Leadenhall Street to copy figures in large folios, recording for long hours cargoes of indigo and other stuff from the East— Lamb was to do this day after day. At best it was a regular task begun every morning and finished in the evening and he had possession of a desk with drawers in which to keep his verses, sonnets to Mrs. Siddons and young Ann Simmons. There would be a day now and then when he could go to the country and live over scenes of his childhood. There were places where he could see pictures. There were the theatres, and the streets with people to look at, and above all there were books at home and those which he might buy at the bookstalls. And sometimes in mornings when business was slack he could write to Coleridge to recall the nights at the Salutation and Cat, to send him new verses or to give him frank criticism of his pieces. The letters to Coleridge continued with frequency until midsummer.

Besides, he was beginning to be something in the world, for Coleridge was enabled to publish a little book of poems by the generosity of friend Cottle of Bristol, and in that volume the preface attributed certain verses in the collection to "Mr. Charles Lamb of the India House." Wasn't he the "Mr. Charles Lamb of the India House"?

There was something to live for after all!

Thoughts such as these must have been passing through the mind of the young clerk as he walked home on the evening of September 22, 1796, and, when he entered the house, came upon a scene which can best be described by the grim report of the inquest in the *Morning Chronicle* for September 26, 1796.

"On Friday afternoon the Coroner and a respectable Jury sat on the body of a Lady in the neighbourhood of Holborn, who died in consequence of a wound from her daughter the preceding day. It appeared by the evidence adduced, that while the family were preparing for dinner, the young lady seized a case knife laying on the table, and in a menacing manner pursued a little girl, her apprentice, round the room; on the eager calls of her helpless infirm mother to forbear, she renounced her first object, and with loud shrieks approached her parent.

"The child by her cries quickly brought up the landlord of the house, but too late—the dreadful scene presented to him the mother lifeless, pierced to the heart, on a chair, her daughter yet wildly standing over her with the fatal knife, and the venerable old man, her father, weeping by her side, himself bleeding at the forehead from the effects of a severe blow he received from one of the forks she had been madly hurling about the room.

"For a few days prior to this the family had observed some symptoms of insanity in her, which had so much increased on the Wednesday evening, that her brother early the next morning went in quest of Dr. Pitcairn—had that gentleman been met with, the fatal catastrophe had, in all probability, been prevented.

"It seems the young Lady had been once before, in her earlier years, deranged, from the harassing fatigues of too much business.—As her carriage towards her mother was ever affectionate in the extreme, it is believed that to the increased attentiveness, which her parents' infirmities called for by day and night, is to be attributed the present insanity of this ill-fated young woman.

"It has been stated in some of the Morning Papers, that she has an insane brother also in confinement—this is without foundation.

"The Jury of course brought in their Verdict, *Lunacy*."

Most of us know a day when a decision is made by us or for us that sets the direction for the rest of our lives. This was the day for Charles Lamb. For him a curtain had rung down on the play now finished, the results of which could not be forgotten and would be present every hour to control the life of the main actor. No one had the faintest suspicion that the daughter's feelings towards her mother were other than those of tender love and supreme devotion. It was as if she had stood by, paralyzed, and seen another commit the act. "The former things are passed away. I have something more to do than feel." Brave words by Charles and truly kept.

Mary was for some months confined in an asylum at Hoxton. Then, on application to the Home Secretary, Charles was allowed to take charge of her, and his guardianship, formally arranged, never ceased, day or night, until his death. Charles took a little house on Chapel Street, Pentonville, and then with the help of an old servant he set up housekeeping for his old father and Aunt Hetty, who had not got on so well with her rich relations and had returned. It was not to be for long. "My poor old aunt, whom you have seen, the kindest, goodest creature to me when I was at school; who used to toddle there to bring me fag, when I, school-boy like, only despised her for it, & used to be ashamed to see her come & sit herself down on the old coal hole steps as you went into the old grammar school, & opend her apron & bring out her bason, with some nice things she had caused to be saved for me—the good creature is now lying on her death bed. I cannot bear to think on her deplorable state. To the shock she received on that our evil day, from which she never completely recovered, I impute her illness. She says, poor thing, she is glad she is come home to die with me. I was always her favourite: 'No after friendship e'er can raise The endearments of our early days, Nor e'er the heart such fondness prove, As when it first began to love.'"

She died the following February.

It was in April that Charles was able to take Mary out of the asylum and find quarters for her elsewhere. He never brought her home while their father was alive. At this time he began going with Mary to the chapel at Hackney, finding relief and comfort in the simple belief of the Unitarians. And he was so under its influence that his letters to Coleridge presenting the dangers of mysticism doubtless had a part in turning Coleridge for a time from his hereditary allegiance to the Church of England. Sundays and holidays he spent with Mary, his days at the East India House and his evenings with "Daddy." How exacting his father had become may be read in Lamb's letter to Coleridge in December 1796.

"I am got home at last, and, after repeated games at Cribbage have got my father's leave to write awhile: with difficulty got it, for when I expostulated about playing any more, he very aptly replied, 'If you won't play with me, you might as well not come home at all.' The argument was unanswerable, and I set to afresh."

Anxious days and nights found Lamb making every effort to bring Mary back from the gloom of insanity, talking with her and above all reading with her as he had done so often in calmer days. Their perseverance and courage were superhuman and were rewarded a hundredfold by periods of convalescence when she was herself again. "The spirit of my mother," she said to him, "seems to descend and smile upon me, bidding me live to enjoy the life and reason which the Almighty had given me."

Charles was showing a new spirit. He turned again to the solace of writing and sent to Coleridge his poems. Those which Coleridge had already published in his collection as well as a dedication were to appear under the title "Poems by Mr. Charles Lamb of the India House" to his part of the volume for a new edition of Coleridge's poems. So the desk at Leadenhall Street had its use in keeping Charles to his work and his mind from thoughts which were heavy to bear.

Coleridge had moved to Nether Stowey and was asking his old schoolmate at Christ's Hospital to visit him and his wife and to see the baby, David Hartley. The visit was set for the autumn of 1796 but plans in Lamb's office made necessary postponement of the trip and it was not until months later that the visit was actually made.

With rare eagerness Lamb writes to Coleridge in June 1797: "I discern a possibility of my paying you a visit next week. May I, can I, shall I, come so soon? Have you *room* for me, *leisure* for me, and are you all pretty well? Tell me all this honestly—immediately. And by what *day*-coach could I come soonest and nearest to Stowey? A few months hence may suit you better; certainly me as well. If so, say so. I long, I yearn, with all the longings of a child do I desire to see you, to come among you—to see the young philosopher, to thank Sara for her last year's invitation in person—to read your tragedy—to read over together our little book—to breathe fresh air—to revive in me vivid images of 'Salutation scenery.' "

We can imagine, then, the excitement of Lamb starting that July morning in the coach for Bristol. As it developed, the trip was really something to be excited about, for he was not only going to see the Coleridges but he was going to make some new friends—it was really to be a memorable meeting. How much had happened in the eighteen months since he saw Coleridge! The tragedy in his own family, the death of Aunt Hetty and the decision to keep Mary near him, and for Coleridge—marriage, a son, some work begun which might lead somewhere!

Would he like Sara? How would Coleridge look? Would it be the same as in those more carefree evenings at the Salutation and Cat?

This is what he found: a little house, which Tom Poole had got for his new friend, and certainly not too big for the three Coleridges and a guest, "a miserable hovel," Coleridge afterwards called it. The rooms were low, the stairs difficult and the kitchen too small, according to the oft-repeated complaints of Sara, but there was a spring of clear water at the front door and an acre of pleasant ground about the house. In his usual impulsive manner Coleridge was everything, farmer, gardener, cook, nurse, and doubtless much in the way in any capacity. Can such a difficult combination—a very realistic, practical housewife and a very absent-minded and impractical husband—be made to work? What Lamb's thoughts were on this subject we should much like to know.

The greeting was most generous. Lamb liked Sara and Sara liked him and even better Charles took a great fancy to the "minute philosopher," David Hartley, who was just then cutting his teeth. Almost immediately an accident happened. "Dear Sara accidentally emptied a skillet of boiling milk on my foot which confined me during the whole time of Lamb's stay." Perhaps it was just as well, for with the talkative Coleridge on their country walks they would not have had half the opportunity to get so well acquainted.

There are some new people in the neighbourhood and Lamb will meet them too. The Wordsworths, for instance. What had Wordsworth been doing? Born in the little village of Cockermouth in the Lake District in 1770, he was therefore two years older than Coleridge and five years older than Lamb. After rather hard years of boyhood, he went to Cambridge in 1787. He spent four years at the University and immediately afterwards took a short holiday in the Alps, travelled in France for almost two years and was won over to the side of the Revolution. A passionate affair with Annette Vallon resulted in the birth of a daughter. Returning to England, he occupied himself with the writing of poetry which was published in 1793 as

An Evening Walk and *Descriptive Sketches*. Unable to decide upon a career, he was greatly unsettled in his mind on account of political affairs in France and the confusion in the application of ideas of liberty. All this threw him into a mood of great depression which was much relieved by the steadying influence of his sister Dorothy. Fortunately a legacy of £900, and some tutoring of the son of Basil Montagu, supplemented by financial and moral support from Dorothy, brought Wordsworth a greater sense of security and induced him to lease a farmhouse at Racedown. Here from 1795 to 1797 he occupied himself with writing.

Some of Wordsworth's poems had reached Coleridge at Cambridge and their Revolutionary implications had pleased him, but it was not until 1795 that the two young poets met. Acquaintance developed into a close friendship and later, when Coleridge took the little house at Nether Stowey in early 1797, William and Dorothy Wordsworth rented Alfoxden so that they might be in the neighbourhood. Dorothy came to have a great admiration for Coleridge. Perhaps it might have developed into something more. For her brother her affection was as nearly perfect as a human relationship can be. In more recent years the publication of her *Journal* and other memoirs have added to the stature of Dorothy and we have come to have an even higher regard for her assistance to her brother. It is futile, but interesting, to conjecture what Coleridge might have been with the steadying hand of Dorothy Wordsworth.

This is what Coleridge wrote of her: "Wordsworth and his exquisite sister are with me. She is a woman, indeed! in mind I mean, and heart; for her person is such, that if you expected to see a pretty woman, you would think her rather ordinary: if you expected to see an ordinary woman, you would think her pretty! but her manners are simple, ardent, impressive. In every motion, her most innocent soul outbeams so brightly, that who saw would say, 'Guilt was a thing impossible in her.' Her information various. Her eye watchful in minutest observation of nature: and her taste, a perfect electrometer."

And here is what Dorothy thought of him: "You had a great loss in not seeing Coleridge. He is a wonderful man. His conversation teems with soul, mind and spirit. Then he is so benevolent, so good tempered, and cheerful, and, like William, interests himself so much about every little trifle. At first I thought him very plain—that is, for about three minutes; he is pale, thin, has a wide mouth, thick lips, and not very good teeth, longish loose-growing half-curling rough black hair. But if you hear him speak for five minutes you think no more of them. His eye is large and full, and not very dark, but grey, such an eye as would receive from a heavy soul the dullest expression; but it speaks every emotion of his animated mind: it has more of the 'poet's eye in a fine frenzy rolling' than I ever witnessed. He has fine dark eyebrows and an overhanging forehead."

When it was decided that Lamb was to visit the Coleridges, it was quite natural that the Wordsworths should be asked to drop in. And they did soon after the arrival of the guest from London. On this particular afternoon it would have been a great privilege to look in upon the interesting group but we should probably have been like the neighbours, a bit curious, if not critical, of the somewhat unconventional actions of these newcomers into the vicinity. The day would come, however, when these same curious neighbours would point with pride to the cottage where this meeting had taken place and tell of the things said and done there!

Coleridge could not go on the walks, so at home, nursing his injury, he wrote the lines, now famous, "This Lime-tree Bower My Prison," in part a lament upon his misfortune but primarily a tribute to his guest. It was unfortunate that he should address him as "gentle-hearted Charles," an epithet which nettled Lamb and, when the lines were published, brought forth an irritated request that the words be blotted out in the next printing and substituted by "drunken dog, ragged-head, seld-shaven, odd-eyed, stuttering, or any other epithet which truly and properly belongs to the gentleman in question."

Lamb went back to London, stopping on the way in Hampshire for two or three days to see the Southeys. A perfect "bread-and-butter letter" he wrote to the Coleridges! There was just one thing forgotten—Lamb had left his great-coat; "is it not ridiculous that I sometimes envy that great-coat lingering so cunningly behind?" It took months, well on into the winter, for Coleridge to send the coat back.

A few weeks after Lamb left Nether Stowey, Coleridge, William and Dorothy set out for a walk over the Quantock Hills to visit the country about Linton. Sara stayed at home with young David Hartley; our own guess is that was her preference. To meet the cost of the trip, about four pounds, they agreed to write a poem together. The world knows about that trip and its influence upon the "Ancient Mariner" and the others of the *Lyrical Ballads* published next year.

Lamb returned to the house in Chapel Street, Pentonville. At home there was now, after the death of his mother and Aunt Hetty, only his father, since brother John had gone elsewhere to live. Mary, released from Hoxton and living in Hackney, would not be with him until after her father had died. The day at the office, a game of cribbage in the evening with a lonely imbecile father, week-end visits to Mary—that was Lamb's week. There was not much to look forward to. Yes, there was the chance of permanent employment at the East India House and best of all a hope, if only a hope, that Mary would be better. Would it be strange and unnatural if he was depressed and irritable on that Monday morning when he returned to his desk? Coleridge and Wordsworth were so fortunate, writing, talking, walking—just the sort of life for a young man who wished above all to be a poet. We who can read the whole record are not so certain that the advantage was to be with those at Nether Stowey.

Besides, he found a new friend. Charles Lloyd, son of a Birmingham banker, had been living with Coleridge to be near a sage who could give him inspiration for his poetry. Coming to London at the suggestion of Coleridge, Lloyd settled at the Bell and Mouth to be near Lamb. Lloyd was a Quaker—the Bell and Mouth was well known as the centre for Quakerism—and was therefore the more welcome as Lamb was then, and always, devoted to members of that faith, and besides both had come to have a great admiration for the poet Cowper.

That Lamb had reached a greater peace and was able to go on writing is evident by the production in 1798 of the little story, *A Tale of Rosamund Gray and Old Blind Margaret.* Like everything else which Lamb wrote, the story, simple and exquisite in expression, has many autobiographical elements along with its signs of youthful imagination.

Blind Margaret, selfish and self-centred, is satisfied to require the constant attention of Rosamund, a beautiful girl of fourteen with apparently no aim in the world but to serve her grandmother. Allan Clare, two years older than she, brings presents to Rosamund and keeps coming more frequently. Naturally, to the great annoyance of the grandmother, the two become infatuated. Young Clare has lost his wealthy parents and is living with his sister Elinor, near the Gray cottage in Widford. A lovely moonlight lures Rosamund outdoors where she is seduced by the villain Matravis. Blind Margaret, in distress over the disappearance of Rosamund, dies. Rosamund, desolate and in disgrace, languishes and dies in the arms of Elinor. Matravis flees and Allan leaves. After years the one who tells the story returns, goes through the village to the cottage, church and churchyard and finds Allan Clare by the grave of his sister.

Little reason for thinking that the author of that story could ever be Elia! Nor is it strange that the story was not well received. And yet Shelley a dozen years later wrote to Leigh Hunt, "What a lovely thing is his *Rosamund Gray!* How much knowledge of the sweetest and deepest parts of our nature in it! When I think of such a mind as Lamb's—when I see how unnoticed remain things of such exquisite and complete perfection—what should I hope for myself if I had not higher objects in view than fame!"

The year 1798 in Lamb's life was interesting for several reasons. There was not much change in the family situation except that Mary late in the preceding year had suffered a long and serious attack and had to be returned to restraint from her lodging in Hackney. Lamb's lines "Written on Christmas Day, 1797" evidently refer to this bereavement and express the question which must have often driven him into perplexity and depression.

> I am a widow'd thing, now thou art gone!
> Now thou art gone, my own familiar friend,
> Companion, sister, helpmate, counsellor!
> Alas! that honour'd mind, whose sweet reproof
> And meekest wisdom in times past have smooth'd
> The unfilial harshness of my foolish speech,
> And made me loving to my parents old,
> (Why is this so, ah, God! why is this so?)
> That honour'd mind become a fearful blank,
> Her senses lock'd up, and herself kept out
> From human sight or converse, while so many
> Of the foolish sort are left to roam at large,
> Doing all acts of folly, and sin, and shame?
> Thy paths are mystery!

It was at this time also that Lamb wrote "The Old Familiar Faces," the best known lines by him and not unworthy of a place in any English anthology. Coleridge asked that Mary should come and live with them—very generous, but as practical as many of his other suggestions. Then ironically a few months later occurred the estrangement between the two friends which is a bit difficult for us to understand but perhaps was largely due to the temperament of Coleridge, who was especially irritable, having increased his use of laudanum to relieve his physical distress. Besides, affairs at home annoyed him and he showed a particular sensitiveness to the relation between Lamb and his new friend Charles Lloyd. Lamb had continued to have the same reverence and affection for "the greater Ajax" but had not done just the proper thing to keep Coleridge happy. Before leaving for Germany in August, Coleridge wrote, "Poor Lamb, if he wants any knowledge, he may apply to me"—he was always calling Lamb "poor"—and Lamb tartly replied with a series of questions under the caption "Theses Quaedam Theologicae." The estrangement was not really deep or long, lasting for about a year, and Charles could truthfully write near the end, "He was my fifty-year-old friend without a dissension." Correspondence ceased until 1800. Southey was the fortunate one to receive letters which would have gone to Coleridge, some of Lamb's best letters.

One incident of the year caused Lamb and his friends some annoyance, although in the thirteen letters for the year there is the only allusion to it in a letter to Southey in November. In the final issue of the *Anti-Jacobin,* July 1798, appeared a satirical poem, "The New Morality," by George Channing, containing these lines:

> And ye five other wandering Bards that move
> In sweet accord of harmony and love,
> C—DGE, S—TH—Y, L—D, and L—BE and Co.
> Tune all your mystic harps to praise Lepaux!

The names can be easily recognised, Coleridge, Southey, Lloyd and Lamb, Lepaux being the high-priest of Theophilanthropy. In the new *Anti-Jacobin Review and Magazine* which followed in August, a part of "The New Morality" was reprinted with a footnote accusing Coleridge of hypocrisy and the desertion of his wife and children, and in the same number there was a cartoon by the famous Gillray representing the prominent English revolutionists worshipping Justice, Philanthropy and Sensibility. Southey, as a donkey, offers a volume of *Sap[p]hics* with a copy of his *Joan of Arc* in his pocket. Behind him, reading a manuscript, *Blank Verse by Toad and Frog,* are a toad and frog, identified in the accompanying key plan as Lloyd and Lamb. Although Coleridge and Southey, in the opinion of the day, may have been appropriate subjects for attack, Lloyd and Lamb could not conceivably be. Lamb did not reply but Lloyd rose to his defence. "The person you have thus leagued in a partnership of infamy with me is Mr. Charles Lamb, a man who, so far from being a democrat, would be the first person to assent to the opinions contained in the foregoing pages: he is a man too much occupied with real and painful duties—duties of high personal self-denial—to trouble himself about speculative matters."

In April 1799, John Lamb, senior, died, and immediately thereafter Charles moved to another house on Chapel Street where he could bring Mary to live with him. In this year Thomas Manning, who had already been introduced to Lamb, came to have a prominent place in Lamb's life and the series of letters was begun which are unsurpassed for their good humour, variety of information and chatty criticism. In the autumn Coleridge returned from Germany and lived for a time in London with his wife and young Hartley, and the close relationship between the Lambs and Coleridges was re-established. Although there are few significant incidents in this year, Lamb's fortunes seemed brighter: he was relieved of the responsibility of his father, he had Mary with him, he was again in close relations with Coleridge, he found a new friend who interested him much. He was trying his hand at something he had wanted to do, writing a play, and finally affairs at the India House were going well, for he was now receiving a more respectable salary and had even better prospects.

Of all years before the appearance of *Elia* in 1820, 1800 has most letters to show Lamb and his interests in a circle of friends, widening with the introduction of the famous William Godwin, of whom we shall hear often, and John Rickman, "the finest fellow to drop in o' nights." More than half of the forty letters of this year are addressed to the new friend Manning and they carry us through the year with bits of family news—the death of the aged servant Hetty and Mary's long illness—with special comment on two old books, Percy's *Reliques of Ancient Poetry* and Burton's *Anatomy of Melancholy,* the latter of which had a great influence on Lamb's work, and finally with a copy of his new play, now rejected.

His neighbours' curiosity about Mary, Charles had already felt. "Nor is it the least of our evils that her case and all our story is so well known around us. We are in a manner *marked*." Fortunately, a friend, John Gutch, a former Christ's Hospital boy, offered rooms in Southampton Buildings and by summer Charles and Mary were happily settled there. Charles found refreshment in a four-days' vacation in Hertfordshire, and two days at Oxford to visit the Gutch family. "Unluckily, it was not a family where I could take Mary with me, and I am afraid there is something of dishonesty in any pleasures I take without *her*."

They were not to remain quiet in the Southampton Buildings. Neighbours began to look askance and Gutch very adroitly made it easy for them to move by Lady Day of the next year, this time to Mitre Court, Temple. It was going back home for Charles and Mary, and within the precincts of the old monastery they were to live the next sixteen years where Charles had spent his first twenty years.

In this period Lamb was especially occupied by writing for the magazines and newspapers. For the years 1801-1804 he had connections with the *Albion,* the *Morning Chronicle* and the *Morning Post,* but the result was not satisfactory either to employers or contributor. In an Elia essay, "Newspapers Thirty-five Years Ago," he has left us some of the flavour of his activity in producing jokes at the rate of sixpence per joke.

"In those days every Morning Paper, as an essential retainer to its establishment, kept an author, who was bound to furnish daily a quantum of witty paragraphs. Sixpence a joke—and it was thought pretty high too—was Dan Stuart's settled remuneration in these cases. The chat of the day, scandal, but, above all, *dress,* furnished the material. The length of no paragraph was to exceed seven lines. Shorter they might be, but they must be poignant.

"A fashion of *flesh,* or rather *pink*-coloured hose for the ladies, luckily coming up at the juncture when we were on our probation for the place of Chief Jester to S.'s Paper, established our reputation in that line. We were pronounced a 'capital hand.' O the conceits which we varied upon *red* in all its prismatic differences! from the trite and obvious flower of Cytherea, to the flaming costume of the lady that has her sitting upon 'many waters.' Then there was the collateral topic of ankles. What an occasion to a truly chaste writer, like ourself, of touching that nice brink, and yet never tumbling over it, of a seemingly ever approximating something 'not quite proper;' while, like a skilful posture-master, balancing betwixt decorums and their opposites, he keeps the line, from which a hair's-breadth deviation is destruction; hovering in the confines of light and darkness, or where 'both seem either;' a hazy uncertain delicacy; Autolycus-like in the Play, still putting off his expectant auditory with

'Whoop, do me no harm, good man!' But, above all, that conceit arrided us most at that time, and still tickles our midriff to remember, where, allusively to the flight of Astræa—*ultima Cœlestûm terras reliquit*—we pronounced—in reference to the stockings still that 'MODESTY, TAKING HER FINAL LEAVE OF MORTALS, HER LAST BLUSH WAS VISIBLE IN HER ASCENT TO THE HEAVENS BY THE TRACT OF THE GLOWING INSTEP.' This might be called the crowning conceit: and was esteemed tolerable writing in those days.

"But the fashion of jokes, with all other things, passes away; as did the transient mode which had so favoured us. The ankles of our fair friends in a few weeks began to reassume their whiteness, and left us scarce a leg to stand upon."

For the next few years, 1802-1805, new friends are introduced, Holcroft, author of *The Road to Ruin;* the Burney family, consisting of Captain James, son of Dr. Burney who wrote the well-known *History of Music* and brother of Fanny Burney; his wife Sarah Burney, the probable original for "Sarah Battle" by Elia; and son Martin; and most important of all, William Hazlitt, in 1804, who had already painted Coleridge's portrait. The holiday trips for this period were taken to the Coleridges at Keswick in August 1802, to the Isle of Wight and Portsmouth in July 1803, to Richmond in August 1804.

John Woodvil, the play which Kemble rejected in 1800, was published early in 1802 and, as expected, entailed a loss of about twenty-five pounds for its author. But Lamb was not daunted by the refusal of his first dramatic effort; he started another and was occupied in the theatrical affairs of Holcroft and Godwin. Perhaps more significant was his venture into juvenile literature, *The King and Queen of Hearts,* first of a group known as the Copperplate Series, very slight in itself, but perhaps notable in giving the author confidence of an ability to write for young readers.

Mary called 1805 a "sad and dreary year"—and for two special reasons. First, because of a return of her illness which lasted longer than usual and left brother and sister greatly depressed, and second, because of a tragic event which brought the Lambs and Wordsworths even more closely together. In a severe storm at sea the East India Company's *Earl of Abergavenny* sank on a night in February, and the captain, John Wordsworth, was drowned. John was the beloved brother of William. Grief over the incident was deepened by the first report that John had made no effort to save himself. The efforts of Charles and Mary in collecting accounts from survivors successfully proved that there was no foundation for the disturbing rumours.

The letters are as usual the best, and almost the only, source for incidents in Lamb's life in 1806. To Hazlitt he writes with enthusiasm of some paintings which he has recently seen, especially his favourites Leonardo and Titian. To Manning, sailing for China—he was away eleven years—he says, "I didn't know what your going was till I shook a last fist with you, and then 'twas just like having shaken hands with a wretch on the fatal scaffold, and when you are down the ladder, you can never stretch out to him again." Not inferior in quality or interest are the letters of this year written by Mary to Dorothy Wordsworth, to Mrs. Clarkson, and best of all, to Sarah Stoddart. The Lambs had met the Clarksons in the Lake District in 1802 on their visit to the Coleridges, and the two families had become intimate. Thomas Clarkson was the famous anti-slavery agitator, whose *History of the Slave Trade* was published in 1808. Coleridge came back from Malta and stayed for a time with the Lambs, causing much concern to Mary and other friends because he did not intend to return to his wife.

Hopes and ambitions led to the performance of *Mr. H——* in December, and to a failure which for a moment was a crushing blow but resulted in calling forth latent courage and new resolves. The account of this performance and failure is given in another chapter of this book.

From the year 1807 we have only four letters by Charles and one by Mary. Perhaps this small number may be partly due to the severe routine which both were under in finishing the *Tales from Shakespear,* published early in the year, *Mrs. Leicester's School,* and in the strenuous reading for the *Specimens of English Dramatic Poets* and the copying of the quotations. The visit to the Clarksons at Bury St. Edmunds which was enjoyed so heartily had an unfortunate sequel in an attack of Mary's illness, so severe that she had to go to the asylum at Hoxton.

In 1808 were published the *Specimens* and *The Adventures of Ulysses;* Coleridge gave his first series of lectures; and Hazlitt and Sarah Stoddart were married, with Lamb and Mary standing by. Because of Sarah's difficulty in deciding on which William to marry, Mary's hesitation in selecting the proper dress and Charles's good humour—this wedding on Sunday, May Day, at St. Andrew's Church, is probably better known than any other similar occasion.

From 1809-1817 Lamb and his sister lived at No. 4 Inner Temple Lane. In many ways this was his happiest and most successful period. There was not much to show in the way of writing—the two small volumes of poetry by Charles and Mary published by Mrs. Godwin; two little juvenile pieces in verse (1811), *Prince Dorus* and *Beauty and the Beast;* two worthy contributions, "On the Genius and Character of Hogarth" and "The Tragedies of Shakespeare," in 1810 to Leigh Hunt's *Reflector;* "Confessions of a Drunkard," written in 1813 for Leigh Hunt's *Examiner; On the Melancholy of Tailors* for John Scott's *Champion,* and an excellent review of Wordsworth's *Excursion* for Gifford's *Quarterly Review* in 1814; and during the last months of this period the collection of his work which was published in two volumes in 1818. There was not much of significance in the

WILLIAM WORDSWORTH
Courtesy New York Public Library Print Room

MARY LAMB AT SEVENTY AND CHARLES AT FIFTY-NINE
From the painting by Francis Stephen Cary, National Portrait Gallery

way of formal writing. For these nine years we have few letters, in all ninety-six, of which about a dozen were by Mary—no letter at all for 1813 and only three for 1812. Personally important for the Lambs were the deaths of George Burnett and Robert Lloyd, both of whom had become very close to Charles and Mary, visits to Cambridge and to the Hazlitts at Winterslow, the close association with Hazlitt, Wordsworth, Barnes, Editor of the *Times,* and Coleridge. Coleridge settled finally in 1815 at Dr. Gillman's in Highgate with hopes of recovering from the opium habit.

Of significance in literary history were the beginning of Crabb Robinson's *Diary* in 1811, the meeting of Lamb and Talfourd, his subsequent biographer and first collector of his letters, and his association with "Barry Cornwall," who also was to become an admiring biographer.

1815: to us that year stands for Napoleon and Waterloo. Neither is mentioned by Lamb in his letters but one characteristic observation to Southey is recorded. "After all, Bonaparte is a fine fellow, as my barber says, and I should not mind standing bareheaded at his table to do him service in his fall. They should have given him Hampton Court or Kensington, with a tether extending forty miles round London."

The small number of letters and the literary unproductiveness of this period may be due in part to the work at the office. "I am cruelly engaged and like to be. On Friday I was at office from 10 in the morning (two hours dinner except) to 11 at night, last night till 9. My business and office business in general has increased so. I don't mean I am there every night, but I must expect a great deal of it. I never leave till 4—and do not keep a holyday now once in ten times, where I used to keep all red letter days, and some fine days besides which I used to dub Nature's holydays."

There are reasons for grouping the next seven years, 1818-

1825. For the first five, Charles and Mary lived at No. 20 Russell Street, Covent Garden, which they liked for its nearness to the theatres. Lamb predicted that Mary could see things from the windows and they had not been there a day before she saw a thief caught and taken off to court. From 1823-1826, they had a cottage in Colebrook Row, Islington, afterwards called "Elia," their first residence out of the city. The first important event was the publication in 1818 of the *Works,* of which it may be said that this proved unique in containing only one piece, "The Old Familiar Faces," for which the author is now remembered. The two volumes were appreciated but with nothing of the reception which he had after the Elia essays had appeared two years later. There were holiday trips to the country, the death of his close friend Admiral Burney, and Lamb's proposal to the actress Fanny Kelly and her rejection in 1819, which are described elsewhere in this book.

1820 was a full year in the life of Charles Lamb. It was a year of much visiting. The Wordsworths were in London in June and then after a trip to the Continent were back in November. Lamb saw much of Crabb Robinson, made the usual annual visit to Coleridge at Highgate and saw many friends, especially Stoddart, Godwin, Talfourd, Ayrton, and made a new one, Thomas Allsop. Allsop was the wealthy silk merchant who found an easy approach to Lamb's heart through his liking of game. And so regularly there were presents of hare and pheasant, fish and pig, for Lamb's table in such profusion that Lamb was to remark: "I have almost forgotten butcher's meat as plebeian."

In July the Lambs went for a few days to Cambridge. Other trips to Cambridge had brought new friends and new experiences and were a refreshment in the routine of Lamb's domestic and office existence. This visit was notable first because they found Crabb Robinson there occupied with legal affairs—and what could be more welcome?—and then because they came to know the little motherless Emma Isola, aged eleven, daughter of Charles Isola, an administrative officer of the University, and granddaughter of Augustino Isola, an Italian, who had settled in Cambridge and who numbered Wordsworth among his pupils. The charming girl won the hearts of Charles and Mary at once. They asked her to come to see them. This she did on the following Christmas, making a new world for both of them and leading to her adoption in 1823 as their daughter. We can imagine that Lamb might have said at the end of his life that the happiest circumstance that ever befell him was the discovery of Emma Isola. Probably it was a reason for Lamb immortalizing the season in his Elia essay "Rejoicings upon the New Year's Coming of Age."

At this time Lamb was working on his first contributions to the *London Magazine* and here at Cambridge he wrote, or prepared to write, the Elia essay to which in his usual whimsical way of concealment he gave the title, "Oxford in the Vacation." After their return from Cambridge, Mary had an unusually severe attack but in September she was well again and busy as ever with her social affairs, taking up the relations with good friends at the theatre, at dinners and at the art galleries.

For reasons which we can only surmise there are but few letters written in 1820. One of Mary's letters is addressed to Fanny Kelly and its joyful enthusiasm furnishes no sign of the disappointment which must have come to both Charles and Mary over the rejection of Charles's proposal of marriage a few months before. Besides a number of unimportant short notes, there are two letters to Coleridge, one about Charles Lloyd, whom Lamb blames for interfering with his friendship with several persons, and one very frankly reproaching Coleridge for taking his books from his library, especially books lent to him; one letter to Joseph Cottle containing the now well-known observation about Byron, "It was quite a mistake that I could dislike anything you should write against Ld Byron, for I have a thorough aversion to his character, and a very moderate admiration of his genius—he is great in so little a way—to be a Poet is to be The Man, the whole Man—not a petty portion of occasional low passion worked up into a permanent form of Humanity."

The loss by death of other friends was followed in 1821 by the death of his brother John who, though he had failed Charles in crises, was nevertheless his brother and dear to him. The trip to France which Lamb had always wished to make was a great disappointment and saddened for him by a serious attack of Mary's illness on the way. However, new friends were still being made, friends who remained to the end: Henry F. Cary, Thomas Hood, Bernard Barton, Theodore Hook, Robert Bloomfield, P. J. Patmore and William Hone. Then almost suddenly at last came the offer from the East India Company of retirement on a generous pension, so delightfully described in the Elia essay "The Superannuated Man" and presented more fully in a later chapter of this volume.

From 1826-1834 the Lambs lived outside of London, first at Enfield for six years and then at Edmonton. Part of this time they had a house of their own and for a part they were in lodgings. When Lamb was retired, at first he went about with a sense of relief and freedom and the "perpetual holidays" dazzled him. It was too good to be true. Four hundred and fifty pounds a year, with nine pounds deducted towards a pension for Mary if she should outlive him—that was wonderful! All the things he had wanted to do he would now have time for. He could take as many walks as he had longed to take. He could read in the British Museum during office hours, something he had often wished to do. He could see his friends and write many letters. Letters written during the remaining nine years constitute almost half the complete collection, and for each of the two years 1827 and 1833 we have as many as seventy.

Then came the reaction. Strangely he began to yearn for the old desk at the office, for the daily meetings and chats with his friends there and for the folios which during more than thirty years he had helped to fill with figures. The illnesses of Mary were all too frequent and lasted longer than formerly. There was one bright spot—Emma Isola was developing into a very attractive young woman. Charles gave her lessons in Latin and Mary worked with French in order to teach her the language. And Emma in return introduced Charles and Mary to her own language, Italian, and the three together "scrambled" through Dante's "Inferno." All three went out together to dinner with friends and enjoyed visits to the theatre. Then, of course, the inevitable happened. Edward Moxon, the young publisher, fell in love with Emma.

For a time Charles took rooms in town and worked regularly at the British Museum making extracts from the Garrick collection of Elizabethan plays for Hone's *Every-Day Book*. He wrote his "Popular Fallacies" for the *New Monthly Magazine* and many verses for albums of his friends. For Moxon he collected his *Album Verses* as the young publisher's first offering in 1830, and a short play *Satan in Search of a Wife* followed in 1831. In 1833 Moxon published the *Last Essays of Elia*.

Meantime every attention was given to Emma, who married Moxon in 1833 and went off to Paris for her honeymoon. Mary was gravely affected by Emma's marriage, but clever Mrs. Walden, to whose keeping Charles had entrusted Mary in his absence, sensing an attack, took a glass of wine and suggested a toast "to the health of Mr. and Mrs. Moxon." The words were an electric shock and Mary was restored to her senses. That evening, wrote Lamb in his first letter to the bridal pair, they played seven games of piquet together. "We attack Tasso soon."

Some of the old friends came—Talfourd, Cary, Crabb Robinson and George Dyer. Charles resumed his walks, always preferring the old road that led past the Red Lion to London.

Then came the great shock, a shock too hard to bear—the death of Coleridge in July 1834, the end of a great friendship. On his deathbed were found the lines "This Lime-tree Bower My Prison" which Coleridge had written on the occasion of Lamb's memorable visit at Nether Stowey in 1797. By the side of the poem Coleridge had written: "Ch. and Mary Lamb—dear to my heart, yea, as it were, my heart. S. T. C. Aet. 63, 1834. 1797-1834 = 37 years!" He had requested that "small plain gold mourning rings, with my hair," be presented to "my close friend and ever-beloved schoolfellow, Charles Lamb" and "his equally beloved sister, Mary Lamb." Charles was so affected by the news that he could not attend the funeral but a few weeks later he paid a visit to the Gillmans and, asking to see Coleridge's nurse, gave her five guineas.

A few days after the death of Coleridge a young Cambridge student, Fuller Russell, was invited by Lamb to his cottage and many years afterwards Russell wrote the last contemporary account of Charles and Mary together.

"On reaching his cottage—which stood back from the road (nearly opposite the church), between two houses which projected beyond it, and was screened by shrubs and trees I found that he was out, taking his morning's stroll. I was admitted into a small, panelled, and a greatly shaded parlour. The modest room was hung round with engravings by Hogarth in dark frames. Books and magazines were scattered on the table and on the old-fashioned window seat. I chatted awhile with Miss Lamb—a meek, intelligent, very pleasant, but rather deaf elderly lady, who told me that her brother had been gratified by parts of my poem, and had read them to her. 'Elia' came in soon—a short, thin man. His dress was black, and he wore a capacious coat, breeches and gaiters, and a white neck-handker-chief. His dark and shaggy hair and eyebrows, heated face, and very piercing jet-black eyes gave to his appearance a singularly wild and striking expression. The sketch in *Fraser's Magazine* gives a true idea of his dress and figure, but his portraits fail to express adequately his remarkably 'fine Titian head, full of dumb eloquence,' as Hazlitt described it. He grasped me cordially by the hand, sat down, and taking a bottle from the cupboard be-hind him, mixed some rum with water. On another occasion his sister objected to this operation, and he refrained. Presently after he said, 'May I have a little drop now? Only a *leetle* drop?' 'No,' said she, 'be a good boy.' At last, however, he prevailed, and took his usual draught."

Professor Ernest Carson Ross has established in his excellent and scholarly work, *The Ordeal of Bridget Elia,* that Mary suf-fered another attack in November. She had not completely re-covered when Charles had the fall that brought his death. On the morning of December 22, Charles was walking towards a public house, when he tripped over a stone and cut his face. The injury caused him some pain, but he was not considered in dan-ger until erysipelas set in on December 24, and he sank so rapidly that when Talfourd arrived on the twenty-seventh Lamb did not know him. When he was dying, Mary could not be told; she did not understand. He died on December 27, 1834, in his sixtieth year and was buried in Edmonton churchyard in a spot which he had pointed out to Mary on one of their last walks together.

3

And Mary

THE strangest fact in the sad story of Mary Lamb is that, when she was not insane, her good sense and excellent judgement were of great assistance to the friends of Charles Lamb in making decisions. Charles himself never exaggerated when he spoke and wrote of his dependence upon her for advice and sympathy. If ever he acted unwisely, he said, "it was because my guardian angel was away." She was a capable housekeeper, looking after the details of the home, and their well-known reputation as hosts, much appreciated by numerous friends, always included Mary. Many are the references to the evenings in the Lambs' rooms where generous repasts of food and drink prepared by Mary made the Temple a bright spot for many a visitor to London. Then there were evenings at the theatre which both loved, when they went alone or were joined by such close friends as Hazlitt, Robinson, or the Wordsworths. Best of all were the holidays with trips to the Lake District to visit the Coleridges, the Southeys, the Wordsworths; to Winterslow to see the Hazlitts, to the seaside and to Richmond. For these trips great preparations were made and both Charles and Mary looked forward to them with youthful expectancy.

We know almost nothing about Mary Lamb until after the birth of Charles, when she was eleven—just that she attended the little school in Fetter Lane kept by William Bird, where she learned to read, that she loved the Temple Gardens, and, as soon as Charles was big enough, led him to all the nooks and crannies and read for him the inscriptions on the tombs and monuments. We know, too, that she was allowed to browse with Charles among the books of the library of their good friend and landlord, Samuel Salt. Her sketches in *Mrs. Leicester's School* tell of memories of the farm, the manor house and the grandmother and all the simple things associated with country life. When Charles came, life had a new interest, for then she had somebody to take to school and to the theatre, and to go with on holidays.

Her mother, as well as her grandmother, seems to nave been lacking in the tenderness and sympathy which would have been of vital consequence in rearing a child smitten like Mary with a hereditary tendency to madness, but there was no question of Mary's affection and of her devotion to her mother for many years. Charles, who was always keenly sensitive to personal relationship, once wrote to Coleridge with a frankness which he never repeated: "My Mother *never understood* her right. She loved her, as she loved us all, with a Mother's love; but in opinion, in feeling, and sentiment, and disposition, bore so distant a resemblance to her daughter, that she never understood her right. Never could believe how much *she* loved her—but met her caresses, her protestations of filial affection, too frequently with coldness and repulse.—Still she was a good mother, God forbid I should think of her but *most* respectfully, *most* affectionately. Yet she would always love my brother above Mary, who was not worthy of one tenth of that affection, which Mary had a right to claim. But it is my sister's gratifying recollection, that every act of duty and of love she could pay, every kindness (and I speak true, when I say to the hurting of her health, and most probably, in great part to the derangement of her senses) thro' a long course of infirmities and sickness, she could shew her, SHE EVER DID."

For eleven years, from the age of twenty-one to thirty-two,

Mary did her part in the support of the family by her work with the needle as a mantua-maker along with a little girl apprentice as helper. Towards the end of this period in September 1796, the household consisted of the father, John Lamb, who was then in his dotage; an invalid mother; old Aunt Hetty, who was the sister of John Lamb, senior; son John, recovering from a serious accident to his foot, and Charles, who had a few months before been overcome by the worries at home, or perhaps more by his passion for Alice W——n and had spent six weeks in confinement in the Hoxton madhouse. Mary had a load too heavy to carry and she was never the person to shirk. With daily attendance upon a mother who must have been most unsympathetic, and harassed by close application to her needlework, she was strained beyond the limit of her physical endurance.

Then came the inevitable tragedy.

In one moment the lives of both brother and sister took a new direction. They could not go on as before. How were they to meet this crushing blow? Would it make them cringe before a future which might contain other acts of tragedy or overwhelm them with the thoughts of a scene terrible to remember? This was not a new fear. There was something back there in the father's family—no one seemed to know exactly what—something they had lived with for many years, hardly daring to think what form it might take or whom it might strike.

The measure of their characters was to be the courage and good sense with which each confronted the future. They did not conceal or dissemble, they spent no time in idle repining. When Charles accepted from the court the charge of his sister, he, with his whole self, pledged his future, and no one ever kept a religious vow more honestly and with less regret for what he had missed. What might have been an unpleasant, sordid result, embittering both lives and driving friends away, became something as beautiful as a Greek tragedy, with only happy memories and noble friendships, attracting friends by the manner in which it was borne. Others came to realise what it all meant and admired and loved them for it. At the end of life, each perhaps could hardly have wished it had been otherwise—the good days had so outnumbered the bad ones.

With our present knowledge of mental disturbances we are better acquainted with such manifestations as those which afflicted Mary Lamb. A distinguished psychiatrist who is especially interested in this subject has read this chapter and has kindly offered this comment: "As for making a diagnosis I think more evidence should be at hand for the sake of accuracy, but from what is presented I would suspect that her malady was a type of manic-depressive insanity. It is the type that keeps recurring and goes through generations."

There were always premonitory symptoms, irritability, or other change of manner. Charles knew them well and knew that, when they appeared, he must act at once. And then the brother would "take her under his arm to Hoxton Asylum." "It was very affecting," Procter wrote in his *Memoir,* "to meet them, walking together, weeping together, carrying Mary's straight-jacket with them—on this painful mission."

In April 1803, while Coleridge was staying in London to arrange for an edition of the poems of 1796-1797, and was living with the Lambs, Mary had an attack when Coleridge was present. Of this he wrote to his wife, "I had purposed not to speak of Mary Lamb, but I had better write it than tell it. The Thursday before last she met at Rickman's a Mr. Babb, an old friend and admirer of her mother. The next day she smiled in an ominous way, on Sunday she told her brother that she was getting bad, with great agony, on Tuesday morning she laid hold of me with violent agitation and talked wildly about George Dyer. I told Charles there was not a moment to lose, and I did not lose a moment, but went for a hackney-coach and took her to the private mad-house at Hoxton. She was quite calm, and said it was the best to do so. But she wept bitterly two or three times, yet all in a calm way; Charles is cut to the heart."

Of her talk during her insane periods Talfourd has left a description. "Her ramblings often sparkled with brilliant description and shattered beauty. She would fancy herself in the days of Queen Anne or George the First and describe the brocaded dames and courtly manners as though she had been bred among them, in the best style of the old comedy. It was all broken and disjointed so that the hearer could remember little of her discourse, but the fragments were like the jewelled speeches of Congreve, only shaken from their setting. There was sometimes even a vein of crazy logic running through them, associating things essentially most dissimilar, but connecting them by a verbal association in strange order. As a mere physical instance of deranged intellect, her condition was, I believe, extraordinary; it was as if the finest element of the mind had been shaken into fantastic combinations like those of a kaleidoscope."

We are fortunately in possession of a very detailed as well as true and sympathetic description of Mary Lamb, by her longtime friends, the Cowden Clarks. "Miss Lamb bore a strong resemblance to her brother, being in stature under middle height, possessing well-cut features, and a countenance of singular sweetness, with intelligence. Her brown eyes were soft, yet penetrating, her nose and mouth very shapely; while the general expression was mildness itself. She had a speaking-voice, gentle and persuasive; and her smile was her brother's own—winning in the extreme. There was a certain catch, or emotional breathingness in her utterance, which gave an inexpressible charm to her reading of poetry, and which lent a captivating earnestness to her mode of speech when addressing those she liked. This slight check, with its yearning, eager effect in her voice had something softenedly akin to her brother Charles's impediment of articulation: in him it scarcely amounted to a stammer; in her it merely imparted additional stress to the fine sensed suggestions she made to those whom she counselled or consoled. She had a mind at once nobly-toned and practical, making her ever a chosen source of confidence among her friends, who turned to her for consolation, confirmation and advice in matters of nicest moment, always secure of deriving from her both aid and advice. Her manner was easy, almost homely, so quiet, unaffected, and perfectly understanding was it. Beneath the sparing talk and retired carriage, few casual observers would have suspected the ample information and large intelligence that lay comprised there. She was oftener a listener than a speaker. In the modest-havioured woman simply sitting there, taking small share in the general conversation, few who did not know her would have imagined the accomplished classical scholar, the excellent understanding, the altogether rarely-gifted being, morally and mentally, that Mary Lamb was. Her apparel was always of the plainest kind: a black stuff or silk gown, made and worn in the simplest fashion. She took snuff liberally—a habit that had evidently grown out of her propensity to sympathize with and share all her brother's tastes; and it certainly had the effect of enhancing her likeness to him. She had a small, white, and delicately formed hand; and as it hovered above the tortoise-shell box containing the powder so strongly approved by them both, in search of the stimulating pinch, the act seemed yet another link of association between brother and sister, when hanging together over their favourite books and studies."

We are not so sure that Talfourd was right when he wrote "she never shrank from alluding to her mother, when any topic connected with her youth made such a reference natural, but spoke of her as though no fearful remembrance was associated into the image." Emma Isola, not acquainted with the facts, on one occasion asked her why she never spoke of her mother and was answered only with a cry of distress. Probably the question coming so abruptly confronted Mary in a peculiarly painful way with the tragedy. She left one expression which leads us into the world of thoughts which must have been with her many times and also reveals the nobility of her character. "I have no bad terrifying dreams. At midnight when I happen to awake, the nurse sleeping by the side of me, with the noise of the poor mad people around me, I have no fear. The spirit of my mother seems to descend, and smile upon me, and bid me live to enjoy the life and reason which the Almighty has given me—I shall see her again in heaven; she will then understand me better; my Grandmother too will understand me better, and will then say no more, as she used to do, 'Polly, what are those poor crazy moyther'd brains of yours thinking of always?'"

In April after the tragedy Lamb wrote to Coleridge, "I have taken her out of her confinement, and taken a room for her at Hackney, and spend my Sundays, holidays, & c., with her. She boards herself. In one little half year's illness, and in such an illness of such a nature and of such consequences! to get her out into the world again, with a prospect of her never being so ill again—this is to be ranked not among the common blessings of Providence. May that merciful God make tender my heart, and make me as thankful, as in my distress I was earnest, in my prayers."

In June 1805, Lamb wrote to Dorothy Wordsworth and, as always, never failed to make a fair statement about Mary. "Your long kind letter has not been thrown away (for it has given me great pleasure to find you are all resuming your old occupations, and are better) but poor Mary to whom it is addrest cannot yet relish it. She has been attacked by one of her severe illnesses, and is at present *from home*. Last Monday week was the day she left me; and I hope I may calculate upon having her again in a month, or little more. I am rather afraid late hours have in this case contributed to her indisposition. But when she discovers symptoms of approaching illness, it is not easy to say what is best to do. Being by ourselves is bad, and going out is bad. I get so irritable and wretched with fear, that I constantly hasten on the disorder. You cannot conceive the misery of such a fore-sight. I am sure that for the week before she left me, I was little better than light-headed. I now am calm, but sadly taken down, and flat. I have every reason to suppose that this illness, like all her former ones, will be but temporary; but I cannot always feel so. Meantime she is dead to me, and I miss a prop. All my strength is gone, and I am like a [fool, ber]eft of her co-opera-tion. I dare not think, lest I [should think] wrong; so used am I to look up to her [in the least] and the biggest perplexity. To say *all that* [I know of her] would be more than I think any body could [believe or even under]stand; and when I hope to have her well [again with me] it would be sinning against her feelings to go about to praise her; for I can conceal nothing that I do from her. She is older, and wiser, and better, than me, and all my wretched imperfections I cover to myself by resolutely thinking on her goodness. She would share life and death, heaven and hell, with me. She lives but for me. And I know I have been wasting and teazing her life for five years past inces-santly with my cursed drinking and ways of going on. But even in this up-braiding of myself I am offending against her, for I know that she has cleaved to me for better, for worse; and if the balance has been against her hitherto, it was a noble trade.

"I am stupid and lose myself in what I write. I write rather what answers to my feelings (which are sometimes sharp enough) than express my present ones, for I am only flat and stupid."

On their return from a visit to the Clarksons in June 1807, an attack came upon Mary while they were in the stage coach. "You will wish to know how we performed our journey. My sister was tolerably quiet until we got to Chelmsford, where she began to be very bad indeed, as your friends William Knight and his family can tell you when you see them. What I should have done without their kindness I don't know, but among other acts of great attention, they provided me with a waistcoat to confine her arms, by the help of which we went through the rest of our journey. But sadly tired and miserably depressed she was before we arrived at Hoxton."

Between their two longish periods of residence at the Temple while they were temporarily lodged in Southampton Buildings, Mary became overstrained after the moving and change. An attack postponed their trip to the Hazlitts, planned for the mid-summer, but fortunately they were able to make the visit in October and the holiday proved of great benefit to Mary. In "A Farewell to Essay-writing" Hazlitt leaves with us the charming picture: "I used to walk out at this time with Mr. and Miss L——of an evening, to look at the Claude Lorraine skies over our heads, melting from azure into purple and gold, and to gather mushrooms, that sprung up at our feet, to throw into our hashed mutton at supper." And only a few days later Robert Lloyd, brother of Charles Lloyd and a Birmingham bookseller, after several evenings at the Lambs', wrote to his wife, "I spent yesterday with Lamb and his sister—it is sweetly gratifying to see them. . . . If I may use the expression, their union of affection is what we conceive of marriage in Heaven. They are the World *one* to the *other*. They are writing a book of poetry for children together."

To Hazlitt in November 1810, Lamb wrote, "Mary has been very ill indeed since you saw her, that is, as ill as she can be to remain at home. But she is a good deal better now, owing to a very careful regimen, she drinks nothing but water and never goes out, she does not even go to the Captain's. Her indisposition has been ever since that night you left Town, the night Miss W[ordsworth] came; her coming, and that damn'd infernal bitch Mrs. Godwin coming and staying so late that night, so overset her that she lay broad awake all that night, and it was by a miracle that she escaped a very bad illness which I thoroughly expected.—I have made up my mind that she shall never have any one in the house again with her, and that no one shall sleep with her not even for a night, for it is a very serious thing to be always living with a kind of fever upon her, & therefore I am sure you will take it in good part if I say that if Mrs. Hazlitt comes to town at any time, however glad we shall be to see her in the daytime, I cannot ask her to spend a night under our roof. Some decision we must come to, for the harassing fever that we have both been in, owing to Miss Wordsw^s coming, is not to be borne, & I had rather be dead than so alive. However at present owning to a regimen & medicines which Tuthill, who very kindly volunteer'd the care of her, has given her, she is a great deal quieter, though too much harassd by Company, who cannot or will not see how late hours & society teaze her."

In the years 1811 to 1815, Mary was subject to several attacks, each brought on by special worry or overwork, the death of their good friend George Burnett, concern about Coleridge, her exertion over the writing of her article, "On Needle-Work," and other similar exertions.

In October 1815, to Miss Hutchinson, Wordsworth's sister-in-law, Lamb wrote, "I am forced to be the replier to your Letter, for Mary has been ill and gone from home these five weeks yesterday. She has left me very lonely and very miserable. I stroll about, but there is no rest but at one's own fireside, and there is no rest for me there now. I look forward to the worse half being past, and keep up as well as I can. She has begun to show some favorable symptoms. The return of her disorder has been frightfully soon this time, with scarce a six month's interval. I am almost afraid my worry of spirits about the E. I. House was partly the cause of her illness, but one always imputes it to the cause next at hand; more probably it comes from some cause we have no control over or conjecture of. It cuts sad great slices out of the time, the little time we shall have to live together. I don't know but the recurrence of these illnesses might help me to sustain her death better than if we had had no partial separations. But I won't talk of death. I will imagine us immortal, or forget that we are otherwise; by God's blessing in a few weeks we may be making our meal together, or sitting in the front row of the Pit at Drury Lane, or taking our evening walk past the theatres, to look at the outside of them at least, if not to be tempted in. Then we forget we are assailable, we are strong for the time as rocks, the wind is tempered to the shorn Lambs."

In August 1818, Mrs. Leigh Hunt wrote to Mary Shelley, wife of the poet, "You will be sorry to hear poor Miss Lamb is ill again: what a sad thing it is for such an admirable woman. I don't know how it is, but those things seem to fall on the most delightful and amiable of mankind—I don't mean her particular complaint, but distress and uneasiness in general."

In September 1820 Lamb reported to Hazlitt, "The last thing she read was the 'Thursday Nights,' which seem'd to give her unmix'd delight, & she was sorry for what she said to you that night. The Article is a treasure to us for ever." The reference was to Hazlitt's account of Lamb's Thursday parties in the article, "On the Conversation of Authors."

The Lambs went to France in the summer of 1822, sailing from Brighton to Dieppe with an attendant for Mary. Robinson records in his diary, "Lamb in high spirits, Mary rather nervous." Greatly, of course, to her disappointment, she was taken ill on the road at Amiens, and remained there to be nursed. To the Kenneys, with whom Charles had stayed during his visit to Paris, he wrote concerning her return: "Mary got home safe on Friday night. She has suffered only a common fatigue, but as she is weakly, begs me to thank you in both our names for all the trouble she has been to you. She did not succeed in saving Robinson's fine waistcoat. They could not comprehend how a waistcoat, marked Henry Robinson, could be a part of Miss Lamb's wearing apparel. So they seized it for the king, who will probably appear in it at the next levee. Next to yourself, our best thanks to H. Payne." In early September she returned from Paris.

For the next two years there were heartbreaking occasions, with one "exempt year," 1824. There were many seasons such as this one described by Crabb Robinson: "I walked to Enfield and found the Lambs in excellent state—not in high health, but what is far better, quiet and cheerful." And then would come a time of anxiety, an attack extending over a longer period, almost three months in 1829, and on one such occasion Lamb wrote to Barton from a full and sad heart.

"Less than a month I hope will bring home Mary. She is at Fulham, looking better in her health than ever, but sadly rambling, and scarce showing any pleasure in seeing me, or curiosity when I should come again. But the old feelings will come back again, and we shall drown old sorrows over a game at Picquet again. But 'tis a tedious cut out of a life of sixty four, to lose twelve or thirteen weeks every year or two. And to make me more alone, our illtemperd maid is gone, who with all her airs, was yet a home piece of furniture, a record of better days; the young thing that has succeeded her is good and attentive, but she is nothing—and I have no one here to talk over old matters with."

Only a few months before his death Charles wrote Maria

Fryer, an old schoolmate of Emma Isola, a final expression of what Mary had been to him as a comfort in a time of loneliness. "It is no new thing for me to be left to my sister. When she is not violent her rambling chat is better to me than the sense and sanity of this world. Her heart is obscured, not buried; it breaks out occasionally; and one can discern a strong mind struggling with the billows that have gone over it. I could be nowhere happier than under the same roof with her. Her memory is unnaturally strong; and from ages past, if we may so call the earliest records of our poor life, she fetches thousands of names and things that never would have dawned upon me again, and thousands from the ten years she lived before me. What took place from early girlhood to her coming of age principally lives again (every important thing and every trifle) in her brain with the vividness of real presence. For twelve hours incessantly she will pour out without intermission all her past life, forgetting nothing, pouring out name after name to the Waldens as a dream; sense and nonsense; truths and errors huddled together; a medley between inspiration and possession. What things we are! I know you will bear with me, talking of these things. It seems to ease me; for I have nobody to tell these things to now."

At the time of the death of her brother, Mary had an attack which mercifully deprived her of the sense of what had happened. Her friends tried to persuade her to leave Edmonton and go into the city, but for a time she refused, as she wanted to be near the spot where *he* lay beneath the sod where they had stood together and selected their resting-place. When she was well, she used to stroll out every evening to his grave and would contrive to lead thither any friend who came to drink tea with her or to go with her for a walk.

Due to the provisions of her brother, she had no worries about money. She was well looked after, visited by old friends, and spent some happy days remembering Charles. Crabb Robinson records a visit in 1835: " 'Oh, here's Crabby,' she said, not quite herself, 'now this is very kind, not merely good-natured but very, very kind to come and see me in my affliction.' "

After a long illness in 1839 she consented to removal with her nurse, Mrs. James, to the house of her nurse's sister in St. John's Wood, where she died in 1847 at the age of eighty-two, surviving her brother by thirteen years.

Mary Lamb wrote almost as good letters as her brother. It is difficult to select one which shows best her good sense and understanding, combined with humour and sympathy. She seems to have been liked almost equally by women and men. Her relation with Sarah Stoddart is as characteristic as any. A letter of 1803 is full of advice that Sarah might well have followed:
"My dear Sarah,

"I returned home from my visit yesterday, and was much pleased to find your letter; for I have been very anxious to hear how you are going on. I could hardly help expecting to see you when I came in; yet, though I should have rejoiced to have seen your merry face again, I believe it was better as it was—upon the whole; and, all things considered, it is certainly better you should go to Malta. The terms you are upon with your Lover does (as you say it will) appear wondrous strange to me; however, as I cannot enter into your feelings, I certainly can have nothing to say to it, only that I sincerely wish you happy in your own way, however odd that way may appear to me to be. I would begin now to advise you to drop all correspondence with William; but, as I said before, as I cannot enter into your feelings and views of things, *your ways not being my ways,* why should I tell you what I would do in your situation? So, child, take thy own ways, and God prosper thee in them!

"One thing my advising spirit must say—use as little *Secrecy* as possible; and, as much as possible, make a friend of your sister-in-law—you know I was not struck with her at first sight; but, upon your account, I have watched and marked her attentively; and, while she was eating a bit of cold mutton in our kitchen, we had a serious conversation. From the frankness of her manner, I am convinced she is a person I could make a friend of; why should not you? We talked freely about you: she seems to have a just notion of your character, and will be fond of you, if you will let her.

"My father had a sister lived with us—of course, lived with my Mother, her sister-in-law; they were, in their different ways, the best creatures in the world—but they set out wrong at first. They made each other miserable for full twenty years of their lives—my Mother was a perfect gentlewoman, my Aunty as unlike a gentlewoman as you can possibly imagine a good old woman to be; so that my dear Mother (who, though you do not know it, is always in my poor head and heart) used to distress and weary her with incessant and unceasing attention and politeness, to gain her affection. The old woman could not return this in kind, and did not know what to make of it—thought it all deceit, and used to hate my Mother with a bitter hatred; which of course, was soon returned with interest. A little frankness, and looking into each other's characters at first, would have spared all this, and they would have lived, as they died, fond of each other for the last few years of their life. When we grew up, and harmonised them a little, they sincerely loved each other.

"My Aunt and my Mother were wholly unlike you and your sister, yet in some degree theirs is the secret history I believe of all sisters-in-law—and you will smile when I tell you I think myself the only woman in the world who could live with a brother's wife, and make a real friend of her, partly from early observation of the unhappy example I have just given you, and partly from a knack I know I have of looking into people's real characters, and never expecting them to act out of it—never expecting another to do as I would do in the same case. When you leave your Mother, and say, if you never shall see her again, you shall feel no remorse, and when you make a *jewish* bargain with your *Lover,* all this gives me no offence, because it is your nature, and your temper, and I do not expect or want you to be otherwise than you are. I love you for the good that is in you, and look for no change.

"*But,* certainly, you ought to struggle with the evil that does most easily beset you—a total want of politeness in behaviour, I would say modesty of behaviour, but that I should not convey to you my idea of the word modesty; for I certainly do not mean that you want *real modesty;* and what is usually called false, or mock, modesty is [a quality] I certainly do not wish you to possess, yet I trust you know what I mean well enough.

"*Secrecy,* though you appear all frankness, is certainly a grand failing of yours; it is likewise your *brother's,* and, therefore, a family failing—by secrecy, I mean you both want the habit of telling each other at the moment every thing that happens— where you go,—and what you do,—the free communication of letters and opinions just as they arrive, as Charles and I do,— and which is, after all, only the groundwork of friendship. Your brother, I will answer for [it,] will never tell his wife or his sister all that [is in] his mind—he will receive letters, and not [mention it]. This is a fault Mrs. Stoddart can never [tell him of;] but she can, and will, feel it: though, [on] the whole, and in every other respect, she is [very] happy with him. Begin, for God's sake, at the first, and tell her every thing that passes. At first she may hear you with indifference; but in time this will gain her affection and confidence; show her all your letters (no matter if she does not show hers)—it is a pleasant thing for a friend to put into one's hand a letter just fresh from the post. I would even say, begin with showing her this, but that it is written freely and loosely, and some apology ought to be made for it—which I know not how to make, for I must write freely or not at all.

"If you do this, she will tell your brother, you will say; and what then, quotha? It will beget a freer communication amongst you, which is a thing devoutly to be wished—

"God bless you, and grant you may preserve your integrity, and remain unmarried and penniless, and make William a good and a happy wife.

"Your affectionate friend,

"M. Lamb."

Sarah was the sister of Dr. John Stoddart, who had just been appointed the Judge Advocate at Malta. Later she went with her brother and sister-in-law to spend some time with them. At this moment her affections seem to have been centred on a Mr. William Turner; another William was before him and he in turn was to be followed by the successful suitor, William Hazlitt. This letter contains the only reference to Mary's mother in any of her letters.

In her most readable sketch of Mary Lamb in her volume of the *Eminent Women Series,* Anne Gilchrist has given a delightful contrast of the three devoted friends. "Dorothy Wordsworth was just such a friend and comrade to the poet as Mary was to Charles, sharing his passionate devotion to nature as Mary shared her brother's loves, whether for men or books or for the stir and throng of life in the great city. Alike were these two women in being, as De Quincey said of Dorothy, 'the truest, most inevitable and, at the same time, the quickest and readiest in sympathy with either joy or sorrow, with laughter or with tears, with the realities of life, or with the larger realities of the poets.' But unlike in temperament; Dorothy ardent, fiery, trembling with eager impetuosity that embarrassed her utterance; Mary gentle, silent or deliberate in speech. In after-life there was another sad similarity for Dorothy's reason, too, was in the end over-clouded. . . . As great a contrast in most respects to Dorothy Wordsworth, as the whole range of womankind could have furnished, was Mary's other friend and correspondent, Sarah Stoddart, afterwards Mrs. Hazlitt. Sarah was the only daughter of a retired lieutenant in the navy, a Scotchman who had settled down on a little property at Winterslow near Salisbury which she ultimately inherited. She was a young lady with a business-like determination to marry and with many suitors; but, far from following the old injunction to be off with the old love before being on with the new, she always cautiously kept the old love dangling till she was quite sure the new was the more eligible."

It would be no mean accomplishment to succeed as the indispensable helpmeet of Charles Lamb, but, much more than that, Mary was a writer in her own name. Her letters, only second in interest to those of her brother, are charmingly human and humorous; her verses, most of which were for children, are the equal of those of Charles; and her share of the work done in co-operation with him, *Mrs. Leicester's School* and *Tales from Shakespear,* does not suffer in comparison with his.

A word may properly be said of her essay on needle-work, her only attempt to address adult readers. She does not treat the subject as an art but as a *factor* in social life, and pleads both for the sake of the bodily welfare of the many thousands of women who have to earn their bread by it and of the mental well-being of those who have not so to do, that it should be regarded, like any other mechanical work, as a thing to be done for hire and that what a woman does work at should be real work, something which yields a return either of mental or of pecuniary gain. Her original point of view as well as her style give an indication of what she might have done had circumstances been different.

In a public recognition of her qualities, she has been included in a series of *Eminent Women,* with such famous persons as George Eliot, George Sand, Margaret Fuller, Harriet Martineau, Mary Wollstonecraft and Madame de Staël. Her surprise to be named in such a list may be imagined.

4

The East India House

THE East India House stretched along Leadenhall Street just beyond Grace Church Street and around the corner to Lime Street, a gloomy structure with a portico of Ionic pillars. Its pediment contained a shield above the sculptured figures of Eastern commerce, dominated by Britannia, with Europe on a horse on her right and Asia on a camel at her left. Within the massive walls of this structure were conducted the affairs of the East India Company. The Company possessed a charter bearing the seal of Queen Elizabeth dated December 31, 1600, by which it was given license to trade with India and the East Indies. It began in glorious days and in extent and importance became a fair rival of the Empire itself. In many ways its history is the history of the British Empire. From those days when Elizabethan adventurers sailed the seven seas, the East India agent brought back from strange and hitherto unknown lands the wealth of "Ormus and of Ind," precious stores, fabrics, dyes, spices and other articles of trade which built the commerce of England for more than two centuries. That was what the Company stood for to a realistic Englishman. No other corporation has had a career more crowded with romance, intrigue and daring adventure. To one with imagination and a desire for exploring, here was a challenge to inflame the boldest dreamer.

According to general belief, the vaults of the building contained treasures of gold and countless curiosities from all parts of the Eastern world. Years after Lamb's time, chains and fetters were found in the dungeons, and narrow passages and concealed posterns were discovered which may have been used for the victims of the press gangs that were trapped, drugged and shipped secretly down the river on their way to India.

In this building, upstairs, was the accountants' office, a large room divided into compartments, called compounds, in each of which sat six clerks, one of these Lamb himself. The meaning of the word *compound* was asked one day and Lamb replied that it was "a collection of Simples." It is pleasing to know that the desk which Lamb used for thirty-three years became with the increasing fame of Elia an object of great interest to visitors and had to be moved to another part of the building so that there would be less obstruction to the routine of business.

Charles wrote later, perhaps too modestly, of his youthful accomplishments, or lack of accomplishments, in arithmetic and geography and commented most unfavorably on his penmanship, but evidently his defects were not of a sufficiently serious nature to prevent his being selected for and continuing in the clerkship.

Work consisted of copying the results of the sales. At that time it was the custom of the Company to have every three months large auctions of the cargoes which came from the East. These sometimes lasted for many days and were attended by the big traders in sessions which were conducted much like our stock-exchange operations. A technique was developed by which the buyers by nods and winks concluded their sales and large amounts were transferred—in tea, the most popular article, the sales amounted on one occasion to the then high figure of eight and one-half million pounds. The clerks were very busy at these auctions which, as Lamb has recorded in his letters, sometimes lasted far into the night.

The innumerable folios in which he put down figures Lamb often described as containing most of his written work. To our great regret, the ledgers were later destroyed, and admirers of Lamb, especially from America, searching for any scrap of his work have sought in vain for it here.

We can imagine some of the thoughts which he must have had in an environment of such fruitful suggestiveness. Rare and fragrant spices, whence had they come? Finest silks, where had they been spun? The excitement of procuring, trading, shipping, the encounters with robbers, pirates, adventurers—is it likely that all this could have failed to move the young clerk making innumerable entries in heavy ledgers?

If there were active periods, there were also seasons when business was easy and Lamb had time for his letters and his other writing. As evidence of the strictness of the rules of the House, as well as an indication of the regularity of Lamb's office habits, we may read his letter to Manning which tells of the sad plight of Tommy Bye.

"The E. I. H. has been thrown into a quandary by the strange phenomenon of poor Tommy Bye, whom I have known man and mad-man twenty-seven years, he being elder here than myself by nine years and more. He was always a pleasant, gossiping, half-headed, muzzy, dozing, dreaming, walk-about, inoffensive chap; a little too fond of the creature—who isn't at times? but Tommy had not brains to work off an over-night's surfeit by ten o'clock next morning, and unfortunately, in he wandered the other morning drunk with last night, and with a superfœtation of drink taken in since he set out from bed. He came staggering under his double burthen, like trees in Java, bearing at once blossom, fruit, and falling fruit, as I have heard you or some other traveller tell, with his face literally as blue as the bluest firmament; some wretched calico that he had mopped his poor oozy front with had rendered up its native dye, and the devil a bit would he consent to wash it, but swore it was characteristic, for he was going to the sale of indigo, and set up a laugh which I did not think the lungs of mortal man were competent to. It was like a thousand people laughing, or the Goblin Page. He imagined afterwards that the whole office had been laughing at him, so strange did his own sounds strike upon his *non*sensorium. But Tommy has laughed his last laugh, and awoke the next day to find himself reduced from an abused income of £600 per annum to one-sixth of the sum, after thirty-six years' tolerably good service. The quality of mercy was not strained in his behalf; the gentle dews dropt not on him from heaven."

The regularity with which Lamb went to the office was of such common observation that it was said that one could set one's watch by Lamb's leaving home in the morning. However absorbing the previous evening had been, whatever his indulgences in smoking and drinking, the next morning found him always at Leadenhall. His health was never rugged, he was not a sturdy man, but the care which he took of himself, besides the constant watchfulness of Mary, made it possible for him to carry on so consistently that we have no record of extended absence on account of illness.

For one who liked London as Charles Lamb did, there was always something interesting on the way between home and office. He wrote his friend Manning who had gone to France, "I must be told if any building in Paris as at all comparable to St. Paul's, which, contrary to the usual mode of that part of our nature called admiration, I have looked up to with unfading wonder, every morning at ten o'clock, ever since it has lain on my way to business. At noon I casually glance upon it, being hungry; and hunger has not much taste for the fine arts. Is any night-walk comparable to a walk from St. Paul's to Charing Cross, for lighting and paving, crowds going and coming without respite, the rattle of coaches, and the cheerfulness of shops?"*

* Letter, February 1802.

With a person so alert and observing and so quaint in appearance and, doubtless to many, so eccentric in his actions, there must have been many amusing experiences which he recounted with delight to his friends in the evenings. One day while passing through Leadenhall market, he accidentally stepped on the foot of a butcher, who in anger picked up a cleaver and started after him. Lamb darted through the back door of the East India House into his room, where he sank into a chair. "Whatever's the matter?" asked one of the clerks. "And what else is to be expected," was the reply, "when a Lamb goes trotting into a market?"

Although Lamb enjoyed his holidays and sometimes wrote as if they were the best part of the year, and although he complained at times of the long hours of tedious copying, nevertheless his letters show little annoyance and certainly great enjoyment of some of the humorous characters who shared his life of routine. He liked his fellow clerks, was a favourite among them and has written many delightful sketches of them. When he finally left the House, he kept up his acquaintance with some of his old associates and spoke with regret of going back to the office and finding another person's hat on his peg.

The one letter in which Lamb wrote of his fellow clerks and their doings went to another member of the India House, John Chambers, in 1818.

"DEAR C.,

"I steal a few minutes from a painful and laborious avocation, aggravated by the absence of some that should assist me, to say how extremely happy we should be to see you return clean as the cripple out of the pool of Bethesda. That damn'd scorbutic—how came you by it? ... You are now fairly a damaged lot; as Venn would say, One Scratched. You might play Scrub in the *Beaux' Stratagem*. The best post your friends could promote you to would be a scrubbing post. 'Aye, there's the rub.' I generally get tired after the third rubber. But you, I suppose, tire twice the number every day. First, there's your mother, she begins after breakfast; then your little sister takes it up about Nuncheon time, till her bones crack, and some kind neighbour comes in to lend a hand, scrub, scrub, scrub, and nothing will get the intolerable itch (for I am persuaded it is the itch) out of your penance-doing bones. A cursed thing just at this time, when everybody wants to get out of town as well as yourself. Of course, I don't mean to reproach you. You can't help it, the whoreson tingling in your blood. I dare say you would if you could. But don't you think you could do a little work, if you came? as much as D[odwell] does before 12 o'Clock. Hang him, there he sits at that cursed *Times*—and latterly he has had the *Berkshire Chronicle* sent him every Tuesday and Friday to get at the County news. Why, that letter which you favored him with, appears to me to be very well and clearly written. The man that wrote that might make out warrants, or write Committees. There was as much in quantity written as would have filled four volumes of the Indigo appendix; and when we are so busy as we are, every little helps. But I throw out these observations merely as innuendos. By the way there's a Doctor Lamert in Leadenhall Street, who sells a mixture to purify the blood. No. 114 Leadenhall Street, near the market. But it is necessary that his patients should be on the spot, that he may see them every day. There's a sale of Indigo advertised for July, forty thousand lots—10,000 chests only, but they sell them in quarter chests which makes 40,000. By the bye a droll accident happened here on Thursday, Wadd and Plumley got quarrelling about a kneebuckle of Hyde's which the latter affirmed not to be standard; Wadd was nettled at this, and said something reflecting on tradesmen and shopkeepers, and Plumley struck him. . . . Friend is married; he has married a Roman Catholic, which has offended his family, but they have come to an agreement, that the boys (if they have children) shall be bred up in the father's religion, and the

THE INDIA HOUSE IN LAMB'S DAY

From *Ackermann's Repository of Arts*

ST. DUNSTAN'S CHURCH, FLEET STREET, DURING CHARLES
LAMB'S BOYHOOD

From *Ackermann's Repository of Arts*

girls in the mother's, which I think equitable enough. . . . I am determined my children shall be brought up in their father's religion, if they can find out what it is. Bye is about publishing a volume of poems which he means to dedicate to Matthie. Methinks he might have found a better Mecænas. They are chiefly amatory, others of them stupid, the greater part very far below mediocrity; but they discover much tender feeling; they are most like Petrarch of any foreign Poet, or what we might have supposed Petrarch would have written if Petrarch had been born a fool! Grinwallows is made master of the ceremonies at Dandelion, near Margate; of course he gives up the office. 'My Harry' makes so many faces that it is impossible to sit opposite him without smiling. Dowley danced a Quadrille at Court on the Queen's birthday with Lady Thynne, Lady Desbrow, and Lady Louisa Manners. It is said this performance was graceful and airy. Cabel has taken an unaccountable fancy into his head that he is Fuller, member for Sussex. He imitates his blunt way of speaking. I remain much the same as you remember, very universally beloved and esteemed, possessing everybody's good-will, and trying at least to deserve it; the same steady adherence to principle, and correct regard for truth, which always marked my conduct, marks it still. If I am singular in anything it is in too great a squeamishness to anything that remotely looks like a falsehood. I am call'd Old Honesty; sometimes Upright Telltruth, Esq., and I own it tickles my vanity a little. The Committee have formally abolish'd all holydays whatsoever—for which may the Devil, who keeps no holydays, have them in his eternal burning workshop. When I say holydays, I mean Calendar holydays, for at Medley's instigation they have agreed to a sort of scale by which the Chief has power to give leave of absence, viz.:—

"Those who have been 50 years and upwards to be absent 4 days in the year, but not without leave of the Chief.

35 years and upward, 3 days,
25 years and upward, 2 days,
18 years and upward, 1 day,

which I think very Liberal. We are also to sign our name when we *go* as well as when we *come,* and every quarter of an hour we sign, to show that we are here. Mins and Gardner take it in turn to bring round the book—O here *is* Mins with the Book—no, it's Gardner—'What's that, G.?' 'The appearance book, Sir' (with a gentle inclination of his head, and smiling). 'What the devil is the quarter come again?' It annoys Dodwell amazingly; he sometimes has to sign six or seven times while he is reading the Newspaper."

One of the traditions of the India House was an annual feast free to all the men who worked there. Most of these celebrations Lamb attended but in later years occasionally he used the day for an outing in the country. "Last Saturday was the grand feast day of the India House Clerks. I think you must have heard Charles talk of his yearly turtle feast," Mary wrote. He "borrowed" the Monday as well as that Saturday and he and Mary had a memorable trip to Cambridge.

One day in 1804 a young Oxford student by the name of Thomas De Quincey made a trip to London with the purpose of meeting the author of a play, *John Woodvil,* which he had picked up the year before in a bookshop in Oxford. Most fortunately he wrote many years afterwards the account of the visit, and the rich experiences of a single day have seldom been read with as much enjoyment by so many admirers of both the subject described and the author.*

"But first let me describe my brief introductory call upon him at the India House. I had been told that he was never to be

---

* *The Collected Writings of Thomas De Quincey,* edited by David Masson, Vol. III.

found at home except in the evenings; and to have called then
would have been, in a manner, forcing myself upon his hospitalities, and at a moment when he might have confidential friends
about him; besides that, he was sometimes tempted away to the
theatres. I went, therefore, to the India House; made inquiries
amongst the servants; and, after some trouble (for *that* was early
in his Leadenhall Street career, and possibly he was not much
known), I was shown into a small room, or else a small section
of a large one (thirty-four years affects one's remembrance of
some circumstances), in which was a very lofty writing-desk,
separated by a still higher railing from that part of the floor on
which the profane—the laity, like myself—were allowed to approach the *clerus,* or clerkly rulers of the room. Within the railing sat, to the best of my remembrance, six quill-driving gentlemen; not gentlemen whose duty or profession it was merely to
drive the quill, but who were then driving it—*gens de plume,*
such *in esse,* as well as *in posse*—in act as well as habit; for, as if
they supposed me a spy sent by some superior power to report
upon the situation of affairs as surprised by me, they were all
too profoundly immersed in their oriental studies to have any
sense of my presence. Consequently, I was reduced to a necessity
of announcing myself and my errand. I walked, therefore, into
one of the two open doorways of the railing, and stood closely
by the high stool of him who occupied the first place within the
little aisle. I touched his arm, by way of recalling him from his
lofty Leadenhall speculations to this sublunary world; and, presenting my letter, asked if that gentleman (pointing to the address) were really a citizen of the present room; for I had been
repeatedly misled, by the directions given me, into wrong rooms.
The gentleman smiled; it was a smile not to be forgotten. This
was Lamb. And here occurred a *very, very* little incident—one
of those which pass so fugitively that they are gone and hurry-
ing away into Lethe almost before your attention can have ar-

rested them; but it was an incident which to me, who happened to notice it, served to express the courtesy and delicate consideration of Lamb's manners. The seat upon which he sat was a very high one; so absurdly high, by the way, that I can imagine no possible use or sense in such an altitude, unless it were to restrain the occupant from playing truant at the fire by opposing Alpine difficulties to his descent.

"Whatever might be the original purpose of this aspiring seat, one serious dilemma arose from it, and this it was which gave the occasion to Lamb's act of courtesy. . . . Now, in this situation of Lamb's, the act of descending from his throne, a very elaborate process, with steps and stages analogous to those on horseback—of slipping your right foot out of the stirrup, throwing your leg over the crupper, &c.—was, to all intents and purposes, the same thing as dismounting from a great elephant of a horse. Therefore it both was, and was felt to be by Lamb, supremely ludicrous. On the other hand, to have sat still and stately upon this aerial station, to have bowed condescendingly from this altitude, would have been—not ludicrous indeed; performed by a very superb person and supported by a superb bow, it might have been vastly fine, and even terrifying to many young gentlemen under sixteen; but it would have had an air of ungentlemanly assumption. Between these extremes, therefore, Lamb had to choose;—between appearing ridiculous himself for a moment, by going through a ridiculous evolution which no man could execute with grace; or, on the other hand, appearing lofty and assuming, in a degree which his truly humble nature (for he was the humblest of men in the pretensions which he put forward for himself) must have shrunk from with horror. Nobody who knew Lamb can doubt how the problem was solved: he began to dismount instantly; and, as it happened that the very first *round* of his descent obliged him to turn his back upon me as if for a sudden purpose of flight, he had an excuse for laughing; which he did heartily—saying, at the same time something to this effect: that I must not judge from first appearances; that he should revolve upon me; that he was not going to fly; and other facetiæ, which challenged a general laugh from the clerical brotherhood.

"When he had reached the basis of *terra firma* on which I was standing, naturally, as a mode of thanking him for his courtesy, I presented my hand; which, in a general case, I should certainly not have done; for I cherished, in an ultra-English degree, the English custom (a wise custom) of bowing in frigid silence on a first introduction to a stranger; but, to a man of literary talent, and one who had just practised so much kindness in my favour at so probable a hazard to himself of being laughed at for his pains, I could not maintain that frosty reserve. Lamb took my hand; did not absolutely reject it: but rather repelled my advance by his manner. This, however, long afterwards I found, was only a habit derived from his too great sensitiveness to the variety of people's feelings, which run through a gamut so infinite of degrees and modes as to make it unsafe for any man who respects himself to be too hasty in his allowances of familiarity. Lamb had, as he was entitled to have, a high self-respect; and me he probably suspected (as a young Oxonian) of some aristocratic tendencies. The letter of introduction, containing (I imagine) no matters of business, was speedily run through; and I instantly received an invitation to spend the evening with him. Lamb was not one of those who catch at the chance of escaping from a bore by fixing some distant day, when accidents (in duplicate proportion, perhaps, to the number of intervening days) may have carried you away from the place: he sought to benefit by no luck of that kind; for he was, with his limited income—and I say it deliberately—positively the most hospitable man I have known in this world. That night, the same night, I was to come and spend the evening with him. I

had gone to the India House with the express purpose of accept-
ing whatever invitation he should give me; and, therefore, I
accepted this, took my leave, and left Lamb in the act of resuming his aerial position."

De Quincey continued the vivid description with a report of
the evening at the Lambs' where he met Mary and liked her at
once and where Lamb mystified him and annoyed him by pointing out defects in the poetry of Wordsworth and Coleridge and
made little of their virtues. Especially was De Quincey irritated
by what he considered Lamb's sacrilegious treatment of "The
Ancient Mariner." He went away with a feeling of coolness,
relieved only by the "winning goodness of Miss Lamb." However, not long after this first meeting, De Quincey came to have
a great admiration for Lamb and to realise that on that first
evening he, a more seasoned but not less sympathetic critic,
was really having fun with the young enthusiast from Oxford.

Naturally there were times when Lamb felt the grind. He
had his own slight indispositions, there was always anxiety about
Mary, and he wanted to have more time to read and write. He
wrote to Wordsworth: "If I do but get rid of auditing Ware-
house-keepers Acc^{ts}. and get no worse-harassing task in the
place of it, what a Lord of Liberty I shall be. I shall dance and
skip and make mouths at the invisible event, and pick the thorns
out of my pillow and throw 'em at rich men's night caps, and
talk blank verse, hoity toity, and sing 'A Clerk I was in London
Gay,' ban, ban, Ca-Caliban, like the emancipated monster, and
go where I like, up this street or down that ally. Adieu, and
pray that it may be my luck."*

Ten years later came the great surprise and release, so faithfully described in the Elia essay, "The Superannuated Man":
"Independently of the rigours of attendance, I have ever been
haunted with a sense (perhaps a mere caprice) of incapacity for
business. This, during my latter years, had increased to such a

---

* August 1815.

degree, that it was visible in all the lines of my countenance. My health and my good spirits flagged. I had perpetually a dread of some crisis, to which I should be found unequal. Besides my daylight servitude, I served over again all night in my sleep, and would awake with terrors of imaginary false entries, errors in my accounts, and the like. I was fifty years of age, and no prospect of emancipation presented itself. I had grown to my desk, as it were; and the wood had entered into my soul.

"My fellows in the office would sometimes rally me upon the trouble legible in my countenance; but I did not know that it had raised the suspicions of any of my employers, when, on the 5th of last month, a day ever to be remembered by me, L——, the junior partner in the firm, calling me on one side, directly taxed me with my bad looks, and frankly enquired the cause of them. So taxed, I honestly made confession of my infirmity, and added that I was afraid I should eventually be obliged to resign his service. He spoke some words of course to hearten me, and there the matter rested. A whole week I remained labouring under the impression that I had acted imprudently in my disclosure; that I had foolishly given a handle against myself, and had been anticipating my own dismissal. A week passed in this manner, the most anxious one, I verily believe, in my whole life, when on the evening of the 12th of April, just as I was about quitting my desk to go home (it might be about eight o'clock), I received an awful summons to attend the presence of the whole assembled firm in the formidable back parlour. I thought, now my time is surely come, I have done for myself, I am going to be told that they have no longer occasion for me. L——, I could see, smiled at the terror I was in, which was a little relief to me,— when to my utter astonishment B——, the eldest partner, began a formal harangue to me on the length of my services, my very meritorious conduct during the whole of the time (the deuce, thought I, how did he find out that? I protest I never had the confidence to think as much). He went on to descant on the expediency of retiring at a certain time of life (how my heart panted!), and asking me a few questions as to the amount of my own property, of which I have a little, ended with a proposal, to which his three partners nodded a grave assent, that I should accept from the house, which I had served so well, a pension for life to the amount of two-thirds of my accustomed salary—a magnificent offer! I do not know what I answered between surprise and gratitude, but it was understood that I accepted their proposal, and I was told that I was free from that hour to leave their service. I stammered out a bow, and at just ten minutes after eight I went home—for ever. This noble benefit—gratitude forbids me to conceal their names—I owe to the kindness of the most munificent firm in the world—the house of Boldero, Merryweather, Bosanquet, and Lacy."

It was a natural reaction that Lamb's first feeling of freedom "of being let loose after a forty years' confinement" should give way to a longing for the old routine, his fellow clerks and the old ways. There were deprivations. Now he had to buy his own paper and quill pens; he had used scraps of waste paper for his letters and for many years the House had paid postage for personal mail, both incoming and outgoing. And it did not seem unethical for some of his friends to profit from this custom. Coleridge, one of the recipients of this favour, wrote to Rickman, secretary to the Speaker of the House of Commons, "The East India House has very politely made me a present thro' Mr. Charles Lamb, an *Eminent* in the Indian service, of a hundred or so of pens," and suggested that the House of Commons might supplement this with a gift of sealing wax. Letters intended for Coleridge, Wordsworth and other friends were addressed to Lamb(e)—the added "e" used for identification. It would be interesting to speculate on the gain to literature of this graft on the privileges of the East India House!

That "confinement" had meant much to him and he did not

fail to acknowledge its benefits. He had seen some of his friends without regular habits of daily work and what they were making—or not making—of their lives. It might have saved Coleridge from the decline which set in so early, if he could have had the steadying influence of a daily bit of work, and even Wordsworth, who has been pictured as living an ideal life in the Lake District, might have led a richer and more purposeful existence if he had been more closely associated with people and more accustomed to find a ready piece of work at hand.

Lamb's salary at the India House for the first two years was no pay, with a gratuity of £30 for each of the two years, then £40 per year, then £70, then £80 until 1814 when there was a sudden increase from about £240 to £480. It rose to £700 in 1821 and was £730 in 1825, with a purchasing power of probably three times what it would be today. That was a very respectable salary with the conditions of pension, holidays and general good standing which Lamb had with the Company. But he would have been the superhuman being that some persons have tried to describe him if he had not occasionally felt the grind of the office, "the desk that had worn into his soul."

An indication of the regard in which Lamb was held by the India House is to be found in the minutes of the Court of Directors for March 29, 1825: "That the resignation of Mr. Charles Lamb of the Accountant-General's Office, on account of certified ill-health, be accepted, and, it appearing that he has served the Company faithfully for 33 years . . . he be allowed a pension of £450 . . . per annum." As a lasting testimonial the portrait by Henry Meyer, done in the spring of 1826, "the little dark gentleman in knee-breeches with a fine Titian head, full of dumb eloquence," which many persons considered the best, hangs in the India office in Whitehall today commemorating "if not the most assiduous of its clerks, the one who covered its official writing paper with the best and tenderest literature."

5

And Friends

At Christ's Hospital Lamb revealed a characteristic which developed with the years, a capacity for friendship. Boys whom he met there became attached to him for life, and one, Coleridge, an intimate friend almost without a break in the relationship. Lamb was especially attractive to young men and only a few weeks before his death he was sought out by a young Cambridge University student, Fuller Russell, who wrote of an afternoon spent with Lamb at Enfield and has left a delightful account of the occasion. Qualities of open-mindedness, tolerance, humour and sympathy were so strong in his character that a friendship once formed lasted. Brief sketches of some of his friends in the following pages are sufficient to show the wide range and variety of promise and attainment of those who were proud to call him their friend. It was a great tribute to the idea of friendship. The relationship was not based on a mere liking for literature. Tastes were varied. Whenever one came who was sincere, without pose or affectation, he found a place. No one who could boast merely of money or position was welcome. The qualities of Lamb were admirably supplemented by those of Mary, who often furnished the spark to enkindle the fire of a continuing friendship. Although Charles Lamb was a man's man, he was proud of friendship with women, who were welcome to the circle not alone because they were congenial to Mary. Lamb liked them too—Dorothy Wordsworth, Sarah Stoddard, afterwards Mrs. William Hazlitt, Fanny Kelly, Mary

Hutchinson, Mary Shelley, Louisa Holcroft and Victoria Novello Clarke. It is difficult to think of another English writer
who had bound to him so many men and women of such varied
qualities and attainments.

Of his distinguished contemporaries in literary achievement,
besides Coleridge and Wordsworth and in addition to those
more fully described in the following pages, Lamb knew more
or less intimately Richard Brinsley Sheridan the dramatist;
John Keats the poet; William Harrison Ainsworth the novelist;
Thomas De Quincey; Thomas Holcroft, dramatist and author
of *The Road to Ruin;* James Sheridan Knowles, dramatist and
author of the famous play, *Virginius;* William Hone, whose
Every-Day Book, Table Book and *Year Book* were widely circu-
lated; Walter Savage Landor; Thomas Love Peacock; and the
American poet, Nathaniel Parker Willis. He saw Shelley once,
met Walter Scott once at breakfast, Christopher North at an
inn (and was delighted to discover that the great Scotchman
liked porter, too), and Thomas Moore and Samuel Rogers at a
famous dinner given by Thomas Monkhouse.

The sketches that follow are arranged in the order in which
each person described met Charles Lamb, as nearly as may be
discovered.

ROBERT SOUTHEY

Of the three poets with whom Lamb was intimately associated, Coleridge, Wordsworth and Southey, the last is in some
ways the most interesting. Southey was born in Bristol only a
few months before Charles Lamb. His father was an unsuccessful linendraper, his mother a despotic person who seemed to
have no great affection for her family. Young Robert was sent
to the Westminster School, and on to Oxford through the help
of his uncle. He intended to take up law after the University

but an interest in literature, especially Shakespeare, Beaumont and Fletcher, *The Faerie Queene,* and translations of Ariosto and Tasso, led him to an enthusiasm for writing, especially romances. Carried away by the French Revolution, he began an epic on Joan of Arc, which was published in 1796. For almost fifty years he read and wrote continuously and furiously. As a result, there was a quantity of writing so great and so varied that probably only a small part of his romances, plays, poems and reviews will ever be reprinted. However, much in his works was better than second-rate, and the quality of his prose has not been exceeded. Byron's verdict that "Southey's prose is perfect," in the sense that it is simple and sound, has not been contradicted.

Southey met Coleridge in June 1794 and early in the next year he was introduced by him to Lamb, who was then twenty years old. Meantime events had happened in the relations between Southey and Coleridge. Both became interested in a scheme to establish a community on the banks of the Susquehanna River, near Philadelphia. The members of the Pantisocracy, the name given to their Utopia, were to earn their living by tilling the soil, while their wives were to look after the homes and children. Coleridge and Southey brought Robert Lovell into the scheme and the three married sisters; Lovell married Mary Fricker, Coleridge, Sara, and Southey, Edith. The enterprise failed before it left the shores of England, and the relationship among the men had no more tangible results of an idealistic nature.

After wandering from place to place on the continent, especially in Portugal, Southey returned to England and, influenced by Coleridge, who had come to know Wordsworth, settled at Keswick in the Lake District. So Greta Hall became his home for the rest of his life. He gathered about him a large library, rare manuscripts and material on Portuguese and Spanish history, which was not exceeded in quantity and value by any other library in England. Although it became an almost ideal home for a man of letters, poet and critic, it witnessed great sadness in the death of his son Herbert in 1816, from which shock Southey really never recovered, and later in the death of his daughter Edith. His last years were cast in deepest gloom by the insanity of his wife and finally his own, from which in 1843 he was fortunately relieved by death.

Lamb's friendship with Southey, beginning in 1795, lasted until the end of Lamb's life with no estrangement, except on one occasion. The letters which we have from Lamb to Southey (we have only one of those which Southey must have written to Lamb) number only twenty-three. There is reason to believe there must have been other letters, especially before 1798. The first are of that year and the numbers in successive years attest the relative intimacy of the relationship: in 1798, eight; in 1799, six; in 1804, 1814, 1815, 1818, 1823, 1825, 1830 and 1833, there is only one letter for each year except 1830, when there are two. All these letters are interesting and important. The first two years of letters, 1798 and 1799, follow the two years in which Lamb's letters are almost entirely to Coleridge. For this period Southey took Coleridge's place as the one to whom he wrote intimately. After 1800 there was never the same degree of friendship, although each continued his admiration for the other.

The first letters show the sympathetic and critical spirit which marked his frank discussion of Southey's work. Lamb was already a mature critic, and when we realise that he was only twenty-three and that his reading had all been on his own account, and not the required reading of a university, we cannot fail to get the measure of Lamb's reading powers and critical genius. He wrote what he thought, selecting words and lines in Southey's writing for which he suggested improvement. Probably there exists nowhere more intelligent criticism, criticism which does not lose itself in philosophical theorising and speculation, than is to be found in these letters to Southey. They reveal a continuous interest in the affairs of Southey and his family. Each has something of a personal nature or some favourite story or shows some trait of Lamb. "I was at Hazlitt's marriage, and had liked to have been turned out several times during the ceremony. Any thing awful makes me laugh. I misbehaved once at a funeral. Yet I can read about these ceremonies with pious and proper feelings."

Reference has been made to the one break in the friendship between Lamb and Southey. Southey wrote a review of a work by Grégoire on Deism in France. The article, with the title "Progress of Infidelity," appeared in the *Quarterly Review* for January 1823. It contained this passage: "Unbelievers have not always been honest enough thus to express their real feelings: but this we know concerning them, that when they have renounced their birthright of hope, they have not been able to divest themselves of fear. From the nature of the human mind this might be presumed, and in fact it is so. They may deaden the heart and stupefy the conscience, but they cannot destroy the imaginative faculty. There is a remarkable proof of this in 'Elia's Essays,' a book which wants only a sounder religious feeling to be as delightful as it is original."

This criticism by Southey would hardly seem to have justified Lamb's heavy castigation, but, remembering the temper which existed among the journals of that day, we have reason to believe that his anger was directed largely toward Christopher North. His quarrel with the *Quarterly* had begun in 1811 when, in a review of the works of the dramatist Ford, edited by Weber, Lamb was described as a "poor maniac." Later he was humiliated by the treatment which his review of Wordsworth's *Excursion* received, and on several other occasions his patience had been strained to the uttermost.

Before Lamb had read the offending article, but only heard of it, he was disposed to treat it with that silence which would have been dignified. On the tenth of July he wrote Bernard Barton:

"Southey has attacked Elia on the score of infidelity in the Quarterly article, 'Progress of Infidels.' I had not, nor have, seen the Monthly. He might have spared an old friend such a construction of a few careless flights, that meant no harm to religion. If all his UNGUARDED expressions on the subject were to be corrected——

"but I love and respect Southey—and will not retort. I HATE HIS REVIEW, and his being a Reviewer."

But Lamb changed his mind and for the October *London* wrote his long "Letter of Elia to Robert Southey, Esquire," which, on the whole in tone and text, was not worthy of him. He even, and unfortunately, tried to turn the tables on Southey by citing his "unguarded expressions" in ballads of his younger days. That Lamb later was none too proud of this performance is shown by the fact that he included only the concluding paragraphs in the Second Series of *Elia,* as the essay called "The Tombs in the Abbey."

In the letter Lamb mentioned some of his best friends, Talfourd, Wainewright, Cary, Allan Cunningham, Allsop, Gillman, Coleridge, Wordsworth, Monkhouse, Robinson, with especial approbation of Leigh Hunt and Hazlitt whom Southey had treated with considerable harshness.

The publication of this letter produced a sensation in literary circles. Christopher North in *Blackwood's* asked of Lamb, "What is this you are doing? Mr. Southey, having read your *Essays,* wished to pay you a compliment. . . . And with this eulogy you are not only dissatisfied but so irate at the Laureate, that nothing will relieve your bile, but a Letter to the Doctor of seven good pages in 'The London.' "

The *Times* rose to Lamb's defence. The letter, it said, "treats the Laureate with that contempt which his always candid and frequently malignant spirit deserves. When it is considered that Mr. Lamb has been the best friend of Southey, and is besides of particularly kind and peaceable nature, it is evident that nothing but gross provocation could have aroused him to this public declaration of his disgust."

But Southey himself had no relish for controversy with his "best friend." Nothing could have been more generous than his reply, in a letter dated November 19, 1823.

"On Monday I saw your letter in the *London Magazine*, which I had not before had an opportunity of seeing, and I now take the first interval of leisure for replying to it.

"Nothing could be further from my mind than any intention or apprehension of any way offending or injuring a man concerning whom I have never spoken, thought, or felt otherwise than with affection, esteem, and admiration.

"If you had let me know in any private or friendly manner that you felt wounded by a sentence in which nothing but kindness was intended—or that you found it might injure the sale of your book—I would most readily and gladly have inserted a note in the next *Review* to qualify and explain what had hurt you.

"You have made this impossible, and I am sorry for it. But I will not engage in controversy with you to make sport for the Philistines.

"The provocation must be strong indeed that can rouse me to do this, even with an enemy. And if you can forgive an unintended offence as heartily as I do the way in which you have resented it, there will be nothing to prevent our meeting as we have heretofore done, and feeling towards each other as we have always been wont to do.

"Only signify a correspondent willingness on your part, and send me your address, and my first business next week shall be to reach your door, and shake hands with you and your sister. Remember me to her most kindly and believe me—Yours, with unabated esteem and regard."

Lamb's prompt response to this did him credit:

"The kindness of your note has melted away the mist which was upon me. I have been fighting against a shadow. That accursed 'Quarterly Review' had vexed me by a gratuitous speaking, of its own knowledge, that the 'Confessions of a Drunkard' was a genuine description of the state of the writer. Little things, that are not ill meant, may produce much ill. *That* might have injured me alive and dead. I am in a public office, and my life is insured. I was prepared for anger, and I thought I saw, in a few obnoxious words, a hard case of repetition directed against me. I wished both magazine and review at the bottom of the sea. I shall be ashamed to see you, and my sister (though innocent) will be still more so; for the folly was done without her knowledge, and has made her uneasy ever since. My guardian angel was absent at that time.

"I will muster up courage to see you, however, any day next week (Wednesday excepted). We shall hope that you will bring Edith with you. That will be a second mortification. She will hate to see us; but come and heap embers. We deserve it; I for what I've done, and she for being my sister.

"Do come early in the day, by sun-light, that you may see my *Milton.*

"I am at Colebrook Cottage, Colebrook Row, Islington. A detached whitish house, close to the New River, end of Colebrook Terrace, left hand from Sadler's Wells.

"Will you let me know the day before?
"Your penitent
"C. LAMB.

"P. S. I do not think your handwriting at all like Hunt's. I do not think many things I did think."

That thereafter Lamb and Southey remained good friends is

attested by two incidents. When Lamb's *Album Verses* were published in 1830, Southey sent to the *Times* lines addressed to Lamb, of which the following are best remembered:

> Charles Lamb, to those who know thee justly dear
> For rarest genius, and for sterling worth,
> Unchanging friendship, warmth of heart sincere,
> And wit that never gave an ill thought birth,
> Nor ever in its sport infix'd a sting;
> To us who have admired and loved thee long,
> It is a proud as well as pleasant thing
> To hear thy good report, now borne along
> Upon the honest breath of public praise.

And when, in 1835, Moxon began the collection of Lamb's work, Barron Field suggested Southey as the best editor to put it all together.

THOMAS POOLE

Thomas Poole was Coleridge's close friend and benefactor, and in various ways was of great service to English writers of his day. He lived near Bristol and made it possible for Coleridge to take the cottage near him at Nether Stowey. Through Coleridge Lamb became acquainted with Poole, and the two became friends. The few letters to him have to do chiefly with the publication of Coleridge's poems which Lamb was assisting to publish. To Coleridge, Lamb once wrote, "The names of Tom Poole, of Wordsworth and his good sister, with thine and Sara's are become 'familiar in my mouth as household words.'"

WALTER WILSON

Walter Wilson was with Lamb at the East India House. He became a bookseller, inherited some money from John Walter of

the *Times,* and later bought a share of that paper. The few letters to Wilson which are still preserved date from 1801. In one
of them Lamb, probably more candidly than in any other letter,
asks Wilson's forgiveness for being drunk. Almost twenty years
passed before the next extant letter was written, a vivid exposition of the skill of Defoe as a writer of narrative, recording a
lifelong devotion to his work. For the next few years Wilson
was apparently working on the life and works of Defoe and
there must have been some considerable exchange of letters between the two. However, we have only seven letters during that
period. The Defoe publication in three volumes was of superior
quality and became a permanent contribution to the critical
work on the Eighteenth Century. Lamb commented to Wilson,
"It must have interest to divert Mary away so long from her
modern novels." Some personal recollections of Wilson's are in
existence, especially a character sketch of Lamb written in 1836,
giving a side of Lamb of which we have no account elsewhere.

"The propensity of my friend to fun and frolic, would occasionally bring him into scrapes; and his harmless sports termi-
nated sometimes otherwise than he intended. Of some such I
have been myself an eye-witness. But every one knew that there
was not a particle of malignity in his composition; and I am not
aware that any one ever cherished the least feeling of animosity
towards him. Indeed, the reverse of this I have known to be the
case, as soon as the unlucky sufferer had time to recover from his
surprise. He was a good judge of human character, and could
discriminate between the excellencies and the weaknesses that
reside in the same individual. It was one of his leading characteristics to shoot folly as it flies, and his habitual readiness enabled him to grasp the fitting occasion for discharging his arrows
of wit and ridicule, although more in the way of harmless
mirth than of caustic severity. Cheerfulness was a predominant
feature in his character; and he was desirous of imparting that

feeling to others which contributed so materially to his own happiness. He had an instinctive desire for life, and I have heard him say, in his own strong language, when a young man, that he would rather live on board the gallies than not to live at all. He possessed more refinement of mind than of manners, and was ever ready to make ample amends for his indiscretions. In the hilarity of the moment he would sometimes play off his jokes upon his own friends, who knew him too well to take umbrage at such things. . . .

"Some of his frolics, however, were of a more dangerous description. I remember going with him by water upon a party of pleasure to Richmond, accompanied by some of our mutual acquaintances. Upon our return to town, after roaming about the delightful scenery of the neighbourhood, those in the boat found the utmost difficulty in restraining him from the performance of some of his accustomed gambols. Not satisfied with sporting his wit, he was for giving it [vent] by those bodily movements that were quite unsuited to so unsteady a conveyance in the watery element. The consequence was that the boat was within a hair's-breadth of being upset; and if none of us had received any other injury than a ducking I believe he was the only one who would have viewed it in the nature of a sport. He had placed us all, however, in imminent peril; and the contemplation of it after our escape was anything but satisfactory. Availing myself of the privilege of a friend, I wrote to him a letter of remonstrance upon his conduct, descanting at the same time upon some other matters in amicable debate between us. Like the late Rowland Hill, he could not restrain his wit, even upon the most solemn subjects. This I considered offensive, and expressed myself accordingly. His reply, which I have still by me, was just such as might be expected from a right-minded person, whose heart also was in its right place. Characterized by simplicity, by good feeling, and by an excellent judgment, it was calculated to produce all the effect he could desire, and which it did produce. Our friendship did not suffer a momentary inter- ruption; nor am I conscious that so much as an angry word ever passed between us. I always found him the same kind single- hearted creature, and now look back upon our early intercourse with unmixed pleasure and satisfaction."

GEORGE DYER

George Dyer, the son of a watchman, was born in 1755, and so was twenty years older than Lamb. Through the assistance of some generous ladies he was entered at Christ's Hospital where he remained until the age of nineteen. He became a Grecian and went on to Emmanuel College, Cambridge, with a good knowl- edge of Latin and Greek, and acquired a reputation for liking old books and old clothes. He took his degree in 1778 and became an usher in a school at Dedham and later directed an academy at Northampton. He spent some years as tutor of the children of Robert Robinson and wrote his biography, which Wordsworth, for reasons which are not apparent to us, considered one of the best English biographies. At Northampton, when he was thirty- six, Dyer and John Clarke fell in love with the same lady. The two suitors remained friends and many years later John's son, Cowden Clarke, wrote, "When my father died, George Dyer asked for a private conference with me, told me of his youthful attachment for my mother, and inquired whether her circum- stances were comfortable, because in case, as a widow, she had not been left well off, he meant to offer her his hand. Hearing that in point of money she had no cause of concern, he begged me to keep secret what he had confided to me, and he himself never made farther allusion to the subject."

In 1792, the year in which Lamb began work at the East India House, Dyer went to London and took rooms at Clifford's Inn.

Here he stayed for almost fifty years, as Lamb said, "like a dove in the asp's nest"—for lawyers lived at Clifford's Inn. Talfourd speaks of Dyer's "gaunt, awkward form, set off by trousers too short," his "rusty coat" and "straggling hair." Ainger described him as shortsighted and absent-minded, with "the kindest heart and simplest manner imaginable." His poetry was limping, but his prose was acceptable and he turned out countless articles, reviews, biographies for periodicals, pamphlets on religious questions and everything which was original in the one hundred and forty volumes of Valpy's editions of the classics. If there was ever a literary hack, Dyer was the man.

Some well-confirmed stories of his absent-mindedness have come down to us, such as his making tea for breakfast by emptying his snuffbox into the teapot. The publisher Ollier relates that "once when Dyer had been spending the evening at Leigh Hunt's house in Hampstead Heath, he came back a quarter of an hour after leaving. . . . 'What is the matter?' asked Hunt. 'I think, sir,' said Dyer, . . . 'I think I have left one of my shoes behind me.' He had indeed shuffled it off under the table and had not discovered his loss until he had gone a long way." Mary Lamb and Sarah Hazlitt planned to surprise Dyer by mending his arm-chair, which had a hundred holes in it. They sewed up the holes. Dyer's horror may be imagined when it was recorded that every hole held a book.

Quite characteristic was his cancellation of the first five hundred copies of the first volume of his verse because he discovered that on the first page of the sixty-five-page preface he had started with a statement of criticism which was fundamentally wrong. He would listen to no arguments to the contrary; the preface must come out. "It's of great consequence that the world is not misled."

In November 1823, Dyer made the memorable call on Mary Lamb described by Charles in his letter to Mrs. William Hazlitt, and the genesis of the Elia essay "Amicus Redivivus."

"Yesterday week George Dyer called upon us, at one o'clock *(bright noon day)* on his way to dine with Mrs. Barbauld at Newington. He sat with Mary about half an hour, and took leave. The maid saw him go out from her kitchen window; but suddenly losing sight of him, ran up in a fright to Mary. G. D., instead of keeping the slip that leads to the gate, had deliberately, staff in hand, in broad open day, marched into the New River. He had not his spectacles on, and you know his absence. Who helped him out, they can hardly tell; but between 'em they got him out, drenched thro' and thro'. A mob collected by that time and accompanied him in. 'Send for the Doctor!' they said: and a one-eyed fellow, dirty and drunk, was fetched from the Public House at the end, where it seems he lurks, for the sake of picking up water practice, having formerly had a medal from the Humane Society for some rescue. By his advice, the patient was put between blankets; and when I came home at four to dinner, I found G. D. a-bed, and raving, light-headed with the brandy-and-water which the doctor had administered. He sung, laughed, whimpered, screamed, babbled of guardian angels, would get up and go home; but we kept him there by force; and by next morning he departed sobered, and seems to have received no injury."

Leigh Hunt described him: "In a word, he was a sort of better-bred Dominie Sampson—a Goldsmith with the genius taken out of him, but the goodness left—an angel of the dusty heaven of bookstalls and the British Museum," and Hazlitt, in that well-known essay "On the Look of a Gentleman," wrote, "God never put a kinder heart into flesh of man than George Dyer's." Crabb Robinson records in his diary: "I became acquainted about this time with George Dyer. He was one of the best preachers, morally, that ever breathed. He would give away his last guinea."

This strange career did not run the usual course. Poor as a young man, he was made comfortable in his later years by a legacy from Lord Stanhope and was invited into matrimony by a very respectable woman who lived in the same building, so that his last years were very happy.

JOHN RICKMAN

John Rickman, son of a retired clergyman, three years older than Charles Lamb, went to Oxford. He became an eminent statistician and the author of the present system of taking the population census in Great Britain. He held the position of clerk assistant at the Table at the House of Commons which, along with that of Speaker's secretary, he occupied for almost forty years. So distinguished was his record that Joseph Hume, the radical, a member of the House of Commons who had so often been in disagreement with Rickman, made this statement: "I am unwilling to allow this vote to pass without expressing my humble approbation of the conduct of the late Mr. Rickman. I have never known a public officer so modest, so unassuming, possessed of such varied knowledge, respecting the affairs of Parliament, yet so ready to afford every information to others."

An inimitable sketch Lamb communicates to Manning: "Himself hugely literate, oppressively full of information in all stuff of conversation, from matter of fact to Xenophon and Plato—can talk Greek with Porson, politics with Thelwall, conjecture with George Dyer, nonsense with me, and anything with anybody: a great farmer, somewhat concerned in an agricultural magazine—reads no poetry but Shakspeare, very intimate with Southey, but never reads his poetry; relishes George Dyer, thoroughly penetrates into the ridiculous wherever found, understands the *first time* (a great desideratum in common minds)— you need never twice speak to him; does not want explanations, translations, limitations, as Professor Godwin does when you make an assertion: *up* to anything, *down* to everything—what-

JOHN RICKMAN
From the portrait by Samuel Bellin
Engraved by S. Lane. Published in 1843

THOMAS MANNING, 1806
From a bust in the possession of the Rev. L. U. Manning
Courtesy New York Public Library Print Room

ever *sapit hominem*. A perfect *man*. . . . If there be any alloy in
my fortune to have met with such a man, it is that he commonly
divides his time between town and country, having some foolish
family ties at Christchurch, by which means he can only glad-
den our London hemisphere with returns of light."*

It is difficult to discover why a man so eminent in his field
and so closely related to distinguished literary figures of his
time, should seem only to flit through the pages like a literary
ghost, without leaving impression. Lamb had praised him generously, Southey had depended upon him for almost forty years,
Coleridge had admired him, but why has he been forgotten?
Lamb wrote to Manning, "His memory will be to me as the
brazen serpent to the Israelites,—I shall look up to it, to keep me
upright and honest." Coleridge called him a "sterling man" and
Talfourd described him as "the sturdiest of jovial companions."

A biography by Orlo Williams, published in recent years, has
done something to make Rickman less of a ghost. The correspondence between Southey and Rickman lasted from 1800 to
1839 and consisted of more than twelve hundred letters, in which
there are long arguments on history, antiquities, political economy, poor laws and general politics. Reading of this correspondence makes us wonder even more why there should be so little of
political news in Lamb's letters and in his associations with his
friends. Since Rickman was not a person to keep silent about
Parliamentary affairs which he knew intimately, Lamb must
have been well informed about politics. Especially in the year
1813, the East India Company was a subject often discussed in
Parliament—for that year we have not a single letter nor the
record of a single conversation on the subject, showing Lamb's
reluctance to write of politics.

So long as Lamb lived in London, Rickman could be depended
upon to make a hand at whist on Wednesday evenings and take

---

* November 1800.

the responsibility of holding in check some of the noisier and more boisterous members of the party.

GEORGE BURNETT

George Burnett, literary worker of "disorderly mind and ill-regulated life," went to Balliol College, Oxford, where he met Robert Southey and the two undergraduates proposed the plan to which Coleridge later gave the name, Pantisocracy. He became a dissenting minister, a medical student at Edinburgh and succeeded George Dyer as tutor in the Stanhope family. He was one of the publisher's hacks, the principal work to his credit being *Specimens of English Prose-Writers* in three volumes. It is probable that Lamb helped Burnett in this enterprise. He was the cause of worry to John Rickman who got him something to do at the Census Office and then found Burnett could not do it. His death in a workhouse affected Charles and Mary very considerably and according to Coleridge in his letter to Crabb Robinson, "overset my dear, most dear, and most excellent friend and heart's sister, Mary Lamb—and her illness has almost overset me."

THOMAS MANNING

Thomas Manning was born in 1772, three years before Lamb, and was the son of a rector of Norfolk. Owing to ill health in early years, he was not able to enjoy the advantages of a school, but studied the classics and mathematics at home with success and became a disciple of Plato. At Cambridge he continued mathematics and published a work on algebra. He passed his examinations but, on account of strong aversion to oaths and tests, left the University without a degree. However, he remained in Cambridge as a private tutor and Lamb met him in 1799. As Lucas points out, his sense of fun and nonsense was quick, and his intelligence and humour were stimulating to Lamb.

The next year the friendship was consummated by presents from Manning of hare and pheasant. Manning visited the Lambs and they in return went to Cambridge and even considered making the trip to Paris while Manning was living there. Brooding over the mysterious Chinese Empire, Manning decided to study the language and arts of the Chinese and to spend time in China. He sailed from England in the spring of 1806, and Lamb wrote wistfully to him, "I am almost sick when I think that such a hold as I had of you is gone."

In China and Tibet, Manning had a series of unusual experiences. After his long adventures in the East he returned at last in 1817. On the way to England he stopped at St. Helena and talked with Napoleon, who in 1803 had given Manning the only passport issued after the war began. Eleven years had wrought many changes in Manning. For instance, he now had a long beard of which he was very proud. He lived in strict retirement, and Barry Cornwall tells of his curious habit of bringing along a few red pepper pods when he was invited to a meal. He never furnished his cottage, possessed only a few chairs, one carpet and a large library of Chinese books.

Lamb called him a man of a thousand, and wrote of him as "of great power, an enchanter almost, far beyond Coleridge or any man in power of impressing." Henry Crabb Robinson did not see it quite that way. "On my walk with Lamb, he spoke with enthusiasm of Manning. Yet this Manning does nothing. He has travelled in China and has been by and from India to Tibet, yet as far as is known, he has written nothing."

There was something of the Oriental in his make-up. Allsop described him in one of his religious moods: "I think few persons had so great a share of Lamb's admiration, for to few did he vouchsafe manifestations of his *very* extraordinary powers. Once, and once only, did I witness an outburst of his *unembodied* spirit, when such was the effect of his more than magnetic, his magic power (learnt was it in Chaldea, or in that sealed continent to which the superhuman knowledge of Zoroaster was conveyed by Confucius, into which he was the first to penetrate with impunity?), that we were all rapt and carried aloft into the seventh heaven. He seemed to see and to convey to us clearly (I had almost said adequately), what was passing in the presence of the Great Disembodied ONE, rather by an intuition or the creation of a new sense than by words. Verily there are *more things on earth than* are dreamt of in our philosophy. I am unwilling to admit the influence this wonderful man had over his auditors, as I cannot at all convey an adequate notion or even image of his extraordinary and very peculiar powers."

Manning left nothing to sustain Lamb's high opinion of him, but he was a good talker and somehow drew from Lamb many of his best letters. Some letters from Manning, fortunately preserved by Lamb, passed after Lamb's death into the care of the Manning family. They were sold at auction in 1900 and printed later in a small volume, edited by P. P. Howe. These letters are in no way striking or unusual beyond revealing his taste, which Lamb humorously commented upon. . . . "My opinion of the second volume of *Lyrical Ballads,* except that I think it is utterly absurd from one end to the other." . . . "I peruse the Coleridgian and Wordsworthian letters. Sheer nonsense, by God!" . . . "I wonder Coleridge (who I know is a poet—I don't know that W. is not) but I'll be damned if that be poetry he has passed upon us in the second volume (—I say I wonder Coleridge can be taken in by such foolish stuff)."

Lamb's letters to Manning are the most varied and delightful and extend over the longest period of any of his letters to any one of his friends. They tell of visits to Cambridge, of varying interests in books, of the doings of Godwin, Coleridge and the

Lloyds. Some of the letters went to Manning in China, and
they are among the best because they tell of things going on
among friends in London, of the *Lyrical Ballads,* of new lodgings, of Lamb's experiences with magazines, of his delight in
the haunts of London, of Mary's illnesses, the plays of Holcroft and Godwin, and all the other incidents of their lives. His
gossip about friends, descriptions of new ones, reports on the
finding of some book that he likes—was there ever better chat-
ter in friendly letters? Lamb liked to tell him of the books and
authors he discovered.

"I am reading Burnet's Own Times. Did you ever read that
garrulous, pleasant history? He tells his story like an old man
past political service, bragging to his sons on winter evenings
of the part he took in public transactions, when his 'old cap was
new.' Full of scandal, which all true history is. No palliatives,
but all the stark wickedness, that actually gives the *momentum*
to national actors. Quite the prattle of age and out-lived importance. Truth and sincerity staring out upon you perpetually
in *alto relievo.* Himself a party man—he makes you a party
man. None of the damned philosophical Humeian indifference, so cold, and unnatural, and inhuman! None of the
damned Gibbonian fine writing, so fine and composite! None
of Mr. Robertson's periods with three members. None of Mr.
Roscoe's sage remarks, all so apposite, and coming in so clever,
lest the reader should have had the trouble of drawing an
inference...."*

"I am afraid 'tis the reading of Chaucer has misled you; his
foolish stories about Cambuscan and the ring, and the horse of
brass. Believe me, there's no such things, 'tis all the poet's
invention; but if there were such *darling* things as old Chaucer
sings, I would *up* behind you on the Horse of Brass, and frisk
off for Prester John's Country. But these are all tales; a Horse

* March 1800.

of Brass never flew, and a King's daughter never talked with Birds!"*

William Godwin, famous as a political and miscellaneous writer, was born in 1756 and was therefore nineteen years older than Charles Lamb. Young Godwin grew up with a tender affection for his mother but with little regard for his father, who died when William was young. He was educated at Hoxton Academy and was intended for the Non-Conformist ministry. For five years he served as a minister in a Non-Conformist church. He had an ultimate faith that the only salvation for the world was the complete disappearance of all institutions—political, social and religious. He planned to begin reform in London, but it was to be peaceful, as his radicalism was philosophical and contemplated calm discussion without violence as the proper way to effect change. In 1793, Godwin produced his first important book, *Enquiry Concerning Political Justice.* This work exercised a profound influence on the thought of the early Nineteenth Century and ranks along with such books as Milton's *Areopagitica,* Locke's *Essay Concerning Human Understanding,* Rousseau's *Emile* and Tom Paine's *Rights of Man.* Believing in the perfectability of the race, he was opposed to laws which restricted one's property or one's habits of life. Marriage was the worst of all laws and property was the worst of all possessions. In 1794, Godwin published his novel *Caleb Williams,* still with an interest possessed by not a half-dozen books of that day.

In 1797, Godwin married Mary Wollstonecraft, a woman of Irish extraction whose character seemed directly opposite to his own. She and her two sisters were all clever women but with

---

* February 1803.

few opportunities for culture. Although Godwin seems to have had about as little passion as any human being, he had a sincere affection for his wife. Both held the same views regarding the "slavery" of marriage and went through the ceremony only for the sake of possible offspring. On the death of his wife only a few months after a formal marriage he was left with an infant daughter, Mary, later known to the world as the wife of the poet Shelley, and an illegitimate daughter, Fanny, who claimed Imlay for her father. In 1801, Godwin married Mary Clairmont, a widow with two children, a son and Mary Jane, who called herself Claire and became the mistress of Lord Byron and the mother of Allegra. This Mrs. Godwin was an energetic and harsh stepmother, and was not liked by Lamb, who once wrote, "Mrs. Godwin grows every day in disfavour with God and man."

Godwin's influence was chiefly upon the intellectuals of his time. His claim, and it was perhaps justly held, was that he was the first anarchist, before anarchism suggested violence. The only standard which he admitted was the development of the individual by reason and liberty, hence the general welfare of the community. For a number of years Godwin was a marked figure in London society; there was hardly a person of prominence whom he did not know. Fortunately in early life he began to make a daily record which he continued for almost a half-century. That diary is now of greater interest and more read than any part of his one-time popular novels or quite revolutionary writings.

Coleridge, probably about 1800, brought Lamb and Godwin together. The two never became very intimate or sympathetic friends, but they were closely associated for the rest of their lives and some of Lamb's writing was done at the suggestion of Godwin and his wife. We have about a dozen letters with interesting comments on Godwin's play *Antonio* for which Lamb

71910

wrote the epilogue. When produced, the play failed notably, "damned with universal consent," Lamb wrote on the playbill which is preserved, and now is chiefly remembered by Lamb's description of its failure. The letters afford specific directions for the writing of a play from one whose own attempts failed lamentably.

Lamb's letters to Godwin are interesting, but on account of the person to whom they were written they did not have the same whimsical, humorous, human quality without restraint as when he was writing to such friends as Barton, Manning, Dyer, or Coleridge.

Among the people who were attracted to Godwin there were many eccentric characters; some of these gravitated to Lamb. Humorous stories are told of the impression which the "professor," as Lamb often called him, had upon others of the circle. Southey wrote that "one night, Lamb and Fell were at Godwin's when the Philosopher committed the discourtesy of falling asleep; they therefore carried off his brandy, rum, sugar, picked his pockets of everything and made off in triumph."

Coleridge describes a discussion at Godwin's which ended in bad temper, which he attributed to the "grossness and vulgar insanocecity of this dim-headed philosophocide" and to the "glass of punch of most deceitful strength" which Mary Lamb had mixed.

We get this picture of Godwin and his family from a letter from Robert Lloyd to his wife in 1809: "We supped with *Godwin,* and from him I am this moment returned (twelve o'clock). You would, I know, my dear love, have been delighted in beholding his family; he appears to keep no servants, and his children to occupy their places. I was much gratified in seeing the three children of Mrs. Wollstonecraft, two girls and a son. . . . Mrs. Godwin is *not* a pleasant woman, a wife far different from the one you would suppose *such* a man would have selected."

After the failures of Godwin's plays, Godwin became a bookseller and he and his second wife began the publication of books for the young. It was probably Mrs. Godwin who first suggested to Charles and Mary Lamb that they write the *Tales from Shakespear*. At any rate, largely through her persistent efforts, the book was written and published, as well as the *Adventures of Ulysses* by Charles.

Although Godwin in his early life had been a careful manager, for some reason his financial troubles began soon after he became acquainted with Charles Lamb. They went from bad to worse, although they did not grow serious until 1821. Then there was a dispute as to the lease of his house on Skinner Street and after a lawsuit the decision was against Godwin, which forced him to give up the house and go bankrupt. Lamb with his usual thoughtfulness started a subscription to help the Godwin family and topped the list with a contribution of £50.

"Godwin's character was peculiar, and cannot be said to be pleasing." We quote the words of the modern literary historian, George Saintsbury.* "Though regarded (or at least described) by his enemies as an apostle of license, he seems to have been a rather cold-blooded person, whose one passion for Mary Wollstonecraft was at least as much an affair of the head as of the heart. He was decidedly vain, and as decidedly priggish; but the worst thing about him was his tendency to 'sponge'—a tendency which he indulged not merely on his generous son-in-law, Shelley, but on almost everybody with whom he came in contact. It is, however, fair to admit that his tendency (which was probably a legacy of the patronage system) was very widespread at the time; that the mighty genius of Coleridge succumbed to it to a worse extent even than Godwin did; and that Southey himself, who, for general uprightness and independence

---

* *A History of Nineteenth Century Literature (1780-1895)* by George Saintsbury, The Macmillan Co., 1896.

has no superior in literary history, was content for years to live upon the liberality not merely of an uncle, but of a school comrade, in a way which in our own days would probably make men of not half his moral worth seriously uncomfortable."

Though of tremendous influence upon some of his earlier contemporaries, Godwin failed to inspire his immediate friends. There is no reference to him which is highly complimentary. Of all the persons who were associated with Lamb, there was no one with a more outstanding success than Godwin. His philosophical views had been the subject of discussion on the Continent, in England, everywhere in London. His novels had been widely read, and many of the young men of the time hung with bated breath upon the words that dropped from the elder philosopher. Shelley turned to Godwin as his teacher and guide and one of many young men who worshipped at his feet was Bulwer-Lytton whose popular romances were modelled on the works of Godwin, but nowhere in the letters of Lamb or in the diaries of Crabb Robinson do we gain the impression that Godwin was in any degree an eminent person.

One of the best paragraphs in Hazlitt's *Spirit of the Age* describes the passing of Godwin's fame.

"The Spirit of the Age was never more fully shown than in its treatment of this writer—its love of paradox and change, its dastard submission to prejudice and to the fashion of the day. Five-and-twenty years ago he was in the very zenith of a sultry and unwholesome popularity; he blazed as a sun in the firmament of reputation; no one was more talked of, more looked up to, more sought after, and wherever liberty, truth, justice was the theme, his name was not far off:—now he has sunk below the horizon, and enjoys the serene twilight of a doubtful immortality. Mr. Godwin, during his lifetime, has secured to himself the triumphs and the mortifications of an extreme notoriety and of a sort of posthumous fame. His bark, after being tossed

WILLIAM GODWIN

From a drawing by Daniel Maclise

WILLIAM HAZLITT AT THIRTY-FIVE

From an engraving after a miniature by John Hazlitt

in the revolutionary tempest, now raised to heaven by all the fury of popular breath, now almost dashed in pieces, and buried in the quicksands of ignorance, or scorched with the lightning of momentary indignation, at length floats on the calm wave that is to bear it down the stream of time. Mr. Godwin's person is not known, he is not pointed out in the street, his conversation is not courted, his opinions are not asked, he is at the head of no cabal, he belongs to no party in the State, he has no train of admirers, no one thinks it worth his while even to traduce and vilify him, he has scarcely friend or foe, the world makes a point (as Goldsmith used to say) of taking no more notice of him than if such an individual had never existed; he is to all ordinary intents and purposes dead and buried; but the author of *Political Justice* and of *Caleb Williams* can never die, his name is an abstraction in letters, his works are standard in the history of intellect. He is thought of now like any eminent writer a hundred-and-fifty years ago, or just as he will be a hundred-and-fifty years hence."

WILLIAM HAZLITT

At Godwin's house Lamb met William Hazlitt. Holcroft and Coleridge were there that evening and, according to Hazlitt, they were disputing fiercely on the subject, "Man as he is, and man as he ought to be." "Give me," said Lamb, "man as he ought not to be." Thus a friendship began which lasted until the death of Hazlitt in 1830. After Lamb's visit to the Coleridges in 1797 and Hazlitt's visit the following year, it is rather surprising that the meeting of the two was delayed for six or seven years.

Hazlitt's father, a well-known Dissenter, had gone to America to promote the cause of Unitarianism and to find a freer atmosphere for his religious and philosophical belief. Disappointed in not securing a satisfactory charge, the family returned to England and removed to the village of Wem, ten miles from Shrewsbury, where the Reverend Hazlitt ministered to the little Unitarian chapel.

In this retired spot, young William, Charles's junior by three years, spent most of the time between the ages of ten and twenty. Then came the revelation! A new preacher named Coleridge came to Shrewsbury for a trial sermon and spent the night with the elder Hazlitt. Next morning while Coleridge was in the parlour tying his shoelace, he received the letter from Josiah Wedgwood, with the tender of a pension of £150, if he would renounce the ministry, return to Stowey and be a poet. Young Hazlitt's enthusiasm and excitement over the moving sermon of Coleridge at the Shrewsbury chapel has been everlastingly preserved in one of Hazlitt's most charming essays, "My First Acquaintance with the Poets."

When Coleridge left Wem, it was agreed that Hazlitt was to pay him a visit at Nether Stowey. And this Hazlitt prepared to do. The months of waiting were, indeed, long months, but he had his reward, for the trip to Bristol was wonderful— walking, thinking, reading, capped by days at the house of Coleridge and his wife. There was so much to talk about, and to plan for. Coleridge enjoyed his rôle of sage and counsellor, having arrived at the ripe age of twenty-six and Hazlitt at twenty.

The scene has been described by Hazlitt. "The next day Wordsworth arrived from Bristol at Coleridge's cottage. I think I see him now. He answered in some degree to his friend's description of him, but was more gaunt and Don Quixote-like. He was quaintly dressed (according to the *costume* of that unconstrained period) in a brown fustian jacket and striped pantaloons. There was something of a roll, a lounge, in his gait, not unlike his own Peter Bell. There was a severe, worn pressure of thought about his temples, a fire in his eye (as if he saw something in objects more than the outward appearance), an intense high narrow forehead, a Roman nose, cheeks furrowed by strong purpose and feeling, and a convulsive inclination to laughter about the mouth, a good deal at variance with the solemn, stately expression of the rest of his face."

A little later Hazlitt would paint that face—and Coleridge's and Lamb's, too.

Not until 1799 do we hear again of Hazlitt, when Crabb Robinson writes of him in London. "Another interesting acquaintance I made this period was with William Hazlitt.... At our first interview I saw he was an extraordinary man." The admiration was mutual. Hazlitt introduced Robinson to the poems of Wordsworth, Coleridge, Lamb and Southey, and Hazlitt felt repaid by Robinson's words of appreciation, "I shall never cease to have regard for him for he was the first person who found out that there was anything in me."

We have only nine letters written by Lamb to Hazlitt and, with one unimportant exception, all lie between 1806 and 1810. Knowing the close friendship which existed for more than twenty-five years, we would be safe in expecting many more. The letters are most natural. They have much to do with painting and pictures. Hazlitt had discovered for himself that he was not destined to be a first-rate painter, a Claude or a Titian, and therefore, characteristically, he would not be a painter at all. There was the hoax that Charles Lamb and Joseph Hume originated as to the disappearance of Hazlitt—"he had died by his own hand"—a joke in which we can scarcely see much fun, but it seemed to cause no particular annoyance to anybody except to the Reverend Hazlitt. He wrote in distress and Lamb replied in a very frank way, humbly begging forgiveness for what seems now a foolish performance. There are references to Mary's illnesses and to various domestic interests. So these few letters leave the impression of a very happy relationship. Perhaps the one letter which would be the last we would part with is on the birth of Hazlitt's son. "Well, my blessing and heaven's be upon him, and make him like his father, with something a better temper, and a smoother head of hair: and then all the men and women must love him."*

A tribute to fine qualities of both subject and author is the expression of Lamb in the famous public letter to Southey described earlier in this chapter: "What hath soured him [Hazlitt], and made him to suspect his friends of infidelity towards him, when there was no such matter, I know not. I stood well with him for fifteen years (the proudest of my life), and have ever spoke my full mind of him to some, to whom his panegyric must naturally be least tasteful. I never in thought swerved from him, I never betrayed him, I never slackened in my admiration of him, I was the same to him (neither better nor worse) though he could not see it, as in the days when he thought fit to trust me. At this instant, he may be preparing for me some compliment, above my deserts, as he has sprinkled many such among his admirable books, for which I rest his debtor; or, for any thing I know, or can guess to the contrary, he may be about to read a lecture on my weaknesses. He is welcome to them (as he was to my humble hearth), if they can divert a spleen, or ventilate a fit of sullenness. I wish he would not quarrel with the world at the rate he does; but the reconciliation must be effected by himself, and I despair of living to see that day. But, protesting against much that he has written, and some things which he chooses to do; judging him by his conversation which I enjoyed so long, and relished so deeply; or by his books, in those places where no clouding passion intervenes—I should belie my own conscience, if I said less, than that I think W. H. to be, in his natural and healthy state, one of

---

* October 1811.

the wisest and finest spirits breathing. So far from being ashamed of that intimacy, which was betwixt us, it is my boast that I was able for so many years to have preserved it entire; and I think I shall go to my grave without finding, or expecting to find, such another companion."

There was a real affection between Lamb and Hazlitt. Each sought out the other for special occasions. It is common for the two names to be linked together. Lamb was best man, indeed the *only* man, at Hazlitt's wedding, was at the christening of his young son, was probably the last person whom Hazlitt painted before he laid aside the brush, was one of the very few friends who visited the Hazlitts at Winterslow Hut, was the most de-sired companion for an evening at the theatre or art gallery, and from among so many persons whom Hazlitt had known, stood alone at the deathbed to hear him say after a stormy career, "I have had a happy life."

There was similarity between the two men in their circum-stances, as well as striking differences. Both were from families of the middle class, Hazlitt's perhaps of higher standing, where only three survived from a much larger number of children, in Hazlitt's—John, Margaret and William; in Lamb's—John, Mary and Charles. Both grew up in a Unitarian atmosphere; both liked painting, the theatre, good talk and books; both hated cant; both were the subject of much vilification and misrepre-sentation—but they were not exceptions, for it was a time when personal and public abuse were common and much tolerated. Lamb liked people, strove to get their views and was tolerant of their opinions; his friends included many persons who hated one another and despised their opinions. To Hazlitt tolerance was a bugbear. One of his essays carries the title "On the Pleasure of Hating." His readiness to despise was his weakest point. Lamb accepted people and their faults, was looking for the good in people, found some interest in everybody, found great delight in walking the streets of London to see what he could discover in the faces of people in the crowds. "I can never hate any one that I've once seen." Hazlitt required that his friends must be on his side and go all the way with him. Of course, he quarrelled with everybody at one time or another. He managed with a rather dour face to endure Lamb's neutrality because of Lamb's humour and kindness but it went against the grain. He inherited from his dissenting father strong convictions of liberty; his father had been a sympathiser of the American side in the Revolution and had kept his faith in France.

Hazlitt had a fondness for the abstract, and was sought out by Coleridge for philosophical disputation. Lamb was equally fond of the concrete, was unphilosophically minded—to use a homely expression, he had his feet on the ground. Their interests and fields were extensive, although probably Hazlitt covered more. "I have at least glanced over a number of subjects—painting, poetry, prose, plays, politics, Parliamentary speakers, metaphysical lore, books, men and things." Lamb was considerate in what he said of people, speaking nothing cruel, although he did not hesitate to speak the truth. Hazlitt cared little how it hurt; consideration for others' feelings were words not in his vocabulary.

Besides qualities of the mind both men were endowed in great measure. Hazlitt excelled in range, in gusto, in vigour, in the number of brilliant passages, with an almost volcanic enthusiasm, carrying the reader along, but often leaving him not an admirer of the author or his good friend. Lamb excelled in humour, in kindliness, in sympathy, in greater perfection as an artist in the use of language. If Lamb has had more praise than he deserved, Hazlitt has not had his share. For ourselves, we should not want to give up either. The words of W. E. Henley may be the judgement of those who lay some claim to catholicity of taste. "As a writer, therefore, it is with Lamb that I would bracket him. They are dissimilar, but they go gallantly and naturally together—*par mobile fratrum.* Give us these two, with some ripe Cobbett, a volume of Southey, some Wordsworth, certain pages of Shelley, a good deal of the Byron who wrote letters, and we get the right prose of the time. The best of it all, perhaps, is the best of Lamb. But Hazlitt's, for different qualities, is so imminent and shining a second that I hesitate as to the pre-eminency. Probably the race is Lamb's. But Hazlitt is ever Hazlitt; and at his highest moments Hazlitt is hard to beat, and has not these many years been beaten."*

LEIGH HUNT

When Leigh Hunt first met Lamb we do not know, but it was before 1810 when the *Reflector* was founded. Hunt went to Christ's Hospital in 1791; Lamb had left in 1789. The most precious account of that famous school, the teachers, studies, other boys, dress, and food, is to be found in Hunt's autobiography. A better recollection of school days has seldom been written. In comparison with the Elia essay on the same school, the details of the day's routine are doubtless more accurately portrayed by Hunt than by Lamb. Hunt was not actually at the school while Lamb was there, but he wrote of times when he saw Lamb on visits to the school to talk with old friends.

In 1813, Leigh and his brother John, the printer, were sentenced to imprisonment on account of caustic lines in the *Reflector* regarding the Prince of Wales. Although a few weeks before Lamb had written a satire, which Robinson called "capital lines," entitled "The Triumph of the Whale" for Hunt's weekly *Examiner* about the same "Prince of Whales," no action was ever taken against him. Hunt had called the Prince "a

---

* Introduction to *The Collected Works of William Hazlitt,* edited by A. R. Waller and Arnold Glover, 1902.

corpulent man of fifty . . . a violator of his vow, a libertine over head and ears in disgrace, a despiser of domesticities, a companion of gamblers and demireps." After that, it would seem that two years was a short sentence! Hunt was permitted to move into the infirmary of the prison, according to prison regulations of the time. He papered the walls of his two rooms with a trellis of roses, painted the ceilings with sky and clouds, moved in his bookcases and piano and his family, consisting of his wife and his son Thornton. A daughter was born there. He cultivated a small bit of ground which he railed off, and wrote articles for his paper. Lamb said that his quarters had no counterpart except in fairy tales. Whether because Lamb felt partly responsible, after his own words about the Prince, or whether out of mere kindness, Charles and Mary often visited the Hunts in prison. Leigh greatly appreciated this. "They came to comfort me in all weathers, hail or sunshine, in daylight or in darkness, even in the dreadful frost and snow of the beginning of 1814."

Leigh Hunt was one of the most unpopular men of his day, along with William Hazlitt, both radicals espousing unpopular causes. Lamb consistently defended both men. Never quite of first-rate ability, Hunt was much liked by a few friends. An interesting chapter in literary history is the story of his relationship with Byron and Shelley. Crabb Robinson never liked him, but always found him entertaining.

Procter once wrote, "Leigh Hunt, from temperament, was more alive to pleasant influences (sunshine, freedom for work, rural walks, complimentary words) than the others. All Unitarians, much slandered, good talkers, good books and good friends."

Hazlitt found him a good person to talk to and described him along with some of the best authors of the day:

"Wordsworth sometimes talks like a man inspired on subjects of poetry (his own out of the question)—Coleridge well on every subject, and Godwin on none. To finish this subject, Mrs. M[ontagu]'s conversation is as fine-cut as her features, and I like to sit in the room with that sort of coronet face. What she says leaves a flavour, like fine green tea. H[unt]'s is like champagne, and N[orthcote]'s like anchovy sandwiches. H[aydon]'s is like a game at trapball: L[amb]'s like snap-dragon: and my own (if I do not mistake the matter) is not very much unlike a game at ninepins!"

The publishing ventures of the Hunts included a number of rash printing enterprises such as the *Reflector,* the *Indicator* and the *Examiner.* Each of these magazines contained good material from men who afterwards became famous, and they make us regret that publications starting with great promise could not have continued. In publishing, Leigh Hunt was doubtless of considerable service to Lamb in encouraging him to go on with his efforts to write for the magazines, and he was definitely the cause of the collection of Lamb's works into two volumes and their publication by Ollier in 1818.

The works of Leigh Hunt are not as well known today as those of Lamb and Hazlitt, but they reveal a delightful writer, reader and talker. We have less than a dozen letters written by Lamb to Hunt, and unfortunately none by Hunt to Lamb. There must have been many because the relationship was close not only between Charles and Hunt, but between the two families. The letters are not of special significance but they possess a very human interest. One good letter early in 1825 reveals details of friends and daily life.

"ILLUSTREZZIMO SIGNOR,

"I have obeyed your mandate to a tittle. I accompany this with a volume. But what have you done with the first I sent you?—have you swapt it with some lazzaroni for macaroni? or pledged it with a gondolierer for a passage? Peradventuri the Cardinal Gonsalvi took a fancy to it:—his Eminence has done my Nearness an honour. 'Tis but a step to the Vatican. As you judge, my works do not enrich the workman, but I get vat I can for 'em. They keep dragging me on, a poor, worn mill-horse, in the eternal round of the damn'd magazine; but 'tis they are blind, not I. Colburn (where I recognise with delight the gay W. Honeycomb renovated) hath the ascendency.

"I was with the Novellos last week. They have a large, cheap house and garden, with a dainty library (magnificent) without books. But what will make you bless yourself (I am too old for wonder), something has touched the right organ in Vincentio at last. He attends a Wesleyan chapel on Kingsland Green. He at first tried to laugh it off—he only went for the singing; but the cloven foot—I retract—the Lamb's trotters—are at length apparent. Mary Isabella attributes it to a lightness induced by his headaches. But I think I see in it a less accidental influence. Mister Clark is at perfect staggers! the whole fabric of his infidelity is shaken. He has no one to join him in his coarse insults and indecent obstreperousnesses against Christianity, for Holmes (the bonny Holmes) is gone to Salisbury to be organist, and Isabella and the Clark make but a feeble quorum. The children have all nice, neat little clasped pray-books, and I have laid out 7s. 8d. in Watts's Hymns for Christmas presents for them. The eldest girl alone holds out; she has been at Boulogne, skirting upon the vast focus of Atheism, and imported bad principles in patois French. But the strongholds are crumbling. N. appears as yet to have but a confused notion of the Atonement. It makes him giddy, he says, to think much about it. But such giddiness is spiritual sobriety.

"Well, Byron is gone; and —— is now the best poet in England. Fill up the gap to your fancy. Barry Cornwall has at last carried the pretty A[nne] S[kepper]. They are just in the treacle-moon. Hope it won't clog his wings—gaum, we used to say at school.

"Mary, my sister, has worn me out with eight weeks' cold and toothache, her average complement in the winter, and it will not go away. She is otherwise well, and reads novels all day long. She had had an exempt year, a good year, for which, forgetting the minor calamity, she and I are most thankful.

"Alsager is in a flourishing house, with wife and children about him, in Mecklenburg Square—almost too fine to visit.

"Barron Field is come home from Sydney, but as yet I can hear no tidings of a pension. He is plump and friendly, his wife really a very superior woman. He resumes the bar.

"I have got acquainted with Mr. Irving, the Scotch preacher, whose fame must have reached you. He is a humble disciple at the foot of Gamaliel S.T.C. Judge how his own sectarists must stare when I tell you he has dedicated a book to S. T. C., acknowledging to have learnt more of the nature of faith, Christianity, and Christian Church, from him than from all the men he ever conversed with. He is a most amiable, sincere, modest man in a room, this Boanerges in the temple. Mrs. Montague told him the dedication would do him no good. 'That shall be a reason for doing it,' was his answer. Judge, now, whether this man be a quack.

"Dear H., take this imperfect notelet for a letter; it looks so much the more like conversing on nearer terms. Love to all the Hunts, old friend Thornton, and all.

"C. LAMB."

No one has left so good a description of Lamb among his books as Hunt. "I looked sideways at my Spenser, my Theocritus, and my *Arabian Nights;* then above them at my Italian poets; then behind me at my Dryden and Pope, my romances, and my Boccaccio; then on my left side at my Chaucer, who lay on a writing-desk; and thought how natural it was in C[harles] L[amb] to give a kiss to an old folio, as I once saw him do to Chapman's *Homer.* At the same time I wondered how he could sit in that front room of his with nothing but a few un-

feeling tables and chairs, or at best a few engravings in trim
frames, instead of putting a couple of armchairs into the back-
room with the books in it, where there is but one window.
Would I were there, with both the chairs properly filled, and
one or two more besides! ... His library, though not abounding
in Greek or Latin (which are the only things to help some persons to an idea of literature) is anything but superficial. The
depths of philosophy and poetry are there, the innermost passages of the human heart. It has some Latin too. It has also a
handsome contempt for appearance. It looks like what it is, a
selection made at precious intervals from the book-stalls;—
now a Chaucer at nine and twopence; now a Montaigne or a Sir
Thomas Browne at two shillings; now a Jeremy Taylor; a
Spinoza; an old English Dramatist, Prior, and Sir Philip Sidney;
and the books are 'neat as imported.' The very perusal of the
backs is a 'discipline of humanity.' There Mr. Southey takes
his place again with an old Radical friend: there Jeremy Collier
is at peace with Dryden: there the lion, Martin Luther, lies
down with the Quaker lamb, Sewell: there Guzman d'Alfar-
ache thinks himself fit company for Sir Charles Grandison, and
has his claims admitted. Even the 'high fantastical' Duchess of
Newcastle, with her laurel on her head, is received with grave
honours, and not the less for declining to trouble herself with
the constitutions of her maids."

BASIL MONTAGU

Montagu, son of the Earl of Sandwich, was born in 1765 in
Bedford Square. He was a friend of Crabb Robinson, Godwin,
Wordsworth and Coleridge, whom he frequently entertained.
It was at the Montagus' that absent-minded George Dyer
stepped in to sign the guest book a second time in one after-

noon, as told by Lamb in his Elia essay, "Oxford in the Vacation." The Montagu house was known for its hospitality and was the scene of some big parties, as well as occasions when Hazlitt read his lectures. According to Fanny Kemble, Montagu was known for his "eccentricity, personal beauty and conversation." On one evening Talfourd describes "Basil Montagu, gentle enthusiast in the cause of humanity, pouring into the out-stretched ear of George Dyer some tale of legalized injustice."

BARRON FIELD

Barron Field, devoted to Leigh Hunt, was eight years younger than Lamb and lives today by his place in Lamb's writings. There may have been some blood relation between the Fields and the Lambs, so that it seemed especially appropriate that they should together visit Mackery End, the place where Lamb's great-aunt lived. Field had studied law, had done something in the way of literary editing, especially the plays of the Elizabethan dramatist Heywood, was dramatic critic for the *Times,* became judge of the Supreme Court in New South Wales and later Chief Justice at Gibraltar. He was responsible for an observation on punning which elicited a good pun by Lamb. "Whoever puns, will steal. I always button my pockets when in company with a punster." Someone added, "Punsters have no pockets." "No," said Lamb, "they only carry a ridicule [reticule]."

Field was a guest often at Lamb's parties and has left an account of the last dinner given for Lamb by Talfourd. It was to Field that Lamb once made a most apt remark in refusing to write for publication a description of a collection of portraits of Charles Mathews: "I pretty well know what I can't do."*

---

* October 4, 1827.

HENRY CRABB ROBINSON

Dr. Williams's Library in London has as one of its treasures a number of little brown notebooks. They might easily have been thrown into the waste basket many years ago. By some good fortune they have been preserved and may today be read by anyone who wishes to delve into the life of the half-century which these little books record. They are the day-by-day diary of Henry Crabb Robinson. Robinson never wrote anything which can be called literature, but he has left us something perhaps even better.

Henry Crabb Robinson, the son of a tanner, was born at Bury St. Edmunds in 1775, only a few months after Charles Lamb. At twenty-three, he became a solicitor and a little later inherited sufficient money to make it possible for him to be an "idler." He began his studies at Jena, became foreign correspondent for the *Times,* and was its first war correspondent in the Peninsular War of 1808. He practised as a barrister and for a long time rode the circuit in England. He travelled extensively in Europe, met and talked with people everywhere, was an omniverous reader and loved the theatre.

Although he never held himself to the daily grind, as did Charles Lamb, nevertheless, he was far from being an idler. His diary, begun in 1811, is said to have had its origin in a suggestion by Hazlitt, because of his interest in the diary of Thomas Holcroft. Robinson's diary continued right down to his death in 1867, at the age of ninety-two. Much of what is covered in these entries for fifty-six years has no counterpart anywhere. Hundreds of descriptions of persons and incidents would have been lost if they had not been kept in this manuscript, all written by the hand of Robinson, a large part in a kind of shorthand which is easily deciphered. The diary, chiefly incidents with few phi-

losophical observations, is of permanent interest, for he knew
not only all the people whom Lamb knew in England, but most
of those prominent in philosophy, art and literature in Europe
and he records conversations with them—Herder, Schiller,
Goethe, Schelling, Wieland, von Kotzebue, Benjamin Constant,
the famous Swiss historian von Müller, Schlegel, and most intimately of all, Madame de Staël.

The first entry of the Robinson diary takes us to the Lambs
and tells of discussions as to whether Coleridge was greater
than Wordsworth. It was at Lamb's that Robinson met Coleridge in 1810. The entries for the next twenty years abound in
delightful descriptions of days and evenings at Lamb's, at
Robinson's or at some mutual friend's, or trips that they made
together, especially to the theatre, and the plays they enjoyed.
They saw Kean for the first time in *Richard III*. They saw
Fanny Kelly, Liston, Macready, the Kembles—there is scarcely
an actor or actress of note who is not mentioned. We can share
in the excitement aroused by Napoleon, if we go with Robinson
to the copy-rooms to read the papers, or to overhear a spirited
discussion between Robinson and Hazlitt, the latter ardently
supporting the cause of Bonaparte. We can better appreciate the
intense excitement over the anonymous publication of *Waverley*
and Robinson gives us some of the guesses which were ventured.

We may look in upon Lamb's evenings at home and meet
some of the people whom one would regularly find there.
Robinson had strong prejudices but he liked people. He was a
guest at social occasions of all kinds, and people were glad to go
to his home. We should have scant record of the lectures of
Hazlitt and Coleridge, their manner of delivery and the impression carried away by the audience, if we did not possess the
Robinson diary. A bachelor with comfortable income, he might
have been a figure in the more distinguished Saturday dinners
at Lord and Lady Holland's or at any other house in London or

on the Continent but he preferred the simple and honest evenings at the Lambs', whom he held as his closest friends, including Mary on equal terms. "In that humble apartment," he recorded, "I spent many happy hours, and saw a greater number of excellent persons than I had ever seen collected together in one room."

One entry must suffice to represent the quality of Robinson's recording of the persons with whom he associated. "I dined with the Colliers and spent the evening at Lamb's. I found a large party collected round the two poets,* but Coleridge had the larger number. There was, however, scarcely any conversation beyond a whisper. Coleridge was philosophizing in his rambling way to Monkhouse, who listened attentively—to Manning, who sometimes smiled, as if he thought Coleridge had no right to metaphysicize on chemistry without any knowledge of the subject—to Martin Burney, who was eager to interpose,—and Alsager, who was content to be a listener; while Wordsworth was for a great part of the time engaged tête-à-tête with Talfourd. I could catch scarcely anything of the conversation. I chatted with the ladies. Miss Lamb had gone through the fatigue of a dinner-party very well, and Charles was in good spirits."†

THE COLLIERS

John Dyer Collier, Mrs. Collier and their son, John Payne Collier, were brought into the Lamb circle by Henry Crabb Robinson. Collier was at one time foreign writer of the *Morning Chronicle*. They were often at Lamb's lodgings and were very congenial to both Charles and Mary. They were mindful of Lamb's liking for certain articles of food, especially game

---

* Wordsworth was in London for a few weeks, spending much of his time with Lamb.

† Entry for December 30, 1817.

and meats, and often sent him presents for the table. It came to be the fashion after the fame of the Elia essay to send him pig for roasting. On one occasion the Colliers sent a pig for Lamb's table. Let us hope that the suckling pig was prepared, as Professor Ernest Carson Ross suggests, according to the recipe given in the famous "Dissertation upon Roast Pig." Lamb wrote in thanks: "It was eaten on Sunday and Monday, and doubts only exist as to which temperature it eat best, hot or cold."

To Collier we are indebted for this story: Lamb met Mary Russell Mitford, the writer, at dinner, and "Charles was joked about the charming young Quakeress who had lived in the same street in Pentonville where Lamb had lodged; she generally wore white and somebody present called her 'a white witch.' 'No,' said Lamb, 'if a witch at all, as she lived at the *last house* in our street, she must be the witch of *End-door*.'"

WILLIAM AYRTON

Famous as impresario and musical critic, Ayrton was a favourite member of the parties at Lamb's and Crabb Robinson's. He was the brother-in-law of Samuel James Arnold, manager of the Lyceum Theatre, and brother of Mrs. Paris, at whose house in Cambridge Charles and Mary were introduced to Emma Isola. He acquired considerable reputation for having first produced at the King's Theatre Mozart's *Don Giovanni*. Hazlitt called him the "Will Honeycomb of our set" and brought him into his famous essay "Persons One Would Wish To Have Seen," as proposing Newton and Locke. He had great admiration for the genius of Lamb, who called him "the last and steadiest left me of that little knot of Whist players, that used to assemble weekly for so many years at The Queen's Gate." Although Lamb always denied having any liking for music, he was a close friend of Ayrton, and often was at his house, was equally intimate with Vincent Novello and attended his regular recitals, and was devoted to the singing of the famous tenor Braham.

VINCENT NOVELLO

Vincent Novello, son of an Italian father and an English mother, became a distinguished organist, and is described by Lamb in his Elia essay, "A Chapter on Ears." He founded a publishing business in which he was later joined by Charles Cowden Clarke, who married Victoria, the eldest daughter of Novello. She lived until 1892 and with her husband has left accounts of many amusing incidents of Charles Lamb and Leigh Hunt.

It will be remembered that Clarke was the son of the schoolmaster who established a school at Enfield where John Keats was one of the scholars.

On Sunday evenings the Novello drawing-room became what Lamb's more pretentious lodgings were on Wednesday and Thursday evenings for talk and discussion. Like Lamb, Novello was fond of the theatre, puns and nonsense. The custom, mentioned elsewhere in this book, for the Novellos, Hunts and Lambs to entertain one another was long cherished by the young Victoria with meetings at the theatre or picnics in the fields.

BENJAMIN HAYDON

Although Benjamin Haydon was strictly not a member of the set which frequented Lamb's lodgings, nevertheless he and Lamb were good friends, and Charles and Mary often went to see his pictures. One of the memorable evenings was the famous party* at Haydon's with Lamb and Keats present, which Hay-

---

* *Autobiography* of Benjamin Haydon.

don described with much enthusiasm. Lamb acted like a boy, and some did not see the humour of it.

In his autobiography Haydon described the scene of the christening party of young William Hazlitt, displaying the characteristic impracticality of both Hazlitt and Lamb.

"In the midst of Hazlitt's weaknesses, his parental affections were beautiful. He had one boy. He loved him. He doated on him. He told me one night this boy was to be christened. 'Will ye come on Friday?' 'Certainly,' said I. His eyes glistened. Friday came, but as I knew all parties I lunched heartily first and was there punctually at four. Hazlitt then lived in Milton's house, Westminster, next door to Bentham. At four I came, but he was out. I walked up and found his wife ill by the fire in a bed gown—nothing ready for guests, and everything wearing the appearance of neglect and indifference. I said, 'Where is Hazlitt?' 'Oh dear, William has gone to look for a parson.' 'A parson; why, has he not thought of that before?' 'No, he didn't.' 'I'll go and look for him,' said I, and out I went into the park through Queen's Square and met Hazlitt in a rage coming home. 'Have ye got a parson?' 'No, sir' said he, 'these fellows are all out.' 'What will ye do?' 'Nothing.' So in we walked, Hazlitt growling at all the parsons and the church.

"When we came in we sat down—nobody was come;—no table laid—no appearance of dinner. On my life there is nothing so heartless as going out to dinner and finding no dinner ready. I sat down; the company began to drop in—Charles Lamb and his poor sister—all sorts of odd, clever people. Still no dinner. At last came in a maid who laid a cloth and put down knives and forks in a heap. Then followed a dish of potatoes, cold, waxy and yellow. Then came a great bit of beef with a bone like a battering-ram toppling on all its corners. Neither Hazlitt nor Lamb seemed at all disturbed, but set to work helping each other; while the boy, half clean and obsti-

nate, kept squalling to put his fingers into the gravy. Even
Lamb's wit and Hazlitt's disquisitions, in a large room, wain-
scotted and ancient, where Milton had meditated, could not rec-
oncile me to such violation of all the decencies of life."

THOMAS MASSA ALSAGER

Alsager was one of the leading men in the conduct of the
Times, being especially concerned, Crabb Robinson wrote, "in
all that respects the collection of mercantile and foreign news."
He did more than perhaps any man of his day to promote the
study and performance of classical chamber music. Lamb called
him Al-singer, adding that that name suited him better than
Al-sager. Many and varied occasions brought them together
and Lamb once excused himself from calling upon Alsager by
saying that Alsager's house in Mecklenburg Square was "almost
too fine to visit."

THOMAS NOON TALFOURD

Of all the friends of Charles Lamb, the one who has perhaps
given us the most precious contribution was Thomas Noon Talfourd, first biographer and collector of Lamb's letters. We first
hear of him as a youth of eighteen whom Crabb Robinson reports as coming to see him regarding "economical arrange-
ments" for the study of law. An entry in the *Diary* for February 25, 1813, states: "This day a Mr. Talfourd called. . . . he has
been for some time Dr. Valpy's* head boy, and wishes, for a
few years, to occupy himself by giving instruction or otherwise
so as to be no encumbrance to his father, who has a large family. He is a very promising young man indeed. No great

* Valpy was a publisher of the *Pamphleteer* and a long series of classics for
which George Dyer did most of the hack work.

powers of conversation and public speaking, not without the faults of his age, but with so much apparent vigour of mind, that I am greatly mistaken if he do not become a distinguished man." The prediction came true. Young Talfourd put himself under the tutelage of the great lawyer, Joseph Chitty, took lodgings in the Temple and settled down to a life of great industry and accomplishment. He possessed to an unusual degree the ability to make friends and only a few months passed before he became acquainted with Lamb, Hazlitt and through them with all their friends. He was a good talker and card player and soon appears in the entries of the Robinson *Diary* as a regular attendant of Lamb's evenings at home.

It would seem almost as fortunate an event as the famous evening when Boswell was introduced to Johnson, that William Evans, an officer in the East India House, asked Talfourd to have dinner with him to meet Lamb. "My duties at the office," wrote the future biographer, "did not allow me to avail myself of this invitation to dinner, but I went up at ten o'clock, through a deep snow, palpably congealing into ice, and was amply repaid when I reached the hospitable abode of my friend. There was Lamb, preparing to depart, but he stayed half an hour in kindness to me and then accompanied me to our common home—the Temple. . . . He took my arm and we walked to the Temple, Lamb stammering out fine remarks as we walked; and when we reached his staircase, he detained me with an urgency which would not be denied, and we mounted to the top story, where an old petted servant, called Becky, was ready to receive us. We were soon seated beside a cheerful fire; hot water and its better adjuncts were before us; and Lamb insisted on my sitting with him while he smoked 'one pipe,'—for alas! for poor human nature—he had resumed his acquaintance with his 'fair traitress.' . . . It was two o'clock before we parted, when Lamb gave me a hearty invitation to renew my visit at pleasure; but two or three months elapsed before I saw him again."

The "next time" was the famous occasion when Lamb rushed into his office and hurried him out to meet the "person whom in all the world I venerated most" with the words, "Wordsworth, give me leave to introduce to you my only admirer."

Talfourd was at once made welcome in the circle of Lamb and his friends and became the devoted friend and admirer of Charles and Mary. On the publication of the letters and life, he dedicated the volumes to Mary with the words, "To Mary Anne Lamb, these letters, the memorials of many years which she spent with the writer in undivided affection, of the sorrows and joys she shared, of the genius which she cherished, and of the excellence which she best knew, are respectfully and affectionately dedicated by the Author." To his first child Talfourd gave the name Charles Lamb Talfourd.

Talfourd left as his contribution to the literature of his day, beside his valuable researches in the letters and life of Charles Lamb, poems, four tragedies, and many critical and miscellaneous essays. He became a knight, sergeant, and judge and was the original of the rising young lawyer of Gray's Inn, Tommy Traddles, in Charles Dickens' *David Copperfield*.

BRYAN WALLER PROCTER

Procter, commonly known among contemporary poets as "Barry Cornwall," met Lamb in 1817 at Leigh Hunt's house. A young solicitor, he was twelve years younger than Lamb, leading a gay life about town, taking lessons from the boxer, Tom Cribb, with little definite purpose in life. Lamb's influence gave him a more serious turn, and as a consequence he wrote *Marcian Colonna* and *A Sicilian Story* and later a memoir of Lamb. Some of the most intimate and touching incidents have been recorded in this simple and sympathetic account of the Lambs and their friends and of Charles's devotion to Mary. Particularly vivid are the descriptions of Charles and Mary walking to Hoxton Asylum, of Lamb's Wednesday evenings, and especially of the last dinner given for Lamb by Talfourd.

THOMAS BARNES

Thomas Barnes, a schoolmate of Leigh Hunt at Christ's Hospital, was in the words of Talfourd one of the "soundest and most elegant scholars whom the school ever produced." At Cambridge he obtained high honours and after a time at law and a short service as theatrical critic for the *Examiner* while Hunt was in prison, he went to the *Times*. He became its first great editor and with the aid of a vigorous mind and excellent judgement continued and enlarged the prestige of that powerful newspaper. He was always happy that he could be the critic who first saw the rising star, Edmund Kean, and predicted his "intoxicating success." Barnes was highly esteemed by Lamb. "I well remember him," wrote Talfourd, "late one evening in the year 1816, when only two or three friends remained with Lamb and his sister, long after 'we had heard the chimes at midnight,' holding inveterate but delighted controversy with Lamb respecting the tragic power of Dante as compared with that of Shakespeare."

THOMAS HOOD

The later years of Lamb's life were brightened by the introduction of a new friend, Thomas Hood, in 1821, who wrote a memorable description of his first meeting with Lamb at the office of the *London Magazine*. Hood had great affection for Lamb and said that he revered him more than any other man. And Lamb wrote to Bernard Barton, the Quaker poet, a few years afterwards:

"What a fertile genius (an[d] a quiet good soul withal) is Hood. He has 50 things in hand, farces to supply the Adelphi for the season, a comedy for one of the great theatres, just ready, a whole entertainment by himself for Mathews and Yates* to figure in, a meditated Comic Annual for next year, to be nearly done by himself.—You'd like him very much." Hood explained his industry by saying, he "had to be a lively Hood for a livelihood."

The Lambs and the Hoods became close friends, lived near each other for a time and had many picnics together after which they frequently went to the theatre. One of Lamb's best known poems, "On an Infant Dying as soon as Born," was written on the occasion of the death of the Hood child. In the summer of 1827, Hood, who had skill as an artist, made a sketch of Mary Lamb getting over a stile. Lamb sent the drawing to William Hone, suggesting that without Hood's knowledge, it might be engraved and reproduced in Hone's *Table Book,* illustrating the difficulties in the country about Edmonton and how elderly ladies overcame them. The sketch appeared as a portrait of the wife of John Gilpin, whose famous ride described by Cowper had already become popular. Without Hood's attention, many of Lamb's stories would have been lost. Hood was not merely a maker of poems and jokes; he was also an admirable man of letters and just missed being a first-rate poet. Although only two of his poems are now well known, "The Song of the Shirt" and "The Bridge of Sighs," he wrote many good lines and his complete poems went into fifteen editions in as many years.

THE DIBDINS

Dibdin was a very well-known name in London in the first quarter of the Nineteenth Century. In more recent times there

* Joint managers of the Adelphi.

has been considerable confusion as to the identity of various members of the family because of the similarity in their sur- names and in their literary work. In 1803, when Mary Lamb wrote to Dorothy Wordsworth that they had been seeing at Sadler's Wells *Goody Two Shoes, Jack the Giant Killer* and *Mary of Buttermere,* she was referring to plays of Charles Dib- din, who wrote also *Young Arthur: or, The Child of Mystery, Isn't It Odd,* a novel in three volumes, reminiscent of Sterne's *Tristram Shandy,* and the mock-heroic poem, *The Chessiad.* All these were known to the Lambs. It was the father, Charles Dib- din, also known to Charles Lamb, who was famous as musician, dramatist, actor and song-writer, having connection with both Covent Garden and Drury Lane, and as the author of more than fourteen hundred songs and thirty plays. It was the son, John Bates Dibdin, grandson of the famous song-writer, Charles Dibdin, just mentioned, who became a close friend of Lamb and to whom Lamb wrote some of his most delightful letters. It was this young man who made the discovery of the author- ship of *Elia* and to the sorrow of the Lambs was "carried off by consumption on his return from one of the Azores islands," at the age of twenty-nine.

There was also Thomas John Dibdin, another son of the older Charles, who made a tremendous success in the production of pantomimes, especially *Mother Goose* and the *High-Mettled Racer,* at a time when Lamb was most frequent in attending the theatres. Thomas Frognall Dibdin, the bibliographer for whom many clubs of bibliophiles have been named, for example the Dibdin Club in New York, was a cousin of Charles Dibdin, the father of John Bates Dibdin.

In one of Lamb's amusing letters to his young friend, John Bates Dibdin, he included the lines,

"Because you boast poetic Grandsire,
And rhyming kin, both Uncle and Sire

Dost think that none but their Descendings
Can tickle folks with double endings?
I had a Dad, that would for half a bet
Have put down thine thro' half the Alphabet."

To show that Lamb's boast was not an idle one, we may quote the opening lines of one of John Lamb's annual addresses "to the other forty-nine members of the Friendly Society" at the Devil Tavern:

"Once more we're met, fresh shav'd, look neat and trim,
In health I hope, and sound both wind and limb;
Most chearfully this morn we left our houses,
And here are come, to serve our absent spouces;
For this at night we surely shall be cuddled,
Unless the Devil sends us home quite fuddled."

BERNARD BARTON

Bernard Barton, the Quaker, met Lamb at one of the dinners given by the *London Magazine* for the contributors. Lamb made a joke about the inconsistency of Quakers writing poetry. Lamb had a tender spot for the Quakers, which may explain why he and Barton so quickly became good friends. They fell to talking and for the rest of Lamb's life they were close friends.

Barton was an acceptable poet who wrote on religious topics something after the manner of the American Quaker Whittier. He was devoted to his religion and a faithful worker in a bank. At times he became restive and once was on the point of giving up his work, when Charles Lamb wrote him a frank letter and with rare common sense urged him to retain his position. For that advice which he followed Barton was ever grateful. Barton was the author of several volumes and, when he sent each volume to Lamb, he always received a reply with apt criticism of the verse. Barton's daughter, Lucy, became the wife of

Edward FitzGerald who wrote a valuable account of Lamb.

Fortunately, Barton kept most of the letters of a twelve-year friendship and these are now in the British Museum. There are no better letters written by Lamb and there are few better letters anywhere. They contain searching and sincere criticism of Barton's poetry, a sympathetic point of view on Quaker customs, appreciations of John Fox and Bunyan, intimate details of Lamb's going about his holidays, his walks in London, his moving to Islington and to Enfield, his discovery of the poet Blake, as well as the reports of the illnesses of Mary. What part of the letters which Lamb wrote are preserved we do not know but those which remain are of great variety of interest, showing Lamb a sympathetic critic as well as enthusiastic friend. Expressions which endeared Lamb to Barton are frequent in the letters: "I am like you, a prisoner to the desk"; the warning to Barton not to throw himself on the booksellers but to retain his position in the bank; a note of sympathy, "I wishd for you yesterday. I dined in Parnassus, with Wordsworth, Coleridge, Rogers, and Tom Moore—half the Poetry of England constellated and clustered in Gloster Place!" On Byron's death Lamb wrote: "I never can make out his great *power,* which his admirers talk of. Why, a line of Wordsworth's is a lever to lift the immortal spirit. Byron can only move the Spleen."* . . . "I can no more understand Shelley than you can. His poetry is 'thin sewn with profit or delight.' "†

THOMAS ALLSOP

Allsop was a prosperous silk merchant; his wife was the daughter of the famous actress, Mrs. Jordan. He was a favourite disciple of Coleridge and presented him with a hundred pounds.

* Letter to Barton, May 1824.
† Letter to Barton, August 1824.

The Allsops came to know the Lambs when Charles was doing his first Elia essays and the friendship continued until the death of Charles in 1834 and of Mary in 1847. His letters, conversations and recollections are a treasure of information regarding Coleridge and his friends. Writing many years later of a time when he was in financial trouble, Allsop said, "I have a clear recollection of Miss Lamb's addressing me in a tone acting at once as a solace and support, and after as a stimulus, to which I owe more perhaps, than to the more extended arguments of all others." He attended the funeral of Charles and thirteen years later was one of the few friends who were present at the burial of Mary.

Of about sixty letters to Thomas Allsop many are mere notes of thanks, greetings, and invitations to come to share the many delicious gifts which were sent for Lamb's table, "the shining bird," "those tempting birds," "pheasant," etc.

HENRY FRANCIS CARY

Cary was an Oxford man from Christ Church who took holy orders and held a benefice until his death. His translation of Dante became a classic and went through four editions in his life time. Almost of equally wide recognition was his translation of *The Birds* by Aristophanes. It was through Coleridge that Lamb came to know Cary and, since he held the position as assistant librarian in the British Museum with the rare books under his special charge, Lamb saw much of him during the many hours there selecting plays for his *Specimens*. Lamb called him "the flower of clergymen"; "though he was perhaps as good as Dr. Primrose, he was not so good as Parson Adams."

In the memoir of Cary by his son appears this story: "I remember that a quotation from one of our dramatists provoked a round of puns on the names of various herbs; the last two introduced had been 'mint and anise,' when Lamb sputtered out, 'Now, Cary, it's your turn.' 'It's cumin' was the prompt rejoinder. 'Then I won't make another pun to-day,' stammered Lamb."

Cary wrote the lines for Lamb's tombstone at Edmonton. He himself was buried in Westminster Abbey.

CUNNINGHAM, CLARE and WAINEWRIGHT

The *London Magazine* gave a dinner each month for its contributors. These became famous occasions not only because of the excellence of the food but because of the distinction of the authors brought together. Through these dinners Lamb came to know Allan Cunningham, the Scottish ballad-writer; John Clare, the rural poet of Northamptonshire, who possessed some talent in versifying; best of all, Henry Cary; and perhaps *worst* of all, Thomas Griffiths Wainewright, lover of good pictures and good talk, dilettante, painter, essayist, and forger and poisoner *par excellence*. It pained some of Lamb's friends that he should be on intimate terms with this brilliant coxcomb, but to Lamb's credit it may be said that the evil side of his notorious character was not known until after Lamb's death.

JOHN HOWARD PAYNE

Payne, the American actor and dramatist, was living in Paris and writing plays for the London theatres when the Lambs made their first and only visit to the Continent, which was interrupted by Mary's illness on the road to Paris. James Kenney, the failure of whose play, *A Word for the Ladies,* had so distressed Mary, was also in Paris writing plays. Through him

Lamb met Payne. After Charles's brief visit, Mary was left in the care of the Kenneys and was shown by Payne and Crabb Robinson the sights of the city, including the pictures in the Louvre. On their return to London they were all present at Covent Garden when Payne's play *Clari* was given, in which appeared the now famous lines "Home, Sweet Home."

PETER GEORGE PATMORE

Patmore, father of Coventry, was introduced to Lamb at Hazlitt's lodgings in 1824. He was the second of John Scott, editor of the *London Magazine,* who was killed in the famous duel brought on by the bitter feelings between *Blackwood's* and the *London.* The relations between Lamb and Patmore were close and Patmore has left us in his *My Friends and Acquaintances* some of the best stories about Lamb. Lamb, whose conversational French was scant, on one occasion in ordering an egg bade the waiter bring "eau de vie." The waiter took him at his word. What he brought was so much to Lamb's satisfaction that, Patmore says, the error was repeated.

Another incident, appreciated especially in war-time, records an occasion when Wordsworth was having tea with the Lambs, who were in lodgings at Enfield. At the end of the week the bill included an extra charge of sixpence. On Lamb's inquiring what was meant, the reply was made that the "elderly gentleman [Wordsworth] had taken such a quantity of sugar in his tea."

When Thomas Hood and his wife moved from the country into London, they left with the Lambs a handsome dog named Dash. On every walk, the dog begged to accompany Charles and he could not refuse. But what P. G. Patmore calls Dash's "extravagantly errant nature" caused Charles so much worry that he begged Patmore to take the dog, for, as Mary said, "if we keep him, he'll be the death of Charles!"

EDWARD MOXON

Financed by Samuel Rogers, Moxon established himself as a publisher and put forth as his first book *Album Verses and Other Poems,* by Charles Lamb, in 1830. He took over the *Englishman's Magazine* in 1831, and in the same year published anonymously Lamb's lines, *Satan in Search of a Wife.* In 1835 he issued the second part of Lamb's *Specimens.* He became the publisher of Tennyson. In addition to his activities as publisher he wrote verse, especially sonnets to Emma Isola and Lamb. His marriage to Emma brought great happiness both to Charles and Mary Lamb.

Besides his sonnets Moxon wrote of Lamb in prose. One paragraph touched upon a matter not mentioned by other observers. "He was an admirable Critic, and was always willing to exercise the art he so much excelled in for the fame of others. We have seen him almost blind with poring over the endless and illegible Manuscripts that were submitted to him. On these occasions, how he would long to find out something good, something that he could speak kindly of; for to give another pain (as he writes in a letter now before us) was to give himself greater."

Lamb bequeathed his books to Moxon. However, Moxon did not claim the inheritance until after Mary's death and by that time some of the books had disappeared. He selected about sixty volumes which seemed most worthy of presentation, then destroyed the remainder of the collection. A friend of Moxon induced him to allow the books to be brought to America where they were sold at auction in 1848.

6

Evenings at Home

SOON after the Lambs moved back to the Temple in Mitre Court Buildings in 1801, they more or less formally set apart a special evening each week for their friends to "drop in," to use Charles's favourite phrase of invitation. At first Thursday was named but later Wednesday seemed to suit better, and the practice continued with more or less regularity in the various places where they lived until they moved out of the city to Enfield in 1827. Both Charles and Mary were not at their ease in other people's houses, both were not fond of visiting and, as they grew older, they found it more difficult to leave their own fireside. Besides there was always Mary's comfort to consider and Charles felt more secure at home and could more easily detect an approaching attack and prepare for it.

There was ever something remarkable in Lamb's power of attracting friends and Mary was equally adept in holding them, so that the circle began to widen and include young men of individuality and promise. Two or three would come in almost every evening, those who like Lamb were trying to write, and often an actor after the play, to meet there several of the critics who would review his success or failure at the theatre. So Charles found his time after office hours slipping away and could get done little of the work he wanted to do. Thus it happened—"all great men have public days," he humorously explained—that the custom of observing only Wednesday evenings was established.

There was little formality about the Lambs. Everyone who liked good talk, good company and a little refreshment in food and drink was made welcome at the homy quarters three flights up in the Temple. De Quincey, it will be remembered, was surprised at that first meeting at the East India House to have Lamb ask him to "drop in" and his experience was in no way unique. Wit and good fellowship might have been the motto inscribed over the door. "When a stranger came, it was not asked," said Hazlitt, "has he written anything? We were above that pedantry. If he could take a hand at picquet, he was welcome to sit down. If a person liked anything, if he took snuff heartily, it was sufficient. We abhorred insipidity, affectation and fine gentlemen." Since most of the guests, with the exception of Coleridge, Wordsworth and Southey, lived very near the Temple, they could come with considerable regularity, so that there were usually some whose presence could be depended upon. It would be difficult to imagine a group more varied; Barry Cornwall has assured us that "each was notable for some individual mark or character."

Charles would come home from a long day at the India House, tired and hungry and ready to sit down to a simple meal of steak and fried tripe—a delicacy to him—prepared by Mary and faithful Becky.* To his occasional laments over the monotony of copying figures in the ledgers at the House, Mary listened with her usual serenity, so that soon any ill-temper of Charles disappeared and the fire and a pipe warmed the host into a most agreeable good humour. While Mary darned the socks and Charles read from his beloved Elizabethans aloud to

---

* Becky, the maid, was for many years a part of the Lamb household. Charles said, when she finally left in 1829 after almost fifteen years of service, "Our ill-tempered maid is gone, who with all her airs, was yet a home piece of furniture, a record of better days." She is first mentioned by Lamb in a letter to Coleridge in 1820, but Talfourd wrote of her on his first meeting with Lamb in 1815. She had previously been with the Hazlitts. She is described at length by P. G. Patmore in *My Friends and Acquaintances.*

her, the time soon passed until shortly after nine o'clock. Then there was activity. They pulled the large mahogany table to the side of the room and brought in the roast of mutton, or veal pie, or the "cold joint," with a plentiful supply of punch or porter, swept the hearth, made the fire burn more brightly, and brought out the whist tables with packs of cards and the cribbage board. And the snuffbox was not forgotten for it would be much employed as the evening passed. Then Charles, a small, frail figure dressed in sober black, his head covered with curling black hair, his face humorous and sad, and Mary, homely and practical, kindly and intellectual, her garments simple and old-fashioned, sat down to await the first comers.

The furniture was old-fashioned and worn, the ceiling low, not unstained by traces of "the great plant." The bookshelves sagged with the treasures collected by Lamb after so much thought and saving of precious shillings. On the walls were prints by Hogarth in narrow black frames, with their grim and realistic scenes of a London that was most familiar to those who came to share the hospitality of a hearty English welcome.

Near ten o'clock the first footsteps could be heard ascending the three flights of stairs that led to the upper floors of the old and worn Temple building. More than likely the first to come would be William Godwin. "Professor," Lamb liked to call him. "He is a very well-behaved, decent man; nothing very brilliant about him, or imposing, as you may suppose; quite another guess sort of gentleman from what your Anti-Jacobin Christians imagine him. I was well pleased to find he has neither horns nor claws; quite a tame creature, I assure you. A middle-sized man, both in stature and in understanding." It must have been difficult to think of him as the author of *Caleb Williams* and *Political Justice,* the man once so popular, so terrifying to conservatives, to whose words ardent young revolutionists like Shelley listened with rapt attention. Now he had a shop where he and his wife sold books and, better still, published books for children, among them *Tales from Shakespear, Adventures of Ulysses* and *Mrs. Leicester's School,* destined to become classics for young readers.

Crabb Robinson came often and regularly, that observer and diarist whose daily entries are indispensable to anyone who wishes to know what went on among Lamb's friends. Then came the classical scholar and hack-writer, George Dyer, "a gaunt, awkward man in a very shabby coat, and trousers shrunk so that they showed his bony ankles," so absent-minded and so absorbed in books that he forgot to buy new clothes and even to eat his meals, but with a heart of gold and dear to Charles and Mary Lamb. "I found," wrote Lamb,* "that he had read Shakspere (whom he calls an original, but irregular, genius), but it was a good while ago. . . . He never seem'd even to have heard of Fletcher, Ford, Marlow, Massinger, and the Worthies of Dodsley's Collection." But George Dyer was always welcome, wherever the Lambs happened to be living, and brought with him others of kindred spirit. John Rickman was one of these. "This Rickman lives in our Buildings, immediately opposite our house; the finest fellow to drop in a' nights, about nine or ten o'clock—cold bread-and-cheese time—just in the *wishing* time of the night, when you *wish* for somebody to come in, without a distinct idea of a probable anybody."†

Then came the Burneys—Captain James, wife Sarah and son Martin. The captain's record was well known. He had accompanied Captain Cook on his second and third voyage. When Cook died, Burney had been present, and he returned in command of the famous ship *Discovery*. Martin is described by Southey in a letter to Coleridge: "The captain hath a son—begotten, according to Lamb, upon a mermaid; and thus far is

* Letter to Coleridge, August 1800.
† Letter to Manning, November 1800.

certain, that he is the queerest fish out of water. A paralytic affectation in childhood has kept one side of his face stationary, while the other has continued to grow, and the two sides form the most ridiculous whole you can imagine; the boy, however, is a sharp lad, the inside not having suffered." And later Southey paid him the compliment of saying on the occasion of the re-printing of *Joan of Arc,* "The best omen I have heard of its well-doing is that Martin Burney likes it." Martin became a bar-rister with excellent taste in books, and his honesty and frank-ness in manner and expression made him one of the stimulating talkers at the "Lamb evenings." Procter said he found Martin Burney at the Lambs' more often than anybody else. And since we are reasonably sure that wife Sarah was set in Lamb's eye for the Mrs. Battle of the Elia essay, we shall be amply re-warded by following her during the evening. Her portrait is etched for all time, "sitting bolt upright, neither showing her cards or seeing yours," strong in her devotion to the game and in the expression when necessary of her fixed opinions, as for example her fondness for Pope and especially for *The Rape of the Lock.*

"The broad, burly, jovial bulk of John Lamb," the brother of Charles, sat at one of the tables. John was the "Ajax Telamon" of the clerks at the South Sea House and often introduced some of his favourites to the evenings, although he could never quite understand why Charles had become so famous. Robin-son called his vulgar manners intolerable, Coleridge did not like him and he had knocked Hazlitt down!

In one corner of the room sat Charles Lloyd, earnest and sad, who had worshipped at the shrine of Coleridge, the author of a slender volume of verses, discoursing "of fate, free-will, foreknowledge absolute" with Leigh Hunt, who was a stimulat-ing talker and always a most welcome guest. Basil Montagu would try to enlist sympathy for some one of the many humanitarian causes in which he was so generously interested.

One after another of the guests came "dropping in"—impecunious Ned Phillips, a first-rate hand at whist; Procter, "Barry Cornwall," "candid and affectionate as his own poetry"; Jem White, schoolmate of Charles at Christ's Hospital, clever and of great animal spirit, joyous and companionable, friend of chimney-sweeps, who gave them a feast at Smithfield on the yearly return of the fair of St. Bartholomew; and Thomas Talfourd, who had left D. Valpy's school at Reading and come to live as a young law student in chambers in the Inner Temple. He was devoted to Lamb and became, as all the world knows, his first biographer and collector of his letters. Barnes and Alsager of the *Times* staff came along with Hazlitt, dramatic critic, on his way from the theatre. Now there would be bristling talk because Hazlitt's radical views and his sympathy for Napoleon were well known and it was certain that although some would agree, more would be deeply hostile. But Hazlitt was accustomed to receiving blows and could give lusty ones in return.

Certainly not the least welcome were the actors, of whom one or two always came, Charles Kemble, Liston, and best of all, Fanny Kelly.

On "extra nights" Coleridge or Wordsworth, or both, would arrive and then there would be grand talk indeed. When Wordsworth talked, it was often about his own poems and, although Lamb loved and admired him, he could never resist the temptation to make fun of the poet's egotism and pomposities. "When Coleridge came," Talfourd wrote, "argument, wit, humour, criticism were hushed; the pertest, smartest and the cleverest felt that all were assembled to listen" to his gentle voice, which "suspended *whist* and took with ravishment the thronging audience." He would discourse eloquently and long in a low, gentle voice on Kant, Shakespeare, imagination or some abstract subject in philosophy. On one occasion he is said to have continued without interruption for two hours, Wordsworth occasionally nodding his approval. A little later when Wordsworth was asked whether he understood what Coleridge had been saying, he replied, "Not one syllable of it."

Meanwhile the quiet hostess gave special urging to partake of the cold roast or veal pie with heaps of potatoes, and the jug of porter from the "best tap on Fleet Street." The conversation, now that the card tables were pushed back, became more general and lively. Politics, specially party politics, were seldom debated, although some persons in the room were of the inside circle in political life. Lamb did not like politics as a theme for evening talk and the wishes of the host were respected. The pervading spirit was social and individual progress, the spirit of dreamers and thinkers rather than combatants in the world of affairs.

Literature and art supplied the favoured topics and were discussed with great seriousness and earnestness, with emphasis upon the odd and fantastic and little attention to the works which appeared in the circulating library even when that included such distinguished examples as the Waverley Novels. The Elizabethan age and the Seventeenth Century were the favoured periods, Bunyan was one of the preferred authors, such subjects were popular as the relation of the ancients and moderns, the merits of Raphael and Hogarth, and perhaps more often than other poets, the qualities of Spenser, Milton and Pope. Modern novels found favour with some of the talkers but not with Lamb; he cared little for narrative, even the better novels. Hazlitt agreed, except that he liked *Waverley,* but Leigh Hunt read almost everything in the way of a novel and Mary read even more and stoutly defended on every occasion her preference for stories. Sometimes the talk turned to the play of the evening, with praise for favourite actors or playwrights, and criticism of the stage in general—often stimulated by the presence of some of those actors.

"When the conversation became general," wrote Procter, "Lamb's part in it was very effective. His short clear sentences always produced effect. He never joined in talk unless he understood the subject; then if the matter in question interested him, he was not slow in showing his earnestness; but I never heard him argue or talk for argument's sake. If he was indifferent to the question, he was silent. It was curious to observe the gradations in Lamb's manner to his various guests; although it was courteous to all. With Hazlitt he talked as though they met the subject in discussion on equal terms; with Leigh Hunt he exchanged repartees; to Wordsworth he was almost respectful; with Coleridge he was sometimes jocose, sometimes deferring; with Martin Burney fraternally familiar; with Manning affectionate; with Godwin merely courteous; or, if friendly, then in a minor degree. . . . I never, in all my life, heard so much unpretending good sense talked, as at Charles Lamb's social parties."

For the particular evening for which we have tried to provide the setting, Lamb has suggested the subject, "Persons one would wish to have seen," and Hazlitt has left a remarkably vivid report of the talk.

"On the question being started, A[yrton] said, 'I suppose the two first persons you would choose to see would be the two greatest names in English literature, Sir Isaac Newton and Mr. Locke?' In this A[yrton], as usual, reckoned without his host. Every one burst out a-laughing at the expression of Lamb's face, in which impatience was restrained by courtesy. 'Yes, the greatest names,' he stammered out hastily, 'but they were not persons—not persons.'—'Not persons?' said A[yrton], looking wise and foolish at the same time, afraid his triumph might be premature. 'That is,' rejoined Lamb, 'not characters, you know.

By Mr. Locke and Sir Isaac Newton you mean the "Essay on the Human Understanding" and the "Principia," which we have to this day. Beyond their contents there is nothing personally interesting in the men. But what we want to see any one *bodily* for, is when there is something peculiar, striking in the individuals, more than we can learn from their writings, and yet are curious to know. I dare say Locke and Newton were very like Kneller's portraits of them. But who could paint Shakspeare?'—'Ay,' retorted A[yrton], 'there it is; then I suppose you would prefer seeing him and Milton instead?'—'No,' said Lamb, 'neither. I have seen so much of Shakspeare on the stage and on book-stalls, in frontispieces and on mantel-pieces, that I am quite tired of the everlasting repetition: and as to Milton's face, the impressions that have come down to us of it I do not like; it is too starched and puritanical; and I should be afraid of losing some of the manna of his poetry in the leaven of his countenance and the precisians's band and gown.'—'I shall guess no more,' said A[yrton]. 'Who is it, then, you would like to see "in his habit as he lived," if you had your choice of the whole range of English literature?'

"Lamb then named Sir Thomas Browne and Fulke Greville, the friend of Sir Philip Sidney, as the two worthies whom he should feel the greatest pleasure to encounter on the floor of his apartment in their nightgown and slippers, and to exchange friendly greeting with them. At this A[yrton] laughed outright, and conceived Lamb was jesting with him; but as no one followed his example, he thought there might be something in it, and waited for an explanation in a state of whimsical suspense. Lamb then . . . went on as follows: 'The reason why I pitch upon these two authors is, that their writings are riddles, and they themselves the most mysterious of personages. They resemble the soothsayers of old, who dealt in dark hints and doubtful oracles: and I should like to ask them the meaning of what no mortal but themselves, I should suppose, can fathom. There is Dr. Johnson: I have no curiosity, no strange uncertainty about him; he and Boswell together have pretty well let me into the secret of what passed through his mind. He and other writers like him are sufficiently explicit: my friends, whose repose I should be tempted to disturb (were it in my power), are implicit, inextricable, inscrutable. When I look at that obscure but gorgeous prose composition, the "Urn-burial," I seem to myself to look into a deep abyss, at the bottom of which are hid pearls and rich treasure; or it is like a stately labyrinth of doubt and withering speculation, and I would invoke the spirit of the author to lead me through it. Besides, who would not be curious to see the lineaments of a man who, having himself been twice married, wished that mankind were propagated like trees! As to Fulke Greville, he is like nothing but one of his own "Prologues spoken by the ghost of an old king of Ormus," a truly formidable and inviting personage: his style is apocalyptical, cabalistical, a knot worthy of such an apparition to untie; and for the unravelling a passage or two, I would stand the brunt of an encounter with so portentous a commentator!' . . .

"Some one then inquired of Lamb if we could not see from the window the Temple walk in which Chaucer used to take his exercise; and on his name being put to the vote, I was pleased to find that there was a general sensation in his favour in all but A[yrton], who said something about the ruggedness of the metre, and even objected to the quaintness of the orthography. I was vexed at this superficial gloss, pertinaciously reducing everything to its own trite level, and asked 'if he did not think it would be worth while to scan the eye that had first greeted the Muse in that dim twilight and early dawn of English literature; to see the head round which the visions of fancy must have played like gleams of inspiration or a sudden glory; to watch those lips that "lisped in numbers, for the numbers came"—as by a miracle, or as if the dumb should speak?' . . .

"Lamb put it to me if I should like to see Spenser as well as Chaucer; and I answered, without hesitation, 'No; for that his beauties were ideal, visionary, not palpable or personal, and therefore connected with less curiosity about the man. His poetry was the essence of romance, a very halo round the bright orb of fancy; and the bringing in the individual might dissolve the charm. No tones of voice could come up to the mellifluous cadence of his verse; no form but of a winged angel could vie with the airy shapes he has described.' . . .

"Captain Burney muttered something about Columbus, and Martin Burney hinted at the Wandering Jew; but the last was set aside as spurious, and the first made over to the New World.

"'I should like,' said Mrs. Reynolds,* 'to have seen Pope talk with Patty Blount; and I *have* seen Goldsmith.' Every one turned round to look at Mrs. Reynolds, as if by so doing they could get a sight at Goldsmith. . . .

"'I thought,' said A[yrton], turning short round upon Lamb, 'that you of the Lake School did not like Pope?'—'Not like Pope! My dear sir, you must be under a mistake—I can read him over and over for ever!'—'Why, certainly, the "Essay on Man" must be allowed to be a master-piece.'—'It may be so, but I seldom look into it.'—'Oh, then it's his Satires you admire?'—'No, not his Satires, but his friendly Epistles and his compliments.'—'Compliments! I did not know he ever made any.'—'The finest,' said Lamb, 'that were ever paid by the wit of man. Each of them is worth an estate for life—nay, is an immortality.' . . .

"'What say you to Dryden?'—'He rather made a show of

---

* Lamb's first schoolteacher, pensioned by him until she died in 1832. She *had* seen Goldsmith.

himself, and courted popularity in that lowest temple of Fame, a coffee-shop, so as in some measure to vulgarise one's idea of him. Pope, on the contrary, reached the very *beau ideal* of what a poet's life should be; and his fame while living seemed to be an emanation from that which was to circle his name after death. He was so far enviable (and one would feel proud to have witnessed the rare spectacle in him) that he was almost the only poet and man of genius who met with his reward on this side of the tomb, who realised in friends, fortune, the esteem of the world, the most sanguine hopes of a youthful ambition, and who found that sort of patronage from the great during his lifetime which they would be thought anxious to bestow upon him after his death. Read Gay's verses to him on his supposed return from Greece, after his translation of Homer was finished, and say if you would not gladly join the bright procession that welcomed him home, or see it once more land at Whitehall stairs.'—'Still, said Mrs. Reynolds, 'I would rather have seen him talking with Patty Blount, or riding by in a coronet-coach with Lady Mary Wortley Montagu!'

"Erasmus Phillips, who was deep in a game of piquet at the other end of the room, whispered to Martin Burney to ask if Junius would not be a fit person to invoke from the dead. 'Yes,' said Lamb, 'provided he would agree to lay aside his mask.'

"We were now at a stand for a short time, when Fielding was mentioned as a candidate: only one, however, seconded the proposition. 'Richardson?'—'By all means, but only to look at him through the glass-door of his back-shop, hard at work upon one of his novels (the most extraordinary contrast that ever was presented between an author and his works), not to let him come behind his counter lest he should want you to turn customer, or to go upstairs with him, lest he should offer to read the first manuscript of "Sir Charles Grandison," which was originally written in eight-and-twenty volumes octavo, or get out the letters of his female correspondents, to prove that "Joseph Andrews" was low.'

"There was but one statesman in the whole of English history that any one expressed the least desire to see—Oliver Cromwell, with his fine, frank, rough, pimply face, and wily policy;—and one enthusiast, John Bunyan, the immortal author of the 'Pilgrim's Progress.' It seemed that if he came into the room, dreams would follow him, and that each person would nod under his golden cloud, 'nigh-sphered in heaven,' a canopy as strange and stately as any in Homer.

"Of all persons near our own time, Garrick's name was received with the greatest enthusiasm, who was proposed by Barron Field. He presently superseded both Hogarth and Handel, who had been talked of, but then it was on condition that he should act in tragedy and comedy, in the play and the farce 'Lear' and 'Wildair' and 'Abel Drugger.' What a *sight for sore eyes* that would be! . . .

" 'I should like vastly to have seen Ninon de l'Enclos,' said that incomparable person [Mary Lamb]; and this immediately put us in mind that we had neglected to pay honour due to our friends on the other side of the Channel: Voltaire, the patriarch of levity, and Rousseau, the father of sentiment; Montaigne and Rabelais (great in wisdom and wit); Molière and that illustrious group that are collected round him (in the print of that subject) to hear him read his comedy of the 'Tartuffe' at the house of Ninon; Racine, La Fontaine, Rochefoucauld, St. Evremont, &c.

" 'There is one person,' said a shrill, querulous voice, 'I would rather see than all these—Don Quixote!'

" 'Come, come!' said Hunt; 'I thought we should have no heroes, real or fabulous. What say you, Mr. Lamb? Are you for eking out your shadowy list with such names as Alexander, Julius Cæsar, Tamerlane, or Ghengis Khan?'—'Excuse me,' said Lamb; 'on the subject of characters in active life, plotters and disturbers of the world, I have a crochet of my own, which I beg leave to reserve.'—'No, no! come out with your worthies!' —'What do you think of Guy Fawkes and Judas Iscariot?' Hunt turned an eye upon him like a wild Indian, but cordial and full of smothered glee. 'Your most exquisite reason!' was echoed on all sides; and A[yrton] thought that Lamb had now fairly entangled himself. 'Why, I cannot but think,' retorted he of the wistful countenance, 'that Guy Fawkes, that poor, fluttering annual scarecrow of straw and rags, is an ill-used gentleman. I would give something to see him sitting pale and emaciated, surrounded by his matches and his barrels of gunpowder, and expecting the moment that was to transport him to Paradise for his heroic self-devotion; but if I say any more, there is that fellow Godwin will make something of it. And as to Judas Iscariot, my reason is different. I would fain see the face of him who, having dipped his hand in the same dish with the Son of Man, could afterwards betray Him. I have no conception of such a thing; nor have I ever seen any picture (not even Leonardo's very fine one) that gave me the least idea of it.'—'You have said enough, Mr. Lamb, to justify your choice.'

" 'Oh! ever right, Menenius,—ever right!'

" 'There is only one other person I can ever think of after this,' continued Lamb; but without mentioning a name that once put on a semblance of mortality. 'If Shakespeare was to come into the room, we should all rise up to meet him; but if that person was to come into it, we should all fall down and try to kiss the hem of his garment!' "

Out into the night from the old Temple Buildings they went, each with precious memories of evenings long to be remembered, where were good talk, simple food and drink, wit and good fellowship. Must the new day bring an end to such happy evenings?

7

His Letters

ONLY three years after Lamb's death his friend Thomas Noon Talfourd made a first selection of about one hundred and seventy of his letters. These he edited, omitting many portions with personal references "too sacred for public exposure," weaving a thread of narrative to link them, and explaining allusions not clear to the reader. Mary was still living and every effort was made to keep from her occasions that would cause her to be more depressed or bring on attacks of her illness, now more frequent since the death of her brother.

In 1848, almost twelve years after the first edition, Talfourd made another selection including a few more than one hundred additional letters. The recent death of Mary and the publication in the *British Quarterly Review* of the details of the family tragedy had removed any doubts as to the propriety of publishing the new letters and of inserting passages omitted from the first edition.

From that time to the present, additions have been made until we come to the collections by Canon Ainger and E. V. Lucas. What these two devoted students have contributed in their respective editions can be appreciated only by one who makes a careful examination and comparison of the various publications that preceded them.

Not until 1935 did Lucas have sufficient confidence in the completeness of the collection to publish the three handsome volumes with the title *The Letters of Charles Lamb, to which are added those of his sister Mary Lamb.* It was no longer necessary to make omissions for reasons of personal allusion, but there were incredible difficulties of copyright and some collectors were unwilling to allow the publication of letters in their possession as they believed that unpublished they had a higher market value. His statement in the preface would seem to warrant Lucas in calling this "the first complete edition." "Thus not only do these three volumes contain all the letters in the editions of Talfourd, of Percy FitzGerald, of Bohn's Library, of Ainger, of W. Carew Hazlitt, of Everyman's Library, based on the labours of William Macdonald, of the Boston Bibliophile Society, 1905, and of my own in its latest form, 1912, but also whatever has come to light since their day." This edition contains more than one thousand letters, almost four times the number of the combined first two editions by Talfourd.

It is conceivable that additional letters may be found. After the exciting discoveries in the past century one would hardly dare to predict but rather accept the position of Lucas, who could speak with rare, unparalleled experience. "Such can be the perversity of Fate that it is probable that the mere publication of this book will recall to many memories that box of old papers in the attic which surely had something by a man named Lamb in it."

In one respect certainly Lamb has had the good fortune to have had sensible as well as sympathetic executors, collectors and editors. Talfourd, the first editor, wrote, "There is, indeed, scarcely a note—a 'notelet' (as he used to call his very little letters) Lamb ever wrote, which has not some tinge of that quaint sweetness, some hint of that peculiar union of kindness and whim, which distinguish him from all other poets and humourists." Lucas cheerfully accepted that obligation and we are assured that everything has been retained which throws any light whatsoever on the character of the writer.

Lamb did not conceal his low opinion of his own penmanship. Perhaps it was better than he thought; at any rate the years at the India House effected improvement and, when he took pains, as he frequently did, his letter presented a pleasing appearance. His handwriting was usually clear enough. He confessed to a "bold free hand, and a fearless flourish," whereas his sister "writes such a pimping, mean, detestable hand," indulges in no bold blots, and always makes a fair copy, dotting her i's and crossing her t's, "though she writes a pretty good style, and has some notion of the force of words she is not always so certain of the true orthography of them." Coming from Lamb, this is amusing, for he was capable of distorting familiar words as well as place names and persons and he was not even consistent in his distortions. He would write "volum," "argueer," "tease" and "teaze," "likend" and "likened," "Bonaparte" and "Buonarparte," and certain proper names such as Procter and Hazlitt he consistently spelt wrongly. His punctuation was as unreliable as his spelling.

In the preface to his second edition in 1848, Talfourd spoke of "the appreciation which the letters already published, both in this country and in America—perhaps even more remarkable in America than in England—have attained." There has not been a noticeable lessening of the appreciation in America, which has had as one of its results the purchase of the more important letters which are now in the keeping of American libraries, notably the Henry E. Huntington, the University of Texas, the Folger Shakespeare, the Harvard University and the Pierpont Morgan.

In English the number of those persons whose letters have had a more than local or ephemeral interest is not large, and the differences in their letters are a striking confirmation of the differences of personality, time, taste, political and social conditions. Eminent in any selection is Dean Swift, whose correspondence with Esther Johnson, known as the *Journal to*

Stella, along with six volumes of correspondence published some thirty years ago, revealed characteristics of the man that few people had realised. Not only have these letters added to the stature of the man, but they have also greatly increased our interest in him as a human being. They contain some of the best of his sayings and more striking evidence of his definition that style is proper words in proper places. If they were not marked by distinction in clearness and simplicity, they would not be written by Dean Swift. Besides, they include a great range of subjects and show a skilful adaptation to the particular correspondent; for example, the letters to Pope take on the colour of the artificiality of that Eighteenth-Century poet, the letters to King befit a dignitary of the Church, and the letters to Arbuthnot delightfully picture the kindness of that distinguished doctor as well as the affection which existed between him and Swift. The list of correspondents included the most prominent persons in political and literary life of that time—Bolingbroke, Oxford, Pope, Gay, Addison, Lord Peterborough, Patty Blount, the Duchess of Queensberry and Lady Masham. These letters offer a stirring picture of the political strife and literary activity of a full fifty years. They are characterized by a facility of expression unsurpassed in our history and an irony and humour which were a true revelation. Great would be our loss if we did not have them, but they do not make us love Swift the more.

Cowper had all the qualities of a good letter-writer. Unlike Swift or Walpole or Lamb, he wrote to only a few persons: Lady Hesketh, Joseph Hill, Reverend Unwin, Reverend John Newton, Samuel Rose and William Haley, and no one of them distinguished. Where can we look for better letters, unmatched in our language for simplicity, quiet humour, and charming descriptions of daily life? The little country town of Olney is with us day by day. We know when the jasmine, the honeysuckle, the melons, the broccoli, the cauliflowers all come out;

just how good are the salmon, the mackerel, the turbot, the shrimps and the oysters. And we, too, are concerned about the tame pigeons, the linnet, the crow and the raven and the adventures of Puss. And it is almost like war-time in 1944 when we see how much planning it takes to get new glass for the greenhouse, a new shoebuckle or wood for next winter. Some note is taken of war in America, of the local elections and the publication of books of poetry, but in the main the subject is the simple life of the people of the village. A sense of quiet humour, a tone of melancholy, an emphasis on courage—these are the qualities of Cowper's letters.

For more than sixty-five years Horace Walpole wrote regularly and at length from Strawberry Hill to friends and politicians, poets and women of high social standing—more than three thousand letters. In this unique record the variety of his subjects is as great as his writing periods are frequent. With an amazing display of individuality men and women walk across the stage and leave upon the reader quite definite impressions of their personalities, so distinct that we find ourselves liking or disliking them as we would in real life. A truly wonderful show! One cannot conceive a greater contrast than the difference between Cowper and Walpole in the things they wrote about, the people they wrote to, and the characters revealed of the men doing the writing: Walpole, whose scruples are always a matter of question, whose affectation is always with us; Cowper, whose honesty and integrity no one simply would think of doubting. The Eighteenth Century for us is largely what these letters of Walpole have told us.

Gray has been called the greatest scholar of his day; perhaps he was. His letters are a full, adequate picture of that kind of man. There is no comparable instance of a pure scholar so fully revealed as he. His qualities are those of the academic man drawn into lonely isolation, with the characteristic melancholy, shyness and refusal to throw himself into the confusion of public affairs. There is great and literary interest in his descriptions of his trip to the Continent and his observations on the picturesque and wild in nature are the sure first signs of the taste which was to develop in the Romantic movement. In the main the letters are literary in the sense of being interesting to persons who are interested in books. A question remains whether these letters have made Gray more widely admired or more loved.

It would be difficult to quote from any one who could find better letters for us than E. V. Lucas. He once wrote, "But by the term 'the best letter-writer' we have come to mean the literary man or woman whose correspondence makes the most attractive reading; and here, of course, opinions differ, just as the writers themselves differed: one reader preferring, above all others, those letters in which he sees revealed such treasure as the odd prejudices, the tenderness, the diffidence, and warm heart of Edward Fitz Gerald; another, the resolute and unswerving common sense, cynicism, and humour of Dean Swift; a third, the wistful melancholy and sweet serenity of Thomas Gray; another, the rollicking absurdities and whimsical idiosyncrasy of Lamb; a fifth, the aristocratic disdain and worldly friendliness of Walpole; a sixth, the sympathetic candour, gaiety, and enthusiasms of Keats; and yet another, the comic, mischievous, quizzical, hungry soul of Jane Welsh Carlyle. I have heard each of those named the best English letter-writer; just as I have heard the palm awarded, by those in love with 'divine chit-chat' to William Cowper."*

The date of the first Lamb letter is May 27, 1796; of the last December 22, 1834, only five days before his death. For the first two years eighteen letters of 1796 and thirteen letters of 1797 have been found, all to Coleridge. As we follow the successive

---

* Introduction to *William Cowper's Letters*, Oxford University Press.

years, we become interested in speculating on the causes for large differences in the number of letters for the different years. Surely many letters have been lost. There may have been personal reasons why he did not at times write more regularly, and then some more letters may be discovered later. For example, of 1807 we have five letters; of 1811, six; of 1812, three; of 1813, none; of 1818, nine. It is hard to believe that Lamb wrote in those four years only seventeen letters. Rather it is not much short of a miracle that we have so many letters, when we realise the ease with which books and manuscripts have been lost. There are only nine letters to William Hazlitt, although here was a relationship which lasted more than twenty years, so close that Lamb was the only person at Hazlitt's bedside when he died. But it may be because Hazlitt was in or near London most of those years. Nor does it seem likely that he wrote only six letters to Leigh Hunt, six to George Dyer, eleven to Barron Field, six to Patmore, and nineteen to Crabb Robinson. There are many questions upon which it would be equally interesting to speculate, and perhaps just as futile. That letters of the years after 1819 are more numerous may be explained in part by the growing reputation of Lamb as a writer; for example, he wrote fifty-three letters in 1823; seventy-six in 1827; and seventy in 1833, the year before he died. They were more treasured. Lamb did not keep letters so he had little or nothing to return when he was asked for letters from famous people to him. Others of his friends never kept letters, either. How was it that Coleridge, careless and erratic as he was, did not lose or destroy the letters from Lamb which have been preserved, when Lamb was of the two the more methodical?

There must have been earlier letters than that first one, between January 1795 and May 1796. Lamb was living at 7 Little Queen Street, with his father, now growing imbecile, his mother, Aunt Hetty and his sister Mary. Charles had been for four years

at the East India House. Mary was occupied as a mantua-
maker, doing her work at home, sometimes with the help of a
young apprentice girl. Besides Charles's earnings, there was the
pension from Salt, a slight pension which Aunt Hetty received
and the small earnings from Mary's needlework. The family
was poor, but they were not destitute; the prospect was certainly
brighter than it had been two years before.

At the time of this first letter Lamb was twenty-one, Coleridge twenty-three. After Christ's Hospital, Coleridge went to
Cambridge. Of his life there we know little, not much more
than of his life at Christ's Hospital, which is so sympathetically
described by Leigh Hunt. Something of his Cambridge life we
learn from his companion, Charles Le Grice. We know that
towards the end of the year 1793, whether from dejection, an
affair of love, a slight indebtedness which troubled him, or, perhaps, the instability which was growing upon him, Coleridge
suddenly left Cambridge, went to London and enlisted in the
army as a private under the name of Silas Titus Comerback. He
was in the army for four months when the captain of his company happened to see a Latin quotation inscribed on the walls of
the stable. Such an unusual display of learning piqued the curiosity of the captain, who, when he discovered the authorship,
insisted that Coleridge leave the ranks and return to Cambridge.
He was released in April 1794. In June of that year he met
Robert Southey and in August went to visit him in Bristol,
where he met Southey's friend Robert Lovell and, even more
important, Joseph Cottle. Cottle was one of those men who had
money and were intent to serve as patrons to literary men and
works and this meeting was a piece of good fortune for both
Coleridge and the cause of English literature.

Lovell had already married Mary Fricker. Southey soon became engaged to Edith Fricker, her sister, and in the next year
Coleridge was to marry the other sister, Sara. Coleridge's insta-

bility was never more clearly shown than in his immediate acceptance of a plan which had been worked out by Lovell and Southey to establish a Utopian community on the banks of the Susquehanna in Pennsylvania. The three couples were to go together to America to live an idyllic existence where the men would do the thinking and the small but necessary amount of manual labor, while the women looked after the home and the children.

In September, Coleridge went back to Cambridge, presumably to finish his university work and get his degree. That was not so to be, for after a few months he was again in London talking, talking, trying to find himself in writing, and spending long and happy hours with Lamb at the Salutation and Cat, the tavern almost opposite Christ's Hospital. This was the winter of 1794-1795. Coleridge returned to Bristol, perhaps brought back by Southey, who was beginning to fear that Coleridge was wasting his time and efforts in London. During the year Coleridge continued his writing and in October married Sara Fricker. Apparently the first months of married life were happy for both Coleridge and Sara. He was busy with his poetry but found time to be serviceable as a real family man, showing considerable interest in kitchen and garden.

It was a time for the writing of plays. Moved by the ideals and tragedies of the French Revolution, the three men planned *The Fall of Robespierre,* the first act to be by Coleridge, the second by Southey and the third by Lovell. At the end of the days which were allotted to the writing, Coleridge, as usual, failed to have his act done. Southey's was passable, but Lovell's of no value, and so Southey undertook to do the third act, Coleridge finished his later, and the entire play was afterwards inaugurated in Coleridge's works.

In the spring of 1796 at the age of twenty-four Coleridge made an attempt to enter journalism. His friend Thomas Poole, like

Cottle, was willing to furnish money and the two worked out a plan to publish a paper, to be called *The Watchman*. To secure advance subscriptions Coleridge set out on a tour from Bristol to Sheffield. The account of his experiences of this trip is about the only evidence in the *Biographia Literaria* that Coleridge was possessed of a sense of humour. At any rate he came back with several hundred subscribers who, with a few others that sent in their names later, stayed with the magazine until the last number, the tenth, appeared.

So we have the picture of Lamb and Coleridge at the time of the first letters. They begin with a reference to May, landlord of the Salutation and Cat, where Lamb and Coleridge had spent so many happy evenings in the winter of 1794 and 1795. "Make yourself perfectly easy about May. I paid his bill, when I sent your clothes. I was flush of money, and am so still to all the purposes of a single life, so give yourself no further concern about it. The money would be superfluous to me if I had it." We suppose that when Coleridge left town in January 1795 he could not pay his bill and was required to leave his luggage behind until the money could be sent.

The loneliness which had come over Lamb after his separation from Coleridge, partly because of his blighted attachment for "Alice," and partly because misgivings occasionally troubled Mary and Charles from the taint of madness in the family, had finally led to a breakdown. Again from the first letter: "The 6 weeks that finished last year and began this your very humble servant spent very agreeably in a madhouse at Hoxton—I am got somewhat rational now, and don't bite anyone. But mad I was—and many a vagary my imagination played with me, enough to make a volume if all told. . . . Coleridge, it may convince you of my regards for you when I tell you that my head ran on you in my madness, as much almost as on another Person, who I am inclined to think was the more immediate cause of

my temporary frenzy." Although this is the only attack of the
kind that Lamb is known to have suffered, the note seems to set
the theme as in a Greek chorus of the human drama which
was to be Charles Lamb.

The second letter brings Wordsworth into the picture and he
remains there to the end. With his revolutionary enthusiasm
over, at twenty-six he had settled with his sister Dorothy at
Racedown on the border between Dorset and Somersetshire.

These early letters reveal Lamb's enthusiasm for the books
which he was reading and for the authors whom he had come
to know. At Christ's Hospital both Coleridge and Lamb had
discovered the sonnets of William Bowles. His simplicity and
sincerity, touched with tender melancholy, had appealed to the
boys and their first verses were written under the spell of his
work. The seven years intervening for Lamb had been filled
with discoveries of books and authors of the Seventeenth and
Eighteenth Centuries. He now writes joyfully of finds which he
has been making—*The Compleat Angler,* the eloquence of Sir
Thomas Browne, Robert Burton and Jeremy Taylor, the prose
of Ossian and the poems of Burns and Cowper. His enthusiasm
is not mere feeling; there are a continuing appreciation and a
criticism denoting growth and widening experience. Here was
a young scholar in the best sense, seriously trying to perfect his
criticism not by a study of formal models, but by applying the
touchstone of human life and the possibilities of the written
language. But let no one think that this description adequately
describes the naturalness of these letters, their humorous and
sympathetic references to the little incidents of daily life and
the whims and inconsistencies of people as we see them every
day.

Though we have had signals of warning, we are not prepared,
Coleridge surely could not have been, for the crash which was
to come.

"[P.M. *27th September 1796*]

"My dearest friend—White or some of my friends or the public papers by this time may have informed you of the terrible calamities that have fallen on our family. I will only give you the outlines. My poor dear dearest sister in a fit of insanity has been the death of her own mother. I was at hand only time enough to snatch the knife out of her grasp. She is at present in a mad house, from whence I fear she must be moved to an hospital. God has preserved to me my senses,—I eat and drink and sleep, and have my judgment I believe very sound. My poor father was slightly wounded, and I am left to take care of him and my aunt. Mr. Norris of the Bluecoat school has been very kind to us, and we have no other friend, but thank God I am very calm and composed, and able to do the best that remains to do. Write,—as religious a letter as possible—but no mention of what is gone and done with—with me the former things are passed away, and I have something more to do [than] to feel——

"God Almighty

"have us all in
his keeping.——

"C. LAMB.

mention nothing of poetry. I have destroyed every vestige of past vanities of that kind. Do as you please, but if you publish, publish mine (I give free leave) without name or initial, and never send me a book, I charge you, you[r] own judgment will convince you not to take any notice of this yet to your dear wife.—You look after your family,—I have my reason and strength left to take care of mine. I charge you don't think of coming to see me. Write. I will not see you if you come. God Almighty love you and all of us——"

The tragedy had occurred on the twenty-second, the preceding Thursday. The newspapers printed the account on Monday the twenty-sixth and Charles wrote to Coleridge on the twenty-seventh. Coleridge answered the following day.

"[*28th September 1796.*]

"Your letter, my friend, struck me with a mighty horror. It rushed upon me and stupefied my feelings. You bid me write you a religious letter; I am not a man who would attempt to insult the greatness of your anguish by any other consolation. Heaven knows that in the easiest fortunes there is much dissatisfaction and weariness of spirit; much that calls for the exercise of patience and resignation; but in storms, like these, that shake the dwelling and make the heart tremble, there is no middle way between despair and the yielding up of the whole spirit unto the guidance of faith. And surely it is a matter of joy, that your faith in Jesus has been preserved; the Comforter that should relieve you is not far from you. But as you are a Christian, in the name of that Saviour, who was filled with bitterness and made drunken with wormwood, I conjure you to have recourse in frequent prayer to 'his God and your God,' the God of mercies, and father of all comfort. Your poor father is, I hope, almost senseless of the calamity; the unconscious instrument of Divine Providence knows it not, and your mother is in heaven. It is sweet to be roused from a frightful dream by the song of birds, and the gladsome rays of the morning. Ah, how infinitely more sweet to be awakened from the blackness and amazement of a sudden horror, by the glories of God manifest, and the hallelujahs of angels.

"As to what regards yourself, I approve altogether of your abandoning what you justly call vanities. I look upon you as a man, called by sorrow and anguish and a strange desolation of hopes into quietness, and a soul set apart and made peculiar to God; we cannot arrive at any portion of heavenly bliss without in some measure imitating Christ. And they arrive at the largest inheritance who imitate the most difficult parts of his character, and bowed down and crushed under foot, cry in fullness of faith, 'Father, thy will be done.'

"I wish above measure to have you for a little while here—no visitants shall blow on the nakedness of your feelings—you shall be quiet, and your spirit may be healed. I see no possible objection, unless your father's helplessness prevent you, and unless you are necessary to him. If this be not the case, I charge you write me that you will come.

"I charge you, my dearest friend, not to dare to encourage gloom or despair—you are a temporary sharer in human miseries, that you may be an eternal partaker of the Divine nature. I charge you, if by any means it be possible, come to me.

"I remain, your affectionate,

"S. T. COLERIDGE."

Lamb's reply was equally sincere:

"[P.M. *3rd October 1796.*]

"My dearest friend, your letter was an inestimable treasure to me. It will be a comfort to you, I know, to know that our prospects are somewhat brighter. My poor dear dearest sister, the unhappy and unconscious instrument of the Almighty's judgments to our house, is restored to her senses; to a dreadful sense and recollection of what has past, awful to her mind, and impressive (as it must be to the end of life), but temper'd with religious resignation, and the reasonings of a sound judgment, which in this early stage knows how to distinguish between a deed committed in a transient fit of frenzy, and the terrible guilt of a Mother's murther. I have seen her. I found her this morning calm and serene; far very very far from an indecent forgetful serenity; she has a most affectionate and tender concern for what has happened. Indeed from the beginning, frightful and hopeless as her disorder seemed, I had confidence enough in her strength of mind, and religious principle, to look forward to a time when *even she* might recover tranquillity. God be praised, Coleridge, wonderful as it is to tell, I have never once been otherwise than collected, and calm; even on the dreadful day and in the midst of the terrible scene I preserved a tranquillity, which bystanders may have construed into indifference, a tranquillity not of despair; is it folly or sin in me to say that it was a religious principle that *most* supported me? I allow much to other favorable circumstances. I felt that I had something else to do than to regret; on that first evening my aunt was lying insensible, to all appearance like one dying,—my father, with his poor forehead plaisterd over from a wound he had received from a daughter dearly loved by him, and who loved him no less dearly,—my mother a dead and murder'd corpse in the next room—yet was I wonderfully supported. I closed not my eyes in sleep that night, but lay without terrors and without despair. I have lost no sleep since. I had been long used not to rest in things of sense, had endeavord after a comprehension of mind, unsatisfied with the 'ignorant present time,' and this kept me up. I had the whole weight of the family thrown on me, for my brother, little disposed (I speak not without tenderness for him) at any time to take care of old age and infirmities, had now, with his bad leg, an exemption from such duties, and I was now left alone. One little incident may serve to make you understand my way of managing my mind. Within a day or 2 after the fatal ONE, we drest for dinner a tongue, which we had had salted for some weeks in the house. As I sat down a feeling like remorse struck me,—this tongue poor Mary got for me, and can I partake of it now, when she is far away—thought occurrd and relieved me,—if I give in to this way of feeling, there is not a chair, a room, an object in our rooms, that will not awaken the keenest griefs, I must rise above such weaknesses.—I hope this was not want of true feeling. I did not let this carry me, tho', too far. On the very 2d day (I date from the day of horrors) as is usual in such cases there were a matter of 20 people I do think supping in our room. They prevailed on me to eat *with them* (for to eat I never refused). They were all making merry! in the room,—some had come from friendship, some from busy curiosity, and some from Interest; I was going to partake with them, when my recollection came that my poor dead mother was lying in the next room, the very next room, a mother who, thro' life wished nothing but her children's welfare—indignation, the rage of grief, something like remorse, rushed upon my mind in an agony of emotion,—I found my way mechanically to the adjoining room, and fell on my knees by the side of her coffin, asking forgiveness of heaven, and sometimes of her, for forgetting her so soon. Tranquillity returned, and it was the only violent emotion that mastered me, and I think it did me good.

"I mention these things because I hate concealment, and love to give a faithful journal of what passes within me. Our friends have been very good. Sam Le Grice who was then in town was with me the first 3 or 4 days, and was as a brother to me, gave up every hour of his time, to the very hurting of his health and spirits, in constant attendance and humouring my poor father. Talk'd with him, read to him, play'd at cribbage with him (for so short is the old man's recollection, that he was playing at cards, as tho' nothing had happened, while the Coroner's Inquest was sitting over the way!) Samuel wept tenderly when he went away, for his mother wrote him a very severe letter on his loitering so long in town, and he was forced to go. Mr. Norris of Christ Hospital has been as a father to me, Mrs. Norris as a mother; tho' we had few claims on them. A Gentleman, brother to my Godmother, from whom we never had right or reason to expect any such assistance, sent my father twenty pounds,—and to crown all these God's blessings to our family at such a time, an old Lady, a cousin of my father and Aunt's, a Gentlewoman of fortune, is to take my Aunt and make her comfortable for the short remainder of her days.

"My Aunt is recover'd and as well as ever, and highly pleased at thoughts of going,—and has generously given up the interest of her little money (which was formerly paid my Father for her board) wholely and solely to my Sister's use. Reckoning this we have, Daddy and I, for our two selves and an old maid servant to look after him, when I am out, which will be necessary, £170 or £180 (rather), a year, out of which we can spare £50 or £60 at least for Mary, while she stays at Islington, where she must and shall stay during her father's life for his and her comfort. I know John will make speeches about it, but she shall not go into an hospital. The good Lady of the mad house, and her daughter, an elegant sweet behaved young Lady, love her and are taken with her amazingly, and I know from her own mouth she loves them, and longs to be with them as much.— Poor thing, they say she was but the other morning saying, she knew she must go to Bethlem for life: that one of her brothers would have it so, but the other would wish it not, but be obliged to go with the stream; that she had often as she passed Bedlam thought it likely 'here it may be my fate to end my days—' conscious of a certain flightiness in her poor head oftentimes, and mindful of more than one severe illness of that nature before. A Legacy of £100, which my father will have at Xmas, and this £20 I mentioned before, with what is in the house will much more than set us Clear;—if my father, an old servant maid, and I, can't live and live comfortably on £130 or £120 a year we ought to burn by slow fires, and I almost would, that Mary might not go into an hospital. Let me not leave one unfavourable impression on your mind respecting my Brother. Since this has happened he has been very kind and brotherly; but I fear for his mind,—he has taken his ease in the world, and is not fit himself to struggle with difficulties, nor has much accustomed himself to throw himself into their way,—and I know his language is already, 'Charles, you must take care of yourself, you must not abridge yourself of a single pleasure you have been used to,' &c &c and in that style of talking. But you, a necessarian, can respect a difference of mind, and love what *is amiable* in a character not perfect. He has been very good, but I fear for his mind. Thank God, I can unconnect myself with him, and shall manage all my father's monies in future myself, if I take charge of Daddy, which poor John has not even hinted a wish, at any future time even, to share with me. The Lady at this mad house assures me that I may dismiss immediately both Doctor and apothecary, retaining occasionally an opening draught or so for a while, and there is a less expensive establishment in her house, where she will only not have a room and nurse to herself, for £50 or guineas a year—the outside would be £60—You know by economy how much more, even, I shall be able to spare for her comforts.

"She will, I fancy, if she stays, make one of the family, rather than of the patients, and the old and young ladies I like exceedingly, and she loves dearly, and they, as the saying is, take to her very extraordinarily, if it is extraordinary that people who see my sister should love her. Of all the people I ever saw in the world my poor sister was most and thoroughly devoid of the least tincture of selfishness—I will enlarge upon her qualities, poor dear dearest soul, in a future letter, for my own comfort, for I understand her throughly; and if I mistake not, in the most trying situation that a human being can be found in, she will be found (I speak not with sufficient humility, I fear, but humanly and foolishly speaking) she will be found, I trust, uniformly great and amiable. God keep her in her present mind, to whom be thanks and praise for all His dispensations to mankind.

"LAMB."

It was characteristic of Lamb that even in the depth of great sorrow and discouragement he should be concerned about his "dearest friend." If Coleridge could have heeded these words!

"[P.M. *17th October 1796.*]

"My dearest friend, I grieve from my very soul to observe you in your plans of life veering about from this hope to the other, and settling no where. Is it an untoward fatality (speaking humanly) that does this for you, a stubborn, irresistible concurrence of events? or lies the fault, as I fear it does, in your own mind? You seem to be taking up splendid schemes of fortune only to lay them down again, and your fortunes are an ignis fatuus that has been conducting you, in thought, from Lancaster Court, Strand, to somewhere near Matlock, then jumping across to Dr. Somebody's whose son's tutor you were likely to be, and would to God the dancing demon *may* conduct you at last in peace and comfort to the 'life and labors of a cottager.' You see from the above awkward playfulness of fancy, that my spirits are not quite depressed; I should ill deserve God's blessings, which since the late terrible event have come down in mercy upon us, if I indulged regret or querulousness,—Mary continues serene and cheerful,—I have not by me a little letter she wrote to me, for, tho' I see her almost every day yet we delight to write to one another (for we can scarce see each other but in company with some of the people of the house)...."

And in the next month Lamb expressed again his anxiety. "I am distrest for you, believe me I am; not so much for your painful, troublesome complaint, which, I trust, is only for a time, as for those anxieties which brought it on, and perhaps even now may be nursing its malignity." This was the beginning of Coleridge's neuralgia, the result of worry, chiefly concerning his future, when he began to take laudanum with such disastrous results.

Lamb was never slow in acknowledging how much he owed to his brilliant friend, and was always striving to introduce some comment of sentiment or encouragement. "This has been a sad long letter of business, with no room in it for what honest Bunyan terms heart-work. I have just room left to congratulate you on your removal to Stowey; to wish success to all your projects; to 'bid fair peace' be to that house; to send my love and best wishes, breathed warmly, after your dear Sara, and her little David Hartley."

Nobody understood better than Coleridge the difficulties which beset Lamb in his oft-announced vows to keep from smoke and drink. "Morning," Charles writes him, "is a Girl, and can't smoke—she's no evidence one way or other; and Night is so evidently *bought over,* that *he* can't be a very upright Judge. May be the truth is, that *one* pipe is wholesome, *two* pipes toothsome, *three* pipes noisome, *four* pipes fulsome, *five* pipes quarrelsome; and that's the *sum* on't. But that is deciding rather upon rhyme than reason. . . . After all, our instincts *may* be best. Wine, I am sure, good, mellow, generous Port, can hurt nobody, unless they take it to excess, which they may easily avoid if they observe the rules of temperance."*

Lamb did not hesitate to write frankly to Coleridge what he thought of his poems. It was not always praise nor was it always censure; what he said was not in general terms, but specific indication of word and phrase. It is noteworthy that no critic of the *Lyrical Ballads* of his time came so near giving voice to what have been since accepted as the definite and lasting qualities of these poems. Appreciation so honest and so keen it is a pleasure for us to read it; oases in a desert where seemed to thrive only the review inspired by malice and expressed by cruel invective. From criticism of his contemporaries in letters to them, Lamb turned to authors and books which he had come to know in his extensive reading since school days.

The letters to Coleridge were not all about literary matters.

* Letter to Coleridge, April 1803.

They expressed happiness in recalling Salutation and Cat days, news about mutual friends, his concern for Mary's welfare, all the interests which the young clerk thought his friend would like to hear about.

The value of letters is partly in the revelation of the author and partly in the interest which the author takes in the person to whom he is writing. Is he thinking of the recipient of the letter, or is he merely seeking an opportunity to tell somebody about himself? The letters of Charles Lamb are quite remarkable in their balance in this respect. Not one of those which are preserved is unworthy of the writer. They bring delight to the reader because they are from a person whom we like to hear from, and please us because we like to think ourselves worthy of such attention. The persons described are the kind of people we all come to know, the incidents are those which happen in such circumstances.

Among the most enjoyable of Lamb's letters are those which tell of trips which he took with Mary on his holidays from the India House. Usually he had a month in the summer and two or three days during the year. These both Charles and Mary looked forward to and planned for with the joy of children in school. If the period was longer, they went to see the Hazlitts at Winterslow Hut, the Coleridges and Wordsworths at Nether Stowey in the Lake District, the Clarksons at Bury St. Edmunds, Isle of Wight; to Margate, or best of all to Oxford or Cambridge; if the time was very short, then it must be a place nearer London. "We have already had all the holydays we can have this year. We have been spending our usual summer month at Richmond, from which place we traced the banks of the old Thames for ten and twenty miles, in daily walks or rides, and found beauties which may compare with Ulswater and Windermere. We visited Windsor, Hampton, etc."

A letter addressed to Thomas Manning describes the trip which Charles and Mary made to the Lake District.

"*24th Sept., 1802,* London.

"My dear Manning,

"Since the date of my last letter, I have been a traveller. A strong desire seized me of visiting remote regions. My first impulse was to go and see Paris. It was a trivial objection to my aspiring mind, that I did not understand a word of the language, since I certainly intend some time in my life to see Paris, and equally certainly intend never to learn the language; therefore that could be no objection. However, I am very glad I did not go, because you had left Paris (I see) before I could have set out. I believe, Stoddart promising to go with me another year prevented that plan. My next scheme, (for to my restless, ambitious mind London was become a bed of thorns) was to visit the far-famed Peak in Derbyshire, where the Devil sits, they say, without breeches. *This* my purer mind rejected as indelicate. And my final resolve was a tour to the Lakes. I set out with Mary to Keswick, without giving Coleridge any notice; for my time being precious did not admit of it. He received us with all the hospitality in the world, and gave up his time to show us all the wonders of the country. He dwells upon a small hill by the side of Keswick, in a comfortable house, quite enveloped on all sides by a net of mountains: great floundering bears and monsters they seemed, all couchant and asleep. We got in in the evening, travelling in a post-chaise from Penrith, in the midst of a gorgeous sunshine, which transmuted all the mountains into colours, purple, &c. &c. We thought we had got into Fairy Land. But that went off (as it never came again—while we stayed we had no more fine sunsets); and we entered Coleridge's comfortable study just in the dusk, when the mountains were all dark with clouds upon their heads. Such an impression I never received from objects of sight before, nor do I suppose I can ever again. Glorious creatures, fine old fellows, Skiddaw, &c. I never shall forget ye, how ye lay about that night, like an intrenchment; gone to bed, as it seemed for the night, but promis-

ing that ye were to be seen in the morning. Coleridge had got a
blazing fire in his study; which is a large, antique, ill-shaped
room, with an old-fashioned organ, never played upon, big
enough for a church, shelves of scattered folios, an Æolian harp,
and an old sofa, half-bed, &c. And all looking out upon the last
fading view of Skiddaw, and his broad-breasted brethren: what
a night! Here we stayed three full weeks, in which time I visited Wordsworth's cottage, where we stayed a day or two with
the Clarksons (good people and most hospitable, at whose house
we tarried one day and night), and saw Lloyd. The Wordsworths were gone to Calais. They have since been in London
and past much time with us: he is now gone into Yorkshire to be
married. . . . So we have seen Keswick, Grasmere, Ambleside,
Ulswater (where the Clarksons live), and a place at the other
end of Ulswater—I forget the name—to which we travelled on
a very sultry day, over the middle of Helvellyn. We have clam-
bered up to the top of Skiddaw, and I have waded up the bed
of Lodore. In fine, I have satisfied myself, that there is such a
thing as that which tourists call *romantic,* which I very much
suspected before: they make such a spluttering about it, and toss
their splendid epithets around them, till they give as dim a light
as at four o'clock next morning the lamps do after an illumination. Mary was excessively tired, when she got about half-way
up Skiddaw, but we came to a cold rill (than which nothing
can be imagined more cold, running over cold stones), and with
the reinforcement of a draught of cold water she surmounted it
most manfully. Oh, its fine black head, and the bleak air atop
of it, with a prospect of mountains all about, and about, making
you giddy; and then Scotland afar off, and the border countries
so famous in song and ballad! It was a day that will stand out,
like a mountain, I am sure, in my life. But I am returned (I
have now been come home near three weeks—I was a month
out), and you cannot conceive the degradation I felt at first,

from being accustomed to wander free as air among mountains, and bathe in rivers without being controlled by any one, to come home and *work*. I felt very *little*. I had been dreaming I was a very great man. But that is going off, and I find I shall conform in time to that state of life to which it has pleased God to call me. Besides, after all, Fleet-Street and the Strand are better places to live in for good and all than among Skiddaw. Still, I turn back to those great places where I wandered about, participating in their greatness. After all, I could not *live* in Skiddaw. I could spend a year—two, three years—among them, but I must have a prospect of seeing Fleet-Street at the end of that time, or I should mope and pine away, I know. Still, Skiddaw is a fine creature. My habits are changing, I think: *i.e.* from drunk to sober. Whether I shall be happier or not remains to be proved. I shall certainly be more happy in a morning; but whether I shall not sacrifice the fat, and the marrow, and the kidneys, *i.e.* the night, the glorious care-drowning night, that heals all our wrongs, pours wine into our mortifications, changes the scene from indifferent and flat to bright and brilliant!—O Manning, if I should have formed a diabolical resolution, by the time you come to England, of not admitting any spirituous liquors into my house, will you be my guest on such shameworthy terms? Is life, with such limitations, worth trying? The truth is, that my liquors bring a nest of friendly harpies about my house, who consume me. This is a pitiful tale to be read at St. Gothard; but it is just now nearest my heart. Fenwick is a ruined man. He is hiding himself from his creditors, and has sent his wife and children into the country. Fell, my other drunken companion (that has been: nam hic cæstus artemque repono), is turned editor of a 'Naval Chronicle.' Godwin (with a pitiful artificial wife) continues a steady friend, though the same facility does not remain of visiting him often. That Bitch has detached Marshall from his house, Marshall the man who went to sleep when the

'Ancient Mariner' was reading: the old, steady, unalterable friend of the Professor. Holcroft is not yet come to town. I expect to see him, and will deliver your message. How I hate *this part* of a letter. Things come crowding in to say, and no room for 'em. Some things are too little to be told, *i.e.* to have a preference; some are too big and circumstantial. Thanks for yours, which was most delicious. Would I had been with you, benighted &c. I fear my head is turned with wandering. I shall never be the same acquiescent being. Farewell; write again quickly, for I shall not like to hazard a letter, not knowing where the fates have carried you. Farewell, my dear fellow.

"C. LAMB."*

Wherever Lamb went, he took with him those eyes which some one said "could pick up pins and needles." He was ever looking for the amusing incident or character or listening for a good joke. Early in 1830 Emma Isola grew dangerously ill with "brain fever" at Bury. When she was well enough to travel, Charles went to fetch her home. Returned to Enfield, he wrote kind Mrs. Williams† at the Bury rectory:

"The incidents of our journey were trifling, but you bade me tell them. We had then in the coach a rather talkative Gentleman, but very civil, all the way, and took up a servant maid at Stamford [?Stortsford], going to a sick mistress. To the *latter,* a participation in the hospitalities of your nice rusks and sandwiches proved agreeable, as it did to my companion, who took merely a sip of the weakest wine and water with them. The *former* engaged me in a discourse for full twenty miles, on the probable advantages of Steam Carriages, which being merely problematical, I bore my part in with some credit, in spite of my totally un-engineer-like faculties. But when somewhere about Stanstead he put an unfortunate question to me as to the

---

* Letter to Manning, September 1802.
† April 1830.

'probability of its turning out a good turnip season,' and when I, who am still less of an agriculturist than a steam-philosopher, not knowing a turnip from a potato ground, innocently made answer that I believed it depended very much upon boiled legs of mutton, my unlucky reply set Miss Isola a laughing to a degree that disturbed her tranquillity for the only moment in our journey. I am afraid my credit sank very low with my other fellow-traveller, who had thought he had met a *well-informed passenger,* which is an accident so desirable in a Stage Coach.

"We were rather less communicative, but still friendly, the rest of the way."

To John Bates Dibdin, who was the first to question Lamb as to his authorship of *Elia,* Lamb wrote several delightful letters all of which are fortunately preserved. Dibdin was an invalid, soon to die of tuberculosis. This is from a letter of June 30, 1826:

"Your fair critic in the coach reminds me of a Scotchman who assured me he did not see much in Shakespeare. I replied, I dare say *not.* He felt the equivoke, looked awkward and reddish, but soon returned to the attack, by saying that he thought Burns was as good as Shakespeare: I said that I had no doubt he was—to a *Scotchman.* We exchang'd no more words that day.—Your account of the fierce faces in the Hanging, with the presumed interlocution of the Eagle and the Tyger, amused us greatly. You cannot be so very bad, while you can pick mirth off from rotten walls. But let me hear you have escaped out of your oven. . . . Your business, I take it, is bathing, not baking.

"Let me hear that you have clamber'd up to Lover's Seat; it is as fine in that neighbourhood as Juan Fernandez, as lonely too, when the Fishing boats are not out; I have sat for hours, staring upon a shipless sea. The salt sea is never so grand as when it is left to itself. One cock-boat spoils it. A sea-mew or two improves it. And go to the little church which is a very protestant Loretto, and seems dropt by some angel for the use of a hermit, who was at once parishioner and a whole parish. It is not too big. Go in the night, bring it away in your portmanteau, and I will plant it in my garden. It must have been erected in the very infancy of British Christianity, for the two or three first converts; yet hath it all the appertenances of a church of the first magnitude, its pulpit, its pews, its baptismal font; a cathedral in a nutshell. Seven people would crowd it like a Caledonian Chapel. The minister that divides the word there, must give lumping pennyworths. It is built to the text of two or three assembled in my name. It reminds me of the grain of mustard seed. If the glebe land is proportionate, it may yield two potatoes. Tithes out of it could be no more split than a hair. Its First fruits must be its Last, for 'twould never produce a couple. It is truly the strait and narrow way, and few there be (of London visitants) that find it. The still small voice is surely to be found there, if any where. A sounding board is merely there for ceremony. It is secure from earthquakes, not more from sanctity than size, for 'twould feel a mountain thrown upon it no more than a taper-worm would. Go and see, but not without your spectacles. By the way, there's a capital farm house two thirds of the way to the Lover's Seat, with incomparable plum cake, ginger beer, etc.

"Mary bids me warn you not to read the Anatomy of Melancholy in your present *low way*. You'll fancy yourself a pipkin, or a headless bear, as Burton speaks of. You'll be lost in a maze of remedies for a labyrinth of diseasements, a plethora of cures. Read Fletcher; above all the Spanish Curate, the Thief, or Little Nightwalker, the Wit Without Money, and the Lover's Pilgrimage. Laugh and come home fat. Neither do we think Sir T. Browne quite the thing for you just at present. Fletcher is as light as Soda water. Browne and Burton are too strong potions for an Invalid. And don't thumb or dirt the books. Take care of the bindings. Lay a leaf of silver paper under 'em, as you read them. And don't smoke tobacco over 'em, the leaves will fall in and burn or dirty their namesakes. If you find any dusty atoms of the Indian Weed crumbled up in the Beaum^t and Fletcher, they are *mine*. But then, you know, so is the Folio also. A pipe and a comedy of Fletcher's the last thing of a night is the best recipe for light dreams and to scatter away Nightmares. Probatum est. But do as you like about the former. Only cut the Baker's. You will come home else all crust; Rankings must chip you before you can appear in his counting house. And, my dear Peter Fin Junr., do contrive to see the sea at least once before you return. You'll be ask'd about it in the Old Jewry. It will appear singular not to have seen it. And rub up your Muse, the family Muse, and send us a rhyme or so. Don't waste your wit upon that damn'd Dry Salter. . . . Dry Salters, what a word for this thirsty weather! I must drink after it. Here's to thee, my dear Dibdin, and to our having you again snug and well at Colebrooke. But our nearest hopes are to hear again from you shortly. An epistle only a quarter as agreeable as your last, would be a treat."

On September ninth Lamb wrote to cheer his friend:

"Saturday.   An answer is requested.

"Dear D.,

"I have observed that a Letter is never more acceptable than when received upon a rainy day, especially a rainy Sunday; which moves me to send you somewhat, however short. This will find you sitting after Breakfast, which you will have prolonged as far as you can with consistency to the poor handmaid that has the reversion of the Tea Leaves; making two nibbles of your last morsel of *stale* roll (you cannot have hot new ones on the Sabbath), and reluctantly coming to an end, because when that is done, what can you do till dinner? You cannot go to the Beach, for the rain is drowning the sea, turning rank Thetis fresh, taking the brine out of Neptune's pickles, while mermaids sit upon rocks with umbrellas, their ivory combs sheathed for spoiling in the wet waters foreign to them. You cannot go to the library, for it's shut. You are not religious enough to go to church. O it is worth while to cultivate piety to the gods, to have something to fill the heart up on a wet Sunday! You cannot cast accounts, for your ledger is being eaten up with moths in the Ancient Jewry. You cannot play draughts, for there is none to play with you, and besides there is not a draught board in the house. You cannot go to market, for it closed last night. You cannot look into the shops, their backs are shut upon you. . . . You cannot while away an hour with a friend, for you have no friend round that Wrekin. You cannot divert yourself with a stray acquaintance, for you have picked none up. You cannot bear the chiming of Bells, for they invite you to a banquet where you are no visitant. You cannot cheer yourself with the prospect of a tomorrow's letter, for none come on Mondays. You cannot count those endless vials on the mantlepiece with any hope of making a variation in their numbers. You have counted your spiders: your Bastile is exhausted. You sit and deliberately curse your hard exile from all familiar sights and sounds. Old Ranking poking in his head unexpectedly would just now be as good to you as Grimaldi. Any thing to deliver you from this intolerable weight of Ennui. You are too ill to shake it off: not ill enough to submit to it, and to lie down as a lamb under it. The Tyranny of Sickness is nothing to the Cruelty of Convalescence: tis to have Thirty Tyrants for one. That pattering rain drops on your brain. You'll be worse after dinner, for you must dine at one to-day, that Betty may go to afternoon service. She insists upon having her chopped hay. And then . . . what an interminable afternoon you'll have to go thro'. You can't break yourself from your locality: you cannot say Tomorrow morning I set off for Banstead, by God: for you are book'd for Wednesday. Foreseeing this, I thought a *cheerful letter* would come in opportunely. If any of the little topics for mirth I have thought upon should serve you in this utter extinguishment of sunshine, to make you a little merry, I shall have had my ends. I love to make things comfortable. [*Here is an erasure.*] This, which is scratch'd out was the most material thing I had to say, but on maturer thoughts I defer it.

P. S.—We are just sitting down to dinner with a pleasant party, Coleridge, Reynolds the dramatist, and Sam Bloxam: to-morrow (that is, *today*), Liston, and Wyat of the Wells, dine with us. May this find you as jolly and freakish as we mean to be.

"C. LAMB."

Lamb liked to refer to his being born under the shadow of St. Dunstan's steeple on Lord Mayor's Day as if in some mystic fashion he was endowed by a special London blessing. At any rate it was always with joy that he returned to the city and on occasion when he mentioned it affirmed that "Whittington with his Cat (just emblem of vigilance and a furred gown) never went beyond me in affection which I bear to the citizens."

To Wordsworth* he wrote in answer to an invitation to spend some time with him at Grasmere. "I have passed all my days in London, until I have formed as many and intense local attachments, as any of you mountaineers can have done with dead nature. The Lighted shops of the Strand and Fleet Street, the innumerable trades, tradesmen and customers, coaches, waggons, playhouses, all the bustle and wickedness round about Covent Garden, the very women of the Town, the Watchmen, drunken scenes, rattles—life awake, if you awake, at all hours of the night, the impossibility of being dull in Fleet Street, the crowds, the very dirt & mud, the Sun shining upon houses and pavements, the print shops, the old book stalls, parsons cheap'ning books, coffee houses, steams of soups from kitchens, the panto-

---

* January 1801.

mimes, London itself a pantomime and a masquerade,—all these things work themselves into my mind and feed me, without a power of satiating me. The wonder of these sights impells me into night-walks about her crowded streets, and I often shed tears in the motley Strand from fulness of joy at so much Life.— All these emotions must be strange to you. So are your rural emotions to me. But consider, what must I have been doing all my life, not to have lent great portions of my heart with usury to such scenes?——

"My attachments are all local, purely local. I have no passion (or have had none since I was in love, and then it was the spurious engendering of poetry & books) to groves and vallies. The rooms where I was born, the furniture which has been before my eyes all my life, a book case which has followed me about (like a faithful dog, only exceeding him in knowledge) wherever I have moved—old chairs, old tables, streets, squares, where I have sunned myself, my old school—these are my mistresses."

His devotion to London and his interest in new lodgings are always fully described in letters to his friends.

"I am going to change my lodgings, having received a hint that it would be agreeable, at our Lady's next feast. I have partly fixed upon most delectable rooms, which look out (when you stand a tiptoe) over the Thames and Surrey Hills, at the upper end of King's Bench walks, in the Temple. There I shall have all the privacy of a house without the encumbrance, and shall be able to lock my friends out as often as I desire to hold free converse with my immortal mind; for my present lodgings resemble a minister's levee, I have so increased my acquaintance (as they call 'em), since I have resided in town. Like the country mouse, that had tasted a little of urban manners, I long to be nibbling my own cheese by my dear self, without mouse-traps and time-traps. By my new plan, I shall be as airy, up four pair of stairs, as in the country; and in a garden, in the midst of [that] enchanting, more than Mahometan paradise, London, whose dirtiest drab-frequented alley, and her lowest bowing tradesman, I would not exchange for Skiddaw, Helvellyn, James, Walter, and the parson into the bargain. O! her lamps of a night! her rich goldsmiths, print-shops, toyshops, mercers, hardwaremen, pastry-cooks! St. Paul's Churchyard! the Strand! Exeter Change! Charing Cross, with the man *upon* a black horse! These are thy gods, O London! Ain't you mightily moped on the banks of the Cam! Had not you better come and set up here? You can't think what a difference. All the streets and pavements are pure gold, I warrant you. At least I know an alchemy that turns her mud into that metal,—a mind that loves to be at home in crowds. . . ."

Few letters have conveyed such an intimate and humorous account of the domestic scene as the following one from Mary to little Barbara Betham, aged fourteen.*

"We still live in Temple Lane, but I am now sitting in a room you never saw. Soon after you left us we we[re] distressed by the cries of a cat, which seemed to proceed from the garrets adjoining to ours, and only separated from ours by a locked door on the farther side of my brother's bedroom, which you know was the little room at the top of the kitchen stairs. We had the lock forced and let poor puss out from behind a pannel of the wainscot, and she lived with us from that time, for we were in gratitude bound to keep her, as she had introduced us to four untenanted, unowned rooms, and by degrees we have taken possession of these unclaimed apartments—First putting up lines to dry our clothes, then moving my brother's bed into one of these, more commodious than his own room. And last winter, my brother being unable to pursue a work he had begun, owing to the kind interruptions of friends who were more at leisure

---

* November 1814.

than himself, I persuaded him that he might write at his ease in one of these rooms, as he could not then hear the door knock, or hear himself denied to be at home, which was sure to make him call out and convict the poor maid in a fib. Here, I said, he might be almost really not at home. So I put in an old grate, and made him a fire in the largest of these garrets, and carried in one table, and one chair, and bid him write away, and consider himself as much alone as if he were in a new lodging in the midst of Salisbury Plain, or any other wide unfrequented place where he could expect few visitors to break in upon his solitude. I left him quite delighted with his new acquisition, but in a few hours he came down again with a sadly dismal face. He could do nothing, he said, with those bare whitewashed walls before his eyes. He could not write in that dull unfurnished prison.

"The next day, before he came home from his office, I had gathered up various bits of old carpetting to cover the floor; and, to a little break the blank look of the bare walls, I hung up a few old prints that used to ornament the kitchen, and after dinner, with great boast of what an improvement I had made, I took Charles once more into his new study. A week of busy labours followed, in which I think you would not have disliked to have been our assistant. My brother and I almost covered the wall with prints, for which purpose he cut out every print from every book in his old library, coming in every now and then to ask my leave to strip a fresh poor author—which he might not do, you know, without my permission, as I am elder sister. There was such pasting, such consultation where their portraits, and where the series of pictures from Ovid, Milton, and Shakespear would show to most advantage, and in what obscure corner authors of humbler note might be allowed to tell their stories. All the books gave up their stores but one, a translation from Ariosto, a delicious set of four and twenty prints, and for which I had marked out a conspicuous place! when lo! we found at the moment the scissors were going to work that a part of the poem was printed at the back of every picture. What a cruel disappointment! To conclude this long story about nothing, the poor despised garret is now called the print room, and is become our most favorite sitting room."

An excellent illustration of Lamb's going about in London and visiting the sights and writing of them is his description of an exhibition that interested him in 1800. He is writing to Manning:*

"I wish to God you had made London in your way. There is an exhibition quite uncommon in Europe, which could not have escaped *your genius*,—a LIVE RATTLESNAKE, 10 feet in length, and the thickness of a big leg. I went to see it last night by candle-light. We were ushered into a room very little bigger than ours at Pentonville. A man and woman and four boys live in this room, joint tenants with nine snakes, most of them such as no remedy has been discovered for their bite. We walked into the middle, which is formed by a half-moon of wired boxes, all mansions of *snakes*,—whip-snakes, thunder-snakes, pig-nose-snakes, American vipers, and *this monster*. He lies curled up in folds; and immediately a stranger enters (for he is used to the family, and sees them play at cards,) he set up a rattle like a watchman's in London, or near as loud, and reared up a head, from the midst of these folds, like a toad, and shook his head, and showed every sign a snake can show of irritation. I had the foolish curiosity to strike the wires with my finger, and the devil flew at me with his toad-mouth wide open; the inside of his mouth is quite white. I had got my finger away, nor could he well have bit me with his damn'd big mouth, which would have been certain death in five minutes. But it frightened me so much, that I did not recover my voice for a minute's space. I

* October 1800.

forgot, in my fear, that he was secured. You would have forgot
too, for 'tis incredible how such a monster can be confined in
small gauzy-looking wires. I dreamed of snakes in the night. I
wish to heaven you could see it. He absolutely swelled with
passion to the bigness of a large thigh. I could not retreat without infringing on another box, and just behind, a little devil not
an inch from my back, had got his nose out, with some difficulty
and pain, quite through the bars! He was soon taught better
manners. All the snakes were curious, and objects of terror: but
this monster, like Aaron's serpent, swallowed up the impression
of the rest. He opened his damn'd mouth, when he made at
me, as wide as his head was broad. I hallooed out quite loud,
and felt pains all over my body with the fright."

But the most fun of all is to go through the letters selecting
what you like, a bit of harmless gossip, a new story, description
of a dear friend, expressions of delight in good food, a rainy
Sunday's musings to a friend that can't go out, talk on Christmas, good advice, plain common sense, letters of recommendation, thanks for game for his table, comments on the books discovered or bought, new poems, new plays, anecdotes later to
become Elia essays, inquiry about the dog Dash, thanks for the
little pig—and hundreds more.

Lamb, in the early part of the year 1798, spent two weeks at
the Lloyd home in Birmingham, when he met a very interesting
family consisting of Charles Lloyd the translator, Charles junior, Priscilla who afterwards married Christopher Wordsworth,
and young Robert, to whom Lamb was a friend and helper.

"[*13th November 1798.*]

"Now 'tis Robert's turn.

"MY DEAR ROBERT,

"One passage in your Letter a little displeas'd me. The rest
was nothing but kindness, which Robert's letters are ever brim-

ful of. You say that 'this World to you seems drain'd of all its sweets!' At first I had hoped you only meant to insinuate the high price of Sugar! but I am afraid you meant more. O Robert, I don't know what you call sweet. Honey and the honeycomb, roses and violets, are yet in the earth. The sun and moon yet reign in Heaven, and the lesser lights keep up their pretty twinklings. Meats and drinks, sweet sights and sweet smells, a country walk, spring and autumn, follies and repentance, quarrels and reconcilements, have all a sweetness by turns. Good humour and good nature, friends at home that love you, and friends abroad that miss you, you possess all these things, and more innumerable, and these are all sweet things. . . . You may extract honey from everything; do not go a gathering after gall. The Bees are wiser in their generation than the race of sonnet writers and complainers, Bowles's and Charlotte Smiths, and all that tribe, who can see no joys but what are past, and fill people's heads with notions of the unsatisfying nature of Earthly comforts. I assure you I find this world a very pretty place. My kind of love to all your Sisters and to Thomas—he never writes to me—and tell Susanna I forgive her.

"C. LAMB."

To Robert Southey,* he wrote of books and poetry and introduced a tailor, to whose occupation he liked to profess a special aversion.

"My tailor has brought me home a new coat lapelled, with a velvet collar. He assures me everybody wears velvet collars now. Some are born fashionable, some achieve fashion, and others, like your humble servant, have fashion thrust upon them. The rogue has been making inroads hitherto by modest degrees, foisting upon me an additional button, recommending gaiters; but to come upon me thus, in a full tide of luxury, neither becomes him as a tailor nor the ninth of a man. My meek gentleman

---

* November 1798.

was robbed the other day, coming with his wife and family in a one-horse shay from Hampstead; the villains rifled him of four guineas, some shillings and half-pence, and a bundle of customers' measures, which they swore were bank-notes. They did not shoot him, and when they rode off he addrest them with profound gratitude, making a congee: 'Gentlemen, I wish you good night, and we are very much obliged to you that you have not used us ill!' And this is the cuckoo that has had the audacity to foist upon me ten buttons on a side and a black velvet collar—A damn'd ninth of a scoundrel!"

In a letter to John Rickman in 1801, Lamb alludes to the Widow Clairmont, who with her daughter, destined to meet Byron, had taken the next house to Godwin and is said to have asked on first meeting him, "It is possible that I behold the immortal Godwin?" She began her campaign at once and succeeded.

"I know no more news from here except that the Professor (Godwin) is COURTING. The Lady is a Widow* with green spectacles and one child, and the Professor is grown quite juvenile. He bows when he is spoke to, and smiles without occasion, and wriggles as fantastically as Malvolio, and has more affectation than a canary bird pluming his feathers when he thinks somebody looks at him. He lays down his spectacles, as if in scorn, and takes 'em up again from necessity, and winks that she mayn't see he gets sleepy about eleven o'Clock. You never saw such a philosophic coxcomb, nor any one play the Romeo so unnaturally."

Manning had been in China for nine years. Lamb found it easy to write to him about things at home and there was probably nobody to whom he would rather send a Christmas letter. "DEAR OLD FRIEND AND ABSENTEE,

"This is Christmas-day 1815 with us; what it may be with you

---

* A very disgusting woman. [The footnote is Lamb's.]

I don't know, the 12th of June next year perhaps; and if it should be the consecrated season with you, I don't see how you can keep it. You have no turkeys; you would not desecrate the festival by offering up a withered Chinese bantam, instead of the savoury grand Norfolcian holocaust, that smokes all around my nostrils at this moment from a thousand firesides. Then what puddings have you? Where will you get holly to stick in your churches, or churches to stick your dried tea-leaves (that must be the substitute) in? What memorials you can have of the holy time, I see not. A chopped missionary or two may keep up the thin idea of Lent and the wilderness; but what standing evidence have you of the Nativity?—'tis our rosy-cheeked, homestalled divines, whose faces shine to the tune of *unto us a child;* faces fragrant with the mince-pies of half a century, that alone can authenticate the cheerful mystery—I feel.

"I feel my bowels refreshed with the holy tide—my zeal is great against the unedified heathen. Down with the Pagodas—down with the idols—Ching-chong-fo and his foolish priest-hood! Come out of Babylon, O my friend! for her time is come, and the child that is native, and the Proselyte of her gates, shall kindle and smoke together! And in sober sense what makes you so long from among us, Manning? You must not expect to see the same England again which you left."

The reference to Judge Park's wig in the following letter is to the judge who tried Thurtell, the murderer of William Weare, on January 6 and 7, 1824. Thurtell was hanged on January 9, on a gallows of his own design, and the exhibition was, as always, seen by crowds. A characteristic letter to Bernard Barton:*

"DEAR B. B.,

"Do you know what it is to succumb under an unsurmount-able day mare—a whoreson lethargy, Falstaff calls it—an indis-

---

* January 9, 1824.

position to do any thing, or to be any thing—a total deadness and distaste—a suspension of vitality—an indifference to locality—a numb soporifical goodfornothingness—an ossification all over—an oyster-like insensibility to the passing events—a mind-stupor,—a brawny defiance to the needles of a thrusting-in conscience—did you ever have a very bad cold with a total irresolution to submit to water gruel processes?—this has been for many weeks my lot, and my excuse—my fingers drag heavily over this paper, and to my thinking it is three and twenty furlongs from here to the end of this demi-sheet—I have not a thing to say—nothing is of more importance than another—I am flatter than a denial or a pancake—emptier than Judge Park's wig when the head is in it—duller than a country stage when the actors are off it—a cypher—an O—I acknowledge life at all, only by an occasional convulsional cough, and a permanent phlegmatic pain in the chest—I am weary of the world—Life is weary of me—My day is gone into Twilight and I don't think it worth the expence of candles—my wick hath a thief in it, but I can't muster courage to snuff it—I inhale suffocation—I can't distinguish veal from mutton—nothing interests me—tis 12 o'clock and Thurtell is just now coming out upon the New Drop—Jack Ketch alertly tucking up his greasy sleeves to do the last office of mortality, yet cannot I elicit a groan or a moral reflection—if you told me the world will be at an end to morrow, I should just say, 'will it?'—I have not volition enough to dot my i's—much less to comb my EYEBROWS—my eyes are set in my head—my brains are gone out to see a poor relation in Moorfields, and they did not say when they'd come back again—my scull is a Grub street Attic, to let—not so much as a joint stool or a crackd jordan left in it—my hand writes, not I, from habit, as chickens run about a little when their heads are off—O for a vigorous fit of gout, cholic, tooth ache—an earwig in my auditory, a fly in my visual organs—pain is life—the sharper, the more evidence of life—but this apathy, this death—did you ever have an obstinate cold, a six or seven weeks' unintermitting chill and suspension of hope, fear, conscience, and every thing—yet do I try all I can to cure it, I try wine, and spirits, and smoking, and snuff in unsparing quantities, but they all only seem to make me worse, instead of better—I sleep in a damp room, but it does me no good; I come home late o' nights, but do not find any visible amendment.

"Who shall deliver me from the body of this death?"

The picture mentioned in the following letter to Coleridge was an etching by James Brook Pulham, "desk-fellow" of Lamb at the East India House. The etching, showing Lamb "chatting with his brother clerks," was not liked by Lamb's friends.

"*June 1st, 1826.*

"Dear Coleridge,

"If I know myself, nobody more detests the display of personal vanity which is implied in the act of sitting for one's picture than myself. But the fact is, that the likeness which accompanies this letter was stolen from my person at one of my unguarded moments by some too partial artist, and my friends are pleased to think that he has not much flattered me. Whatever its merits may be, you, who have so great an interest in the original, will have a satisfaction in tracing the features of one that has so long esteemed you. There are times when in a friend's absence these graphic representations of him almost seem to bring back the man himself. The painter, whoever he was, seems to have taken me in one of those disengaged moments, if I may so term them, when the native character is so much more honestly displayed than can be possible in the restraints of an enforced sitting attitude. Perhaps it rather describes me as a thinking man, than a man in the act of thought. Whatever its pretensions, I know it will be dear to you, towards whom I should wish my thoughts to flow in a sort of an undress rather than in the more studied graces of diction.

"I am, dear Coleridge, yours sincerely,

"C. LAMB." . .

This letter to Crabb Robinson describes the death of Randal Norris, Sub-Treasurer and Librarian of the Inner Temple, and lifelong friend of Lamb. Thirty years before, Lamb had written to Coleridge, "Mr. Norris has been as a father to me, and Mrs. Norris as a mother."

"Colebrook Row, Islington,
"*Saturday, 20th Jan., 1827.*

"DEAR ROBINSON,

"I called upon you this morning, and found that you were gone to visit a dying friend. I had been upon a like errand. Poor Norris has been lying dying for now almost a week, such is the penalty we pay for having enjoyed a strong constitution! Whether he knew me or not, I know not, or whether he saw me through his poor glazed eyes; but the group I saw about him I shall not forget. Upon the bed, or about it, were assembled his wife and two daughters, and poor deaf Richard, his son, looking doubly stupefied. There they were, and seemed to have been sitting all the week. I could only reach out a hand to Mrs. Norris. Speaking was impossible in that mute chamber. By this time I hope it is all over with him. In him I have a loss the world cannot make up. He was my friend and my father's friend all the life I can remember. I seem to have made foolish friendships since. Those are the friendships which outlive a second generation. Old as I am waxing, in his eyes I was still the child he knew me. To the last he called me Charley. I have none to call me Charley now. He was the last link that bound me to the Temple. You are but of yesterday. In him seem to have died the old plainness of manners and singleness of heart. Letters he knew nothing of, nor did his reading extend beyond the pages of the 'Gentleman's Magazine.' Yet there was a pride of literature about him from being amongst books (he was librarian), and from some scraps of doubtful Latin which he had picked up in his office of entering students, that gave him very diverting airs of pedantry. Can I forget the erudite look with which, when he had been in vain trying to make out a black-letter text of Chaucer in the Temple Library, he laid it down and told me that—'in those old books, Charley, there is sometimes a deal of very indifferent spelling;' and seemed to console himself in the reflection! His jokes, for he had his jokes, are now ended, but they were old trusty perennials, staple, hearty, that pleased after *decies repetita,* and were always as good as new. One song he had, which was reserved for the night of Christmas-day, which we always spent in the Temple. It was an old thing, and spoke of the flat bottoms of our foes and the possibility of their coming over in darkness, and alluded to threats of an invasion many years blown over; and when he came to the part

> We'll still make 'em run, and we'll still make 'em sweat,
> In spite of the devil and Brussels Gazette!

his eyes would sparkle as with the freshness of an impending event. And what is the 'Brussels Gazette' now? I cry while I enumerate these trifles. 'How shall we tell them in a stranger's ear?' His poor good girls will now have to receive their afflicted mother in an unsuccessful home in an obscure village in Herts, where they have been long struggling to make a school without effect; and poor deaf Richard—and the more helpless for being so—is thrown on the wide world. . . .

"My first motive in writing, and, indeed, in calling on you, was to ask if you were enough acquainted with any of the Benchers, to lay a plain statement before them of the circumstances of the family. I almost fear not, for you are of another Hall. But if you can oblige me and my poor friend, who is now insensible to any favours, pray exert yourself. You cannot say too much good of poor Norris and his poor wife.

"Yours ever,

"CHAS. LAMB."

Dash, a large and handsome dog of a rather curious breed belonging to Thomas Hood, was a special pet of Lamb, who made himself a perfect slave to the dog. Patmore was temporarily keeping the dog which was later returned to its owner.

"Mrs. Leishman's, Chace, Enfield,
[No date: June 1827.]

"DEAR PATMORE,

"Excuse my anxiety—but how is Dash? (I should have asked if Mrs. Patmore kept her rules, and was improving—but Dash came uppermost. The order of our thoughts should be the order of our writing.) Goes he muzzled, or *aperto ore?* Are his intellects sound, or does he wander a little in *his* conversation? You cannot be too careful to watch the first symptoms of incoherence. The first illogical snarl he makes, to St. Luke's with him! All the dogs here are going mad, if you believe the overseers; but I protest they seem to me very rational and collected. But nothing is so deceitful as mad people to those who are not used to them. Try him with hot water. If he won't lick it up, it is a sign he does not like it. Does his tail wag horizontally or perpendicularly? That has decided the fate of many dogs in Enfield. Is his general deportment cheerful? I mean when he is pleased—for otherwise there is no judging. You can't be too careful. Has he bit any of the children yet? If he has, have them shot, and keep *him* for curiosity, to see if it was the hydrophobia. They say all our army in India had it at one time—but that was in *Hyder-*Ally's time. Do you get paunch for him? Take care the sheep was sane. You might pull out his teeth (if he would let you), and then you need not mind if he were as mad as a Bedlamite. It would be rather fun to see his odd ways. It might amuse Mrs. Patmore and the children. They'd have more sense than he! He'd be like a Fool kept in the family, to keep the household in good humour with their own understanding. You might teach him the mad dance set to the mad howl. *Madge Owl-et* would be nothing to him. 'My, how he capers!' [*In the margin is written:*] One of the children speaks this.

"[*Three lines here are erased.*] What I scratch out is a German quotation from Lessing on the bite of rabid animals; but, I remember, you don't read German. But Mrs. Patmore may, so I wish I had let it stand. The meaning in English is—'Avoid to approach an animal suspected of madness, as you would avoid fire or a precipice:'—which I think is a sensible observation. The Germans are certainly profounder than we.

"If the slightest suspicion arises in your breast, that all is not right with him (Dash), muzzle him and lead him in a string (common pack-thread will do; he don't care for twist) to Hood's, his quondam master, and he'll take him in at any time. You may mention your suspicion or not, as you like, or as you think it may wound or not Mr. H.'s feelings. Hood, I know, will wink at a few follies in Dash, in consideration of his former sense. Besides, Hood is deaf, and if you hinted anything, ten to one he would not hear you. Besides, you will have discharged your conscience, and laid the child at the right door, as they say."

After the appearance of "A Dissertation on Roast Pig," a pig was a regular present for Lamb's table, from his friends and admirers. One came from Dodwell, a clerk at the India House whom Lamb celebrated in a charade:

My first is that which infants call their Maker,
My second is that which is best let alone.

"October 7, 1827.

"My dear Dodwell

"Your little pig found his way to Enfield this morning without his feet, or rather his little feet came first, and as I guessed the rest of him soon followed. He is quite a beauty. It was a pity to kill him, or *rather,* as Rice would say, it would have been a pity not to kill him in his state of innocence. He might have lived to be corrupted by the ways of the world, and for all his delicate promise have turned out, like an old Tea Broker you and I remember, a lump of fat rusty Bacon. Bacon was a Beast, my friend at Calne, Marsh, used to say—or was it Bendry? A rasher of the latter still hangs up in Leadenhall. Your kind letter has left a relish upon my taste; it read warm and short as to-morrow's crackling."

This letter is to Edward Moxon, who the following week married Emma Isola.

"[p.m. *24th July 1833.*]

"For god's sake, give Emma no more watches. *One* has turned her head. She is arrogant, and insulting. She said something very unpleasant to our old Clock in the passage, as if he did not keep time, and yet he had made her no appointment. She takes it out every instant to look at the moment-hand. She lugs us out into the fields, because there the bird-boys ask you 'Pray, Sir, can you tell us what's a Clock,' and she answers them punctually. She loses all her time looking 'what the time is.' I overheard her whispering, 'Just so many hours, minutes, &c. to Tuesday—I think St. George's goes too slow'—This little present of Time, why,—'tis Eternity to her—

"What can make her so fond of a gingerbread watch?

"She has spoil'd some of the movements. Between ourselves, she has kissed away 'half past 12,' which I suppose to be the canonical hour in Hanover Sq.

"Well, if 'love me, love my watch' answers, she will keep time to you—

"It goes right by the Horse Guards—

[*On the next page:*]

"DEAREST M.

"Never mind opposite nonsense. She does not love you for the watch, but the watch for you.

"I will be at the wedding, and keep the 30 July as long as my poor months last me, as a festival gloriously.

"Your ever,

"Elia.

"We have not heard from Cambridge. I will write the moment we do.

"Edmonton, 24th July, 3.20 post mer. minutes 4 instants by Emma's watch."

This letter to Mrs. George Dyer, December 22, 1834, is Lamb's last letter. He died five days later. When the book was returned later by Edward Moxon, the leaf was found turned down at the account of Sir Philip Sidney.

"DEAR MRS. DYER,

"I am very uneasy about a *Book* which I either have lost or left at your house on Thursday. It was the book I went out to fetch from Miss Buffam's, while the tripe was frying. It is called Phillip's Theatrum Poetarum; but it is an English book. I think I left it in the parlour. It is Mr. Cary's book, and I would not lose it for the world. Pray, if you find it, book it at the Swan, Snow Hill, by an Edmonton stage immediately, directed to Mr. Lamb, Church-street, Edmonton, or write to say you cannot find it. I am quite anxious about it. If it is lost, I shall never like tripe again.

"With kindest love to Mr. Dyer and all,

"Yours truly,

"C. LAMB."

8

Charles Lamb and the Theatre

AT AN early age Charles Lamb was taken to his first play and his interest in the theatre persisted through life. His devotion to the stage was not merely a passive enjoyment of the play as performed, but was really a satisfaction of impulses in him that resulted in his writing memorable pieces of criticism of plays and actors, essays on principles of the drama and the theatre and other creative work of an original nature. Besides, there were the prologues and epilogues which he furnished for plays written by others, his own personal criticism of many contemporary plays, published and unpublished, and perhaps best of all, the intimate association with many actors and actresses which bore fruit in memorable conversations and numerous delightful stories.

The period was not a proud one in the production of new plays, but it was a golden age of acting and it may well be said that the glamour of London was its theatre. Covent Garden and Drury Lane—these were the names to charm. Around each of these two bright spots there were the darkness and the lowness of London's poor and criminal life but once over the threshold into the fairyland of these theatres, the drab world outside was soon forgotten. The sights and sounds of the city seemed to come to their finest expression in these two theatres. What they must have been to many a charmed enthusiast has been lovingly described by Charles Lamb in his Elia essay, "My First Play."

"At the north end of Cross-court there yet stands a portal,

COVENT GARDEN THEATRE AND BOW STREET IN LAMB'S DAY

From Ackermann's Repository of Arts

DRURY LANE THEATRE, WHEN "MR. H." WAS PRODUCED

From *The Microcosm of London*

of some architectural pretensions, though reduced to humble use, serving at present for an entrance to a printing-office. This old door-way, if you are young, reader, you may not know was the identical pit entrance to old Drury—Garrick's Drury—all of it that is left. I never pass it without shaking some forty years from off my shoulders, recurring to the evening when I passed through it to see *my first play*. The afternoon had been wet, and the condition of our going (the elder folks and myself) was, that the rain should cease. With what a beating heart did I watch from the window the puddles, from the stillness of which I was taught to prognosticate the desired cessation! I seem to remember the last spurt, and the glee with which I ran to announce it. . . .

"I remember the waiting at the door—not that which is left—but between that and an inner door in shelter—O when shall I be such an expectant again!—with the cry of nonpareils, an indispensable play-house accompaniment in those days. As near as I can recollect, the fashionable pronunciation of the theatrical fruiteresses then was, 'Chase some oranges, chase some numparels, chase a bill of the play';—chase *pro* chuse. But when we got in, and I beheld the green curtain that veiled a heaven to my imagination, which was soon to be disclosed—the breathless anticipations I endured! I had seen something like it in the plate prefixed to Troilus and Cressida, in Rowe's Shakespeare—the tent scene with Diomede—and a sight of that plate can always bring back in a measure the feeling of that evening.—The boxes at that time, full of well-dressed women of quality, projected over the pit; and the pilasters reaching down were adorned with a glistening substance (I know not what) under glass (as it seemed), resembling—a homely fancy—but I judged it to be sugar-candy—yet, to my raised imagination, divested of its homelier qualities, it appeared a glorified candy!—The orchestra lights at length arose, those 'fair Auroras!' Once the bell sounded. It was to ring out yet once again—and, incapable of the anticipation, I reposed my shut eyes in a sort of resignation upon the maternal lap. It rang the second time. The curtain drew up—I was not past six years old—and the play was Artaxerxes!

"I had dabbled a little in the Universal History—the ancient part of it—and here was the court of Persia. It was being admitted to a sight of the past. I took no proper interest in the action going on, for I understood not its import—but I heard the word Darius, and I was in the midst of Daniel. All feeling was absorbed in vision. Gorgeous vests, gardens, palaces, princesses, passed before me. I knew not players. I was in Persepolis for the time; and the burning idol of their devotion almost converted me into a worshipper. I was awe-struck, and believed those significations to be something more than elemental fires. It was all enchantment and a dream. No such pleasure has since visited me but in dreams.—Harlequin's invasion followed; where, I remember, the transformation of the magistrates into reverend beldams seemed to me a piece of grave historic justice, and the tailor carrying his own head to be as sober a verity as the legend of St. Denys.

"The next play to which I was taken was the Lady of the Manor, of which, with the exception of some scenery, very faint traces are left in my memory. It was followed by a pantomime, called Lun's Ghost—a satiric touch, I apprehend, upon Rich, not long since dead—but to my apprehension (too sincere for satire), Lun was as remote a piece of antiquity as Lud—the father of a line of Harlequins—transmitting his dagger of lath (the wooden sceptre) through countless ages. I saw the primeval Motley come from his silent tomb in a ghastly vest of white patchwork, like the apparition of a dead rainbow. So Harlequins (thought I) look when they are dead.

"My third play followed in quick succession. It was the Way

of the World. I think I must have sat at it as grave as a judge; for, I remember, the hysteric affectations of good Lady Wishfort affected me like some solemn tragic passion. Robinson Crusoe followed; in which Crusoe, man Friday, and the parrot, were as good and authentic as in the story.—The clownery and pan-taloonery of these pantomimes have clean passed out of my head. I believe, I no more laughed at them, than at the same age I should have been disposed to laugh at the grotesque Gothic heads (seeming to me then replete with devout meaning) that gape, and grin, in stone around the inside of the old Roman Church (my church) of the Templars.

"I saw these plays in the season 1781-2, when I was from six to seven years old. After the intervention of six or seven other years (for at school all play-going was inhibited) I again en-tered the doors of a theatre. That old Artaxerxes evening had never done ringing in my fancy. I expected the same feelings to come again with the same occasion. But we differ from our-selves less at sixty and sixteen, than the latter does from six. In that interval what had I not lost. At the first period I knew nothing, understood nothing, discriminated nothing. I felt all, loved all, wondered all—

        "Was nourished, I could not tell how—
I had left the temple a devotee, and was returned a rationalist. The same things were there materially; but the emblem, the ref-erence, was gone!—The green curtain was no longer a veil, drawn between two worlds, the unfolding of which was to bring back past ages to present a 'royal ghost,'—but a certain quantity of green baize, which was to separate the audience for a given time from certain of their fellow-men who were to come for-ward and pretend those parts. The lights—the orchestra lights —came up a clumsy machinery. The first ring, and the second ring, was now but a trick of the prompter's bell—which had been, like the note of the cuckoo, a phantom of a voice, no

hand seen or guessed at which ministered to its warning. The actors were men and women painted. I thought the fault was in them; but it was in myself, and the alteration which those many centuries—of six short twelvemonths—had wrought in me.—Perhaps it was fortunate for me that the play of the evening was but an indifferent comedy, as it gave me time to crop some unreasonable expectations, which might have interfered with the genuine emotions with which I was soon after enabled to enter upon the first appearance to me of Mrs. Siddons in Isabella. Comparison and retrospection soon yielded to the present attraction of the scene; and the theatre became to me, upon a new stock, the most delightful of recreations."

Lamb's godfather Fielde had been a friend of the Sheridans. To Fielde's house in Holborn young Brinsley Sheridan brought beautiful Marie Linley on her elopement from a school at Bath. In return for many kindnesses and for many years' "nightly illumination of the orchestra and various avenues of that theatre," Fielde was often favoured with complimentary tickets, "box orders" as they were called, and some of these regularly found their way to Charles and Mary. They could not have fallen into better hands.

At Christ's Hospital, the school rules forbad attendance at plays. Lamb realised that the impediment in his speech would be sufficiently serious to prevent his taking orders in the church, and, what was an even greater disappointment as he afterwards admitted, he dare not hope to be an actor. Perhaps that was a reason why he so often befriended the profession and showed a great liking for many actors of his day.

Although we know the names of only a few of the plays which Lamb saw in his early years, at least we have a charming observation in Mary's "Visit to the Cousins" in *Mrs. Leicester's School* of their enjoyment of the theatre and especially of their delight in seeing plays with other happy people. " 'But I hope, my dear Emily, when you're sitting in the playhouse, you will remember that pleasures are far more delightful when they are shared among numbers. If the whole theatre were your own, and you were sitting by yourself to see the performance, how dull it would seem to what you will find it, with so many happy faces around us, all amused with the same thing!' I hardly knew what my mamma meant, for I had never seen a play; but when I got there, after the curtain drew up, I looked up towards the galleries, and into the pit, and into all the boxes, and then I knew what a pretty sight it was to see a number of happy faces. I was very well convinced, that it would not have been half so cheerful if the theatre had been my own, to have sat there by myself. . . . There is nothing in the world so charming as going to a play."

It was natural for Lamb, moved by an enthusiasm in going to the theatre and in reading old plays and in associating with actors, to want to write something himself. Everybody was doing it—Holcroft, Godwin, Coleridge, Wordsworth and Southey. It will be remembered that Lovell, Coleridge and Southey, in addition to their absorption in the Utopian scheme of Pantisocracy, were committed to the writing of a three-act play. The first cooperative effort of Wordsworth and Coleridge consisted of two plays—which were finally completed but not with the collaboration which was first proposed. So we find Lamb beginning a five-act play in blank verse, under the name, *Pride's Cure.* The manuscript was finished by Christmas 1799 and sent to Kemble, then manager of Drury Lane. A little more than a year afterwards, and not sooner so far as we can discover, Lamb made inquiry of Kemble and discovered that the manuscript had been lost. Kemble insisted that Lamb send him another copy. We do not read of any apology—the script was just lost! And Lamb sat down to make a copy by hand. This time the rejection followed promptly just as Coleridge and Southey had predicted, and there was a personal interview in which Kemble told Lamb the play was unsuitable.

In 1802, the play was printed by Lamb at his own expense. Southey made the delightfully frank comment, "Lamb is printing his play which will please you by the exquisite beauty of his poetry, and provoke you by the execrable silliness of his story." How could Lamb, a sensitive writer and critic, of which we find ample evidence in his discerning opinions of the poems of Coleridge and Wordsworth, write a tragedy possessing so few of the requirements of an acting play? It would have been strange if any critic or stage manager had made a different decision. *John Woodvil,* for that was the name finally selected for the play, has a mere suggestion of plot, an improbable story, and the most superficial and conventional portrayal of character. It has some good lines, but as a play to be read or acted Kemble's judgement would seem to be final. For us, however, the piece is to be considered not merely as a play, but as a significant work of a young creative writer. And from that angle it assumes a new interest, for *John Woodvil* would have been a difficult achievement for anyone who had not read widely in Elizabethan drama and who did not possess the growing power of attaining a large and varied vocabulary. Lamb had read Shakespeare, of course, Beaumont and Fletcher, Massinger, Ford and Webster with such result that the English of the Elizabethan age was as natural for him as that of the Georgian period. He could actually think in that language. Godwin reported that he had been searching in the plays of Beaumont and Fletcher to discover a certain quotation, which was to be found in Lamb's *John Woodvil.*

It is not always remembered that the language of Shakespeare was in many ways different from the language of the Georges—and from that of today. Not only had Shakespearean words dropped out but many were used with a different connotation.

If a theatregoer of Lamb's day or our day were carried back by the Time Machine to one of Burbage's performances of Shakespeare, many words and expressions would mean little to him. It is possible that no writer since Lamb has been equally keen and discerning in catching not only the meaning but the special flavour of the word as used by the Elizabethans—as they would have heard it.

Besides the interest aroused by *John Woodvil* as Lamb's work, it had a real importance in giving an opening to Francis Jeffrey who, from his sanctum as editor of the *Edinburgh Review,* was scanning the horizon for some one to belabour among the despised "Lakers." We find in both Jeffrey and Gifford pronouncements and practices to indicate that they would be quick to approve a work which harked back to the old writers. But the chance to scotch one of the new young vipers was too good to miss. It is customary to pass hasty judgement on Jeffrey for his famous criticism of Wordsworth's *Excursion,* "This will not do," but it is not altogether fair to Jeffrey to stop there. He did not like the Romanticists, certainly he did not approve the ways of the group which were sympathetic to the ideas of Wordsworth, Coleridge and Southey. There was almost as great disapproval of these writers by others in the group of Romanticists themselves. Jeffrey had a sincere liking for the Elizabethan writers and held them up as models. He liked their imagery, their richness of imagination and their figurative language so long as it remained, as it did with the Elizabethans, purely decorative. What he could not endure was the introduction of the personal, subjective and moral element. Of his own time he approved Crabbe and all forthright writers of nature, but when Wordsworth or Coleridge used nature as symbol of the subjective individual, bringing in the simple farmer or country girl to point a moral, Jeffrey cried out, "This will not do."

Perhaps we are more tolerant of Francis Jeffrey, who was

really an eminent critic, or perhaps we see the different sides of the man more clearly. Merely for him to direct his criticism to a mediocre play by an author not well known marks a recognition that something new might be on the way. We must conclude that the reception of *John Woodvil* was more than the play warranted; as dramatic literature, it scarcely deserves notice. The critical reviews which it called forth are a striking illustration of the narrowness and limitations of the critics of that period. But for Lamb *John Woodvil* was important. It gave indication of the results of his reading in his Elizabethan favourites and it set him up as a leading proponent for his time of the writers of the Sixteenth and Seventeenth Centuries.

Lamb was not daunted; he turned to the writing of another play. Early in 1806, in one of his early letters to Hazlitt, he wrote: "Have taken a room at *3s* a week, to be in between 5 & 8 at night, to avoid my *nocturnal* alias *knock-eternal* visitors. The first-fruits of my retirement has been a farce which goes to manager tomorrow. *Wish my ticket luck.*"

A few days later Mary Lamb confided in a letter to Sarah Stoddart* that "Charles is gone to finish the farce, and I am to hear it read this night. I am so uneasy between my hopes and fears of how I shall like it, that I do not know what I am doing. I need not tell you so, for before I send this I shall be able to tell you all about it. If I think it will amuse you, I will send you a copy. . . . The said Farce I carried (after many consultations of who was the most proper person to perform so important an office) to Wroughton, the Manager of Drury Lane. He was very civil to me; said it did not depend upon himself, but that he would put it into the Proprietors' hands, and that we should certainly have an answer from them."

On June 11, Wroughton reported: "Sir, Your piece of Mr. H— I am desired to say, is accepted at Drury Lane Theater, by

---

* February 1806.

the Proprietors, and, if agreeable to you, will be brought for-
wards when the proper opportunity serves—the Piece shall be
sent to you for your alterations in the course of a few days, as
the same is not in my Hands but with the Proprietors."

Lamb was to get £200 if the play had a good run and he
hoped for £100 for the copyright.

The happiness which the news of acceptance brought to both
brother and sister was communicated by Mary in her letter to
Sarah Stoddart in July: "The best news I have to send you is,
that the Farce is accepted. That is to say, the manager has written to say it shall be brought out when an opportunity serves. I
hope that it may come out by next Christmas; you must come
and see it the first night; for if it succeeds, it will be a great
pleasure to you, and if it should not, we shall want your consolation. So you must come." And on October 23, she wrote:
"Charles took an emendated copy of his farce to Mr. Wroughton
the Manager yesterday. Mr. Wroughton was very friendly to
him, and expressed high approbation of the farce, but there are
two, he tells him, to come out before it, yet he gave him hopes
that it will come out this season, but I am afraid you will not
see it by Christmas."

A little later during these days when Lamb was offering
consolation to Holcroft for the failure of *The Vindictive Man,*
he sent a characteristic letter to Manning which says a lot about
the new farce and even more about Lamb himself:

"Poor H[olcroft] I fear will feel the disappointment very seriously in a pecuniary light. From what I can learn he has saved
nothing. You and I were hoping one day that he had; but I fear
he has nothing but his pictures and books, and a no very flourishing business, and to be obliged to part with his long-necked
Guido that hangs opposite as you enter, and the game-piece
that hangs in the back drawing-room, and all those Vandykes,
&c.! God should temper the wind to the shorn connoisseur. I

hope I need not say to you, that I feel for the weather-beaten author, and for all his household. I assure you his fate has soured a good deal of pleasure I should have otherwise taken in my own little farce being accepted, and I hope about to be acted—it is in rehearsal actually, and I expect it to come out next week. It is kept a sort of secret, and the rehearsals have gone on privately, lest by many folks knowing it, the story should come out, which would infallibly damn it. You remember I had sent it before you went. Wroughton read it, and was much pleased with it. I speedily got an answer. I took it to make alterations, and lazily kept it some months, then took courage and furbished it up in a day or two and took it. In less than a fortnight I heard the principal part was given to Elliston, who liked it, and only wanted a prologue, which I have since done and sent; and I had a note the day before yesterday from the manager, Wroughton (bless his fat face—he is not a bad actor in some things), to say that I should be summoned to the rehearsal after the next, which next was to be yesterday. I had no idea it was so forward. I have had no trouble, attended no reading or rehearsal, made no interest; what a contrast to the usual parade of authors! But it is peculiar to modesty to do all things without noise or pomp! I have some suspicion it will appear in public on Wednesday next, for W. says in his note, it is so forward that if wanted it may come out next week, and a new melo-drama is announced for every day till then: and 'a new farce is in rehearsal,' is put up in the bills. Now you'd like to know the subject. The title is 'Mr. H.,' no more; how simple, how taking! A great H. sprawling over the play-bill and attracting eyes at every corner. The story is a coxcomb appearing at Bath, vastly rich—all the ladies dying for him—all bursting to know who he is—but he goes by no other name than Mr. H.—a curiosity like that of the dames of Strasburg about the man with the great nose. But I won't tell you any more about it. Yes, I will; but I can't give you an idea how I have done it. I'll just tell you that after much vehement admiration, when his true name comes out, 'Hogs-flesh,' all the women shun him, avoid him, and not one can be found to change their name for him—that's the idea—how flat it is here!—but how whimsical in the farce!"

The performance was given Wednesday, the tenth of December, with Elliston in the title part. It will be recalled that a merry group of friends attended the performance, and vied with the clerks of South Sea House collected by John Lamb, first in cries of approval and later in the hisses in which Lamb himself joined. The next day Lamb wrote to Wordsworth, conveying in calm resignation the news of the play's failure. He bore the disappointment with courage, but he often referred in other years to the hissing.

"Dear Wordsworth,

"Mr. H. came out last night and failed. I had many fears; the subject was not substantial enough. John Bull must have solider fare than a *Letter*. We are pretty stout about it, have had plenty of condoling friends, but after all, we had rather it should have succeeded. You will see the Prologue in most of the Morning Papers. It was received with such shouts as I never witness'd to a Prologue. It was attempted to be encored. How hard! a thing I did merely as a task, because it was wanted—and set no great store by; and Mr. H——!!

"The quantity of friends we had in the house, my brother and I being in Public Offices, &c. was astonishing—but they yielded at length to a few hisses. A hundred hisses—damn the word, I write it like kisses—how different—a hundred hisses outweigh a 1000 Claps. The former come more directly from the Heart—Well, 'tis withdrawn and there is an end.

"Better Luck to us.—C. L.

"11 Dec.—(turn over).

"P. S. Pray when any of you write to the Clarksons, give our kind Loves, and say we shall not be able to come and see them at Xmas—as I shall have but a day or two,—and tell them we bear our mortification pretty well."

The story of the evening has been told by three others who were present. These reports treat of the occasion with sympathy and with individuality of style. Henry Crabb Robinson who had but recently come into the Lamb circle and who liked the theatre as much as the Lambs; Talfourd, to whom every admirer of Lamb is everlastingly indebted; and Hazlitt, friend and boon companion—these were the three. Robinson said:

"By this time I had become acquainted with Charles Lamb and his sister; for I went with them to the first performance of *Mr. H—*. at Covent Garden, which took place in the month of December. The prologue was very well received. Indeed it could not fail, being one of the very best in our language. But on the disclosure of the name, the squeamishness of the vulgar taste in the pit showed itself by hisses; and I recollect that Lamb joined, and was probably the loudest hisser in the house. The damning of this play belongs to the literary history of the day, as its author to the literary magnates of his age."

This is Talfourd's account:

"Wednesday, 10th December, 1806, was the wished-for evening which decided the fate of *Mr. H—* on the boards of Drury. Great curiosity was excited by the announcement; the house was crowded to the ceiling; and the audience impatiently awaited the conclusion of the long, dull, intolerable opera of *The Travellers,* by which it was preceded. At length Mr. Elliston, the hero of the farce, entered, gayly dressed, and in happiest spirits—enough, not too much, elated—and delivered the prologue with great vivacity and success. The farce began; at first it was much applauded; but the wit seemed wire-drawn; and when the curtain fell on the first act, the friends of the author began to fear. The second act dragged heavily on, as second acts of farces will do; a rout at Bath, peopled with ill-dressed and over-dressed actors and actresses, increased the disposition to yawn; and when the moment of disclosure came, and nothing worse than the name *Hogsflesh* was heard, the audience resented the long play on their curiosity, and would hear no more. Lamb, with his sister, sat, as he anticipated, in the front of the pit; and having joined in encoring the epilogue, the brilliancy of which injured the farce, he gave way with equal pliancy to the common feeling, and hissed and hooted as loudly as any of his neighbours. The next morning's playbill contained a veracious announcement, that *the new play of Mr. H— performed for the first time last night, was received by an overflowing audience with universal applause, and will be repeated for the second time tomorrow;* but the stage lamps never that morrow saw. Elliston would have tried again; but Lamb saw at once that the case was hopeless, and consoled his friends with a century of puns for the wreck of his dramatic hopes."

And here is Hazlitt:

"We often make life unhappy in wishing things to have turned out otherwise than they did, merely because that is possible to the imagination which is impossible in fact. I remember when L——'s farce was damned (for damned it was, that's certain) I used to dream every night for a month after (and then I vowed I would plague myself no more about it) that it was revived at one of the Minor or provincial theatres with great success, that such and such retrenchments and alterations had been made in it, and that *it was thought it might do at the other House.* I had heard indeed (this was told in confidence to L.) that *Gentleman* Lewis was present on the night of its performance, and said, that if he had had it, he would have made it, by a few judicious curtailments, 'the most popular little thing that had been brought out for some time.' How often did I conjure up in recollection the full diapason of applause at the end of the *Prologue,* and hear my ingenious friend in the first row of the pit roar with laughter at his own wit! Then I dwelt with forced complacency on some part in which it had been doing well: then we would consider (in concert) whether the long, tedious opera of the *Travellers,* which preceded it, had not tired people beforehand, so that they had not spirits left for the quaint and sparkling 'wit skirmishes' of the dialogue, and we all agreed it might have gone down after a Tragedy, except L. himself, who swore he had no hopes of it from the beginning, and that he knew the name of the hero when it came to be discovered could not be got over. Mr. H—, thou wert damned! Bright shone the morning on the playbills that announced thy appearance, and the streets were filled with the buzz of persons asking one another if they would go to see."

Although Lamb must have chilled when he read the reviews next day, he might have got some consolation from the *Morning Chronicle.* "If the most obnoxious of the puns were struck out and a more interesting concluding scene devised, the piece might be tolerable. . . . Certainly, even as it is, more insipid farces have been endured, and the dissatisfaction with which *Mr. H—* was received seemed greater than the occasion demanded."

The failure of the play, so much discussed in the last century, interested our American dramatic critic, Brander Matthews, who gave his opinion of the cause. "The fatal fault was the keeping of the secret from the spectators. To keep a secret is a misconception of true theatrical effect, an improper method of sustaining dramatic suspense. An audience is interested not in what the end may be, but in the means whereby that end is to be reached. . . . If the audience that night had been slily let into the secret in an early scene, they would have had double enjoyment in watching the futile endeavors of the *dramatis personæ* to divine it, and they would not have been disappointed

wnen Mr. Hogsflesh let slip his full patronymic. Kept in ignorance, the spectators joined the actors in speculation, and when
the word was revealed they were not amused by the disgust of
the actors, so annoyed were they that they had been puzzled
by a vulgar name. Perhaps, too, there was a certain reaction
after the undue expectancy raised by the prologue. Lamb wrote
to Wordsworth that 'the number of friends they had in the
House was astonishing.' Now nothing is so dangerous on the
first night of a new play as a large number of friends in the audience. One is greatly inclined to regret that Lamb did not yield
to Elliston, and let the play be acted again. If it had had a
second chance, the injudicious friends would have been absent,
and the name of the hero would have been noised abroad, and,
once in the possession of this secret, the audience might well
have laughed long and heartily at the hero's misadventures."

During the weeks of acceptance and failure of *Mr. H—* and
the incidents connected with that venture, Charles and Mary
were busy on another project which turned out more successfully, even to the lasting credit of all persons concerned. A few
months before this time Lamb had written some amusing lines,
*The King and Queen of Hearts, Showing how notably the
Queen made her Tarts, and how scurvily the Knave stole them
away: with other particulars belonging thereunto,* to go with
some drawings by William Mulready. This contribution of
Lamb was one of the first of the books to be published by the
Godwins, who, to forestall bankruptcy, had set up a business
for publishing juvenile books. The book was issued at one
shilling plain, and one shilling and sixpence coloured. It is a
bit of irony for us to learn that a copy discovered in 1901, dated
1809, was sold at auction for £226, and later one of the 1806
edition brought £240.

Evidently the success which attended the publication of *The*

King and Queen of Hearts moved Godwin to try something more, and either he or probably Mrs. Godwin, for whom Lamb never concealed his dislike, suggested to Charles and Mary that they together tell the plays of Shakespeare in language within the comprehension of juvenile readers. The idea appealed to the Lambs not only because there appeared a chance for profit, but from their natural desire to help young readers of Shakespeare and young theatregoers.

In May of 1806, Lamb confided to Manning, "[Mary] is doing for Godwin's bookseller twenty of Shakespear's plays, to be made into Children's tales. Six are already done by her, to wit, 'The Tempest,' 'Winter's Tale,' 'Midsummer Night,' 'Much Ado,' 'Two Gentlemen of Verona,' and 'Cymbeline.' 'The Merchant of Venice' is in forwardness. I have done 'Othello' and 'Macbeth,' and mean to do all the tragedies. I think it will be popular among the little people. Besides money. It is to bring in 60 guineas. Mary has done them capitally, I think you'd think."

And Mary in June joyfully wrote to Sarah Stoddart: "My Tales are to be published in separate story-books. . . . I cannot send you them in Manuscript, because they are all in the Godwins' hands; but one will be published very soon, and then you shall have it *all in print.* . . .

"Charles has written Macbeth, Othello, King Lear, and has begun Hamlet; you would like to see us, as we often sit, writing on one table (but not on one cushion sitting), like Hermia and Helena in the Midsummer Night's Dream, or, rather, like an old literary Darby and Joan: I taking snuff, and he groaning all the while, and saying he can make nothing of it, which he always says till he has finished, and then he finds out he has made something of it."

After the farce had been accepted in July, Mary wrote to Sarah Stoddart in Salisbury: "We thank you for your kind invitations, and were half-inclined to come down to you; but after mature deliberation, and many wise consultations, such as you know we often hold, we came to the resolution of staying quietly at home: and during the holiday we are both of us to set stoutly to work and finish the Tales, six of them being yet to do. We thought, if we went anywhere and left them undone, they would lay upon our minds; and that when we returned, we should feel unsettled, and our money all spent beside: and next summer we are to be very rich, and then we can afford a long journey some where, I will not say to Salisbury, because I really think it is better for you to come to us; but of that we will talk another time."

So the work was finished and Lamb was able to tell Manning in December, "Those 'Tales from Shakespear' are near coming out." They appeared some time before January 29, 1807, as Charles on that day sent a copy to Wordsworth. "We have book'd off from Swan and Two Necks, Lad Lane, this day (per Coach) the Tales from Shakespear. You will forgive the plates, when I tell you they were left to the direction of Godwin, who left the choice of subjects to the bad baby [Mrs. Godwin], who from mischief (I suppose) has chosen one from damn'd beastly vulgarity (vide Merch. Venice) where no atom of authority was in the tale to justify it—to another has given a name which exists not in the tale, Nic Bottom, and which she thought would be funny, though in this I suspect *his* hand, for I guess her reading does not reach far enough to know Bottom's Xtian name— and one of Hamlet, and Grave digging, a scene which is not hinted at in the story, and you might as well have put King Canute the Great reproving his courtiers—the rest are Giants and Giantesses. Suffice it, to save our taste and damn our folly, that we left it all to a friend W. G.—who in the first place cheated me into putting a name to them, which I did not mean, but do not repent, and then wrote a puff about their *simplicity,*

&c., to go with the advertisement as in my name! Enough of this egregrious dupery.—I will try to abstract the load of teazing circumstances from the Stories and tell you that I am answerable for Lear, Macbeth, Timon, Romeo, Hamlet, Othello, for occasionally a tail piece or correction of grammar, for none of the cuts and all of the spelling. The rest is my Sister's.—We think Pericles of hers the best, and Othello of mine—but I hope all have some good. As You Like It we like least."

The book bore the title *Tales from Shakespear. Designed for the Use of Young Persons. By Charles Lamb. Embellished with Copper-Plates. In Two Volumes.* Neither did title page nor the preface carry the name of Mary, but Charles never failed to bear testimony to the extent of her assistance and to its superior quality. Not until after many years and a number of printings did Mary's name appear and we can only conjecture why it was not used on the early editions. An admirable preface, as good as the *Tales* themselves, the first part by Mary and the last by Charles, set forth the purpose of the work, with these admirable concluding words: "What these Tales have been to you in childhood, that and much more it is my wish that the true Plays of Shakespear may prove to you in older years—enrichers of the fancy, strengtheners of virtue, a withdrawing from all selfish and mercenary thoughts, a lesson of all sweet and honourable thoughts and actions, to teach you courtesy, benignity, generosity, humanity; for of examples, teaching these virtues, his pages are full."

As the Lambs conceived their project, the plays were to be as little different as possible from the original. Just as in the First Folio, *The Tempest* was the first play. It must have been a happy surprise for young readers to discover that Shakespeare was not so difficult after all. "There was a certain island in the sea, the only inhabitants of which were an old man, whose name was Prospero, and his daughter Miranda, a very beautiful young lady. She came to this island so young, that she had no memory of having seen any other human face than her father's.

"They lived in a cave or cell, made out of a rock; it was divided into several apartments, one of which Prospero called his study; there he kept his books, which chiefly treated of magic, a study at that time much affected by all learned men: and the knowledge of this art he found very useful to him; for being thrown by a strange chance upon this island, which had been enchanted by a witch called Sycorax, who died there a short time before his arrival, Prospero, by virtue of his art, released many good spirits that Sycorax had imprisoned in the bodies of large trees, because they had refused to execute her wicked commands. These gentle spirits were ever after obedient to the will of Prospero. Of these Ariel was the chief."

With a freshness as if the story were being told for the first time, Mary leads us into the scene where Prospero fondly watches and furthers the love affairs of Ferdinand and Miranda. Scenes like the court scene in *The Merchant of Venice* are told with a clarity and precision that makes one wonder how one could have missed so many details in one's own reading or hearing of the original play. It seems easy to tell the story, but that impression of simplicity is a result of the art of translation and conceals the difficulty of selecting the proper details to retain the flavour of the original. The dramatic form has been translated into a tale without loss and without the emergence of the archaic. The authors understood the language of the plays and the characters, and, what was of equal importance, they knew the young readers for whom they were writing. The skill is not in a mere retelling of stories; it is in the pointing of the characters so that they are described and not defined, described with such a humour and understanding that they become bits of living nature. The fun which Charles and Mary must have had in their work has been left for the readers to share.

"Beatrice, who liked not to be left out of any discourse, interrupted Benedick with saying, 'I wonder that you will still be talking, signor Benedick: nobody marks you.' Benedick was just such another rattle-brain as Beatrice, yet he was not pleased at this free salutation; he thought it did not become a well-bred lady to be so flippant with her tongue; and he remembered, when he was last at Messina, that Beatrice used to select him to make her merry jests upon. And as there is no one who so little likes to be made a jest of as those who are apt to take the same liberty themselves, so it was with Benedick and Beatrice. . . ."

Characteristic of Mary's share in the work is such a remark as, "but fathers do not often desire the death of their own daughters, even though they do happen to prove a little refractory." We are sure that no passage gave her more pleasure than her paraphrase of the description of Puck in *A Midsummer Night's Dream:* "Puck, (or as he was sometimes called, Robin Goodfellow) was a shrewd and knavish sprite, that used to play comical pranks in the neighbouring villages; sometimes getting into the dairies and skimming the milk, sometimes plunging his light and airy form into the butter-churn, and while he was dancing his fantastic shape in the churn, in vain the dairy-maid would labour to change her cream into butter: nor had the village swains any better success; whenever Puck chose to play his freaks in the brewing copper, the ale was sure to be spoiled. When a few good neighbours were met to drink some comfortable ale together, Puck would jump into the bowl of ale in the likeness of a roasted crab, and when some old goody was going to drink he would bob against her lips, and spill the ale over her withered chin; and presently after, when the same old dame was gravely seating herself to tell her neighbours a sad and melancholy story, Puck would slip her three-legged stool from under her, and down toppled the poor old woman, and then the old gossips would hold their sides and laugh at her, and swear they never wasted a merrier hour."

With equal good taste, Charles described the character of the Moor, Othello, the baffling Timon and the cunning Iago. "Iago was artful, and had studied human nature deeply, and he knew that all the torments which afflict the mind of man (and far beyond bodily torture), the pains of jealousy were the most intolerable, and had the sorest sting." He leaves us the sad and beautiful tragedy of Romeo and Juliet with, "So did these poor old lords, when it was too late, strive to outgo each other in mutual courtesies." And how charmingly he writes of Cordelia! "Cordelia, who in earnest loved her old father even almost as extravagantly as her sisters pretended to do, would have plainly told him so at any other time, in more daughter-like and loving terms, and without these qualifications, which did indeed sound a little ungracious; but after the crafty flattering speeches of her sisters, which she had seen draw such extravagant rewards, she thought the handsomest thing she could do was to love and be silent. This put her affection out of suspicion of mercenary ends, and showed that she loved, but not for gain; and that her professions, the less ostentatious they were, had so much more of truth and sincerity than her sisters'."

"Macbeth," Charles writes, "had a wife, to whom he communicated the strange prediction of the weird sisters, and its partial accomplishment. She was a bad, ambitious woman, and so as her husband and herself could arrive at greatness, she cared not much by what means. She spurred on the reluctant purpose of Macbeth, who felt compunction at the thoughts of blood, and did not cease to represent the murder of the king as a step absolutely necessary to the fulfilment of the flattering prophecy."

It is a temptation difficult to resist to quote more fully from the story of the murder of Duncan by Macbeth and Lady Macbeth, skilfully leading the reader to the conviction that the murder would not have been accomplished without the connivance of both murderers. The exposition of Lady Macbeth's working upon the mind and will of her husband is a fine bit of recognition of the psychology involved and a fine proof of how it may be presented simply and effectively.

Many pages have been printed to explain Hamlet, but we do not recall a better exposition than this short paragraph:

"The terror which the sight of the ghost had left upon the senses of Hamlet, he being weak and dispirited before, almost unhinged his mind, and drove him beside his reason. And he, fearing that it would continue to have this effect, which might subject him to observation, and set his uncle upon his guard, if he suspected that he was meditating anything against him, or that Hamlet really knew more of his father's death than he professed, took up a strange resolution, from that time to counterfeit as if he were really and truly mad; thinking that he would be less an object of suspicion when his uncle should believe him incapable of any serious project, and that his real perturbation of mind would be best covered and pass concealed under a disguise of pretended lunacy."

Charles and Mary considered it most important that the young reader should be introduced to the old, unfamiliar and richer vocabulary of the Elizabethans, hence they avoided as far as possible words which had come into the language since Shakespeare's time. There was no attempt to reduce the words to one syllable. Though even to an adult reader so many words and phrases in Shakespeare's plays and poetry are confusing, too much would have been lost by dropping words not readily intelligible.

The success of the *Tales* was immediate and a number of editions appeared during Charles's lifetime. It would be impossible to compute the earnings to the publishers. It would be equally difficult to recall another title published in 1808 which today is as popular as the *Tales,* or even read at all. They did their work so well that in the century and a half no successful competitor has appeared, and their tales have been published again and again, in hundreds of editions, and are today recognised as classics.

Few of us realise the difficulty which confronted one who undertook to do what the Lambs did. No one had pointed the way, no one had showed what to do, what not to do. In the Eighteenth Century the text of Shakespeare had been emended, mutilated, given new and strange endings and fanciful interpretations. It was a far different text to look at and read from what we accept now as the words Shakespeare wrote. The real Shakespeare needed to be revived both for the stage and the increasing number of readers. Besides, books for juvenile readers did not take account of content and appearance with a realisation of the likes and dislikes of children. It was a really good fairy that led two artists, so enthusiastic and capable, to a most congenial and perfect piece of collaboration. The task called for a new kind of sympathy and pioneering and this Charles and Mary Lamb possessed to a superlative degree.

Mary mentions in a letter to Sarah Hazlitt, December 10, 1808, a bit of collaboration with Tom Sheridan, the son of the famous Richard Brinsley Sheridan. "Through the medium of Wroughton, there came an invitation and proposal from T. S., that C. L. should write some scenes in a speaking pantomime, the other parts of which Tom now, and his father formerly, have manufactured between them. So, in the Christmas holydays, my brother and his two great associates, we expect, will be all three damned together, that is, I mean, if Charles's share, which is done and sent in, is accepted."

Patmore and others have held the opinion that an unpublished comic opera now in the British Museum is the piece in question and that the handwriting is actually Lamb's, but according to Lucas, who is as good an authority as can be, there is not convincing evidence. It may be by Lamb or the piece may have been destroyed in the burning of Drury Lane in 1809, or it may never have been written at all. We simply do not know.

Lamb turned next to something which sprang from his devotion to the plays of the Elizabethan period. Just when he came to like Elizabethan literature especially we do not know. There is no evidence of his interest in that special period while he was at Christ's Hospital. We know that he and Mary were continually browsing among the old books of the Salt library and his liking may well have been awakened by the folios of his landlord's collection along with a devotion to old books in general.

In the first letters to Coleridge, Lamb writes of copying passages from Beaumont and Fletcher, Massinger and other Elizabethan dramatists for the enjoyment of his friends and doubtless for his pleasure as well. At the time of the family tragedy, he admitted that he destroyed, along with his own verses, "all my books of extracts from Beaumont and Fletcher and a thousand sources." Fortunately in a stronger frame of mind which he regained in time, he began again not only to write verse but to read and copy from the Elizabethans. In December 1806, Mary wrote to Mrs. Clarkson, "My brother sometimes threatens to pass his hollidays in town hunting over old plays at the Museum to extract passages for a work (a collection of poetry) Mr. Wordsworth intends to publish. [Wordsworth must be a slip of the pen, as there is no reason for his name in this connection.] However, I hope before that time arrives, he will be able to borrow the books of some good old collector of those hidden treasures, and thus they can be copied at home and much of Charles' labour and time saved. The Museum is only open during his office hours."

In June 1807 Lamb wrote to the Clarksons, describing the

return after a visit and asking them to forward manuscripts and books which Mary had left behind. "I want in particular the Dramatic Extracts, as my purpose is to make use of the remainder of my holydays in completing them at the British Museum, which will be employment & money in the end."

In the following February he wrote to Manning: "I have done two books since the failure of my farce; they will both be out this summer. The one is a juvenile book—'The Adventures of Ulysses,' intended to be an introduction to the reading of Telemachus! It is done out of the Odyssey, not from the Greek: I would not mislead you; nor yet from Pope's Odyssey, but from an older translation of one Chapman. The 'Shakespear Tales' suggested the doing it. Godwin is in both those cases my bookseller. The other is done for Longman, and is 'Specimens of English Dramatic Poets contemporary with Shakespear.' Specimens are becoming fashionable. We have—'Specimens of Ancient English Poets,' 'Specimens of Modern English Poets,' 'Specimens of Ancient English Prose Writers,' without end. They used to be called 'Beauties.' You have seen 'Beauties of Shakespear?' so have many people that never saw any beauties in Shakespear. Longman is to print it, and be at all the expense and risk; and I am to share the profits after all deductions; *i.e.* a year or two hence I must pocket what they please to tell me is due to me. But the book is such as I am glad there should be. It is done out of old plays at the Museum and out of Dodsley's collection, &c. It is to have notes."

The book was published near the end of 1808 with the title *Specimens of English Dramatic Poets, who Lived About the Time of Shakspeare: with Notes. By Charles Lamb.* As usual with anything which Lamb wrote, he made in the preface a clear and honest statement of the contents of the volume. "More than a third part of the following specimens are from plays which are to be found only in the British Museum and in some scarce private libraries. The rest are from Dodsley's and Hawkins's collections, and the works of Jonson, Beaumont and Fletcher, and Massinger.

"I have chosen wherever I could to give entire scenes, and in some instances successive scenes, rather than to string together single passages and detached beauties, which I have always found wearisome in the reading in selections of this nature.

"To every extract is prefixed an explanatory head, sufficient to make it intelligible with the help of some trifling omissions. Where a line or more was obscure, as having reference to something that had gone before, which would have asked more time to explain than its consequence in the scene seemed to deserve, I have had no hesitation in leaving the line or passage out. Sometimes where I have met with a superfluous character, which seemed to burthen without throwing any light upon the scene, I have ventured to dismiss it altogether. I have expunged, without ceremony, all that which the writers had better never have written, that forms the objection so often repeated to the promiscuous reading of Fletcher, Massinger, and some others.

"The kind of extracts which I have sought after have been, not so much passages of wit and humor, though the old plays are rich in such, as scenes of passion, sometimes of the deepest quality, interesting situations, serious descriptions, that which is more nearly allied to poetry than to wit, and to tragic rather than to comic poetry. The plays which I have made choice of have been, with few exceptions, those which treat of human life and manners, rather than masques, and Arcadian pastorals, with their train of abstractions, unimpassioned deities, passionate mortals, Claius, and Medorus, and Amintas, and Amarillis. My leading design has been, to illustrate what may be called the moral sense of our ancestors. To show in what manner they felt, when they placed themselves by the power of imagination in trying situations, in the conflicts of duty and passion, or the strife of contending duties; what sort of loves and enmities theirs were; how their griefs were tempered, and their full-swoln joys abated: how much of Shakspeare shines in the great men his contemporaries, and how far in his divine mind and manners he surpassed them and all mankind."

The first direct statement of the project was made by Southey, who told Coleridge that he had proposed to the publisher Longman to make a collection "of the scarcer and better old poets, beginning with 'Piers Plowman.' If it be done my name must stand to the prospectus, and Lamb shall take the job and the emolument—for whom in fact I invented it, being a fit thing to be done and he the man fit to do it."

Why Southey in 1804 proposed to his publisher to commission Charles Lamb, aged twenty-nine, to make a selection of poetry may be difficult for us to understand, but evidently Southey was sure of his choice and we really know now that Lamb was the best person who could have been chosen. Because Longman had undertaken a volume of "Specimens" by George Ellis, the hope of a publisher was dropped for the time, but Lamb continued with his selecting.

In a large way Lamb's enthusiasm helped. He had read carefully and widely and had grown in critical stature. Volumes which he had been able to obtain for himself were among his sources; he had borrowed from others; he had been buying books for Wordsworth and Coleridge and these he had read; and besides he was a constant reader at the British Museum.

It was the good fortune of English literature that the task fell into the hands of this enthusiastic artist and was not a case, as sometimes happens, of an idea, excellent in itself, being executed by an inferior workman and the result a mediocrity. The project can be traced in his maturing judgement, his wider experience with the theatre, his enlarged circle of friends interested in the drama, and his constant reading of the plays and copying his favourite selections.

In 1827 Lamb contributed each week to Hone's *Table Book*

an extract similar to those of the original *Specimens*. Off and on for almost twenty years he had been culling from the Garrick collection in the British Museum. For this series he wrote an illuminating preface. "My subsequent leisure has discovered in it [the Garrick collection] a treasure rich and exhaustless. . . . In it is to be found almost every production in the shape of a Play that has appeared in print, from the time of the old Mysteries and Moralities to the days of Crown and D'Urfey. Imagine the luxury to one like me, who, above every other form of Poetry, have ever preferred the Dramatic, of sitting in the princely apartments, for such they are, of poor condemned Montagu House, which I predict will not speedily be followed by a handsomer, and culling at will the flower of some thousand Dramas. It is like having the range of a Nobleman's Library, with the Librarian to your friend. Nothing can exceed the courteousness and attentions of the gentleman who has the chief direction of the Reading Rooms here; and you have scarce to ask for a volume, before it is laid before you." An observation on the courtesy of the attendants which would find favour with untold numbers of readers there since Lamb's day.

As to Lamb's regard for the *Specimens,* probably his favourite work, we read his closing words in the short autobiographical sketch which he prepared for William Upscott, "He also was the first to draw the Public attention to the old English Dramatists."

Since this work of Charles Lamb is not generally known to readers today, some of Lamb's comments are quoted which will show what a good guide and critic he was. For the convenience of the reader, we make no distinction between the original *Specimens* of 1808 and the additional extracts from the Garrick collection, all of which were published together posthumously in 1835. If there have been in either the Nineteenth or the Twentieth Century more pertinent observations, better taste and judgement displayed in making the selections, clearer and more individual appreciation of the qualities of the passages, all expressed in the best of English, we are not aware of them.

Of *Edward the Second:* "The reluctant pangs of abdicating Royalty in Edward furnished hints which Shakspeare scarce improved in his Richard the Second; and the death-scene of Marlowe's king moves pity and terror beyond any scene ancient or modern with which I am acquainted."

Of *The Rich Jew of Malta:* "Shylock in the midst of his savage purpose is a man. His motives, feelings, resentments have something human in them. ... Barabas is a mere monster brought in with a large painted nose to please the rabble."

"This scene [from *The Merry Devil of Edmonton*] has much of Shakspeare's manner in the sweetness and goodnaturedness of it. It seems written to make the reader happy. Few of our dramatists or novelists have attended enough to this. They torture and wound us abundantly. They are economists only in delight. Nothing can be finer, more gentlemanlike, and noble, than the conversation and compliments of these young men."

"Heywood is a sort of *prose* Shakspeare. His scenes are to the full as natural and affecting. But we miss *the Poet,* that which in Shakspeare always appears out and above the surface of *the nature.* Heywood's characters, his Country Gentleman, &c. are exactly what we see (but of the best kind of what we see) in life. Shakspeare makes us believe, while we are among his lovely creations, that they are nothing but what we are familiar with, as in dreams new things seem old: but we awake, and sigh for the difference."

"Heywood's ambition seems to have been confined to the

pleasure of hearing the Players speak his lines while he lived. It does not appear that he ever contemplated the possibility of being read by after-ages. . . . Posterity is bound to take care that a Writer loses nothing by such a noble modesty."

"The insipid levelling morality to which the modern stage is tied down would not admit of such admirable passions as these scenes are filled with. A puritanical obtuseness of sentiment, a stupid infantile goodness, is creeping among us, instead of the vigorous passions, and virtues clad in flesh and blood, with which the old dramatists present us. Those noble and liberal casuists could discern in the differences, the quarrels, the animosities of man, a beauty and truth of moral feeling, no less than in the iterately inculcated duties of forgiveness and atonement. With us all is hypocritical meekness. A reconciliation scene (let the occasion be never so absurd or unnatural) is always sure of applause. Our audiences come to the theatre to be complimented on their goodness. They compare notes with the amiable characters in the play, and find a wonderful similarity of disposition between them. We have a common stock of dramatic morality out of which a writer may be supplied without the trouble of copying it from originals within his own breast. To know the boundaries of honour, to be judiciously valiant, to have a temperance which shall beget a smoothness in the angry swellings of youth, to esteem life as nothing when the sacred reputation of a parent is to be defended, yet to shake and tremble under a pious cowardice when that ark of an honest confidence is found to be frail and tottering, to feel the true blows of a real disgrace blunting that sword which the imaginary strokes of a supposed false imputation had put so keen an edge upon but lately; to do, or to imagine this done in a feigned story, asks something more of a moral sense, somewhat a greater delicacy of perception in questions of right and wrong, than goes to the writing of two or three hackneyed sentences about the laws of honour as opposed to the laws of the land, or a common-place against duelling."

"The old play-writers are distinguished by an honest boldness of exhibition; they show every thing without being ashamed. If a reverse of fortune be the thing to be personified, they fairly bring us to the prison-gate and the alms-basket. A poor man on our stage is always a gentleman; he may be known by a peculiar neatness of apparel, and by wearing black. Our delicacy, in fact, forbids the dramatizing of Distress at all. It is never shewn in its essential properties; it appears but as the adjunct to some virtue, as something which is to be relieved, from the approbation of which relief the spectators are to derive a certain soothing of self-referred satisfaction. We turn away from the real essences of things to hunt after their relative shadows, moral duties: whereas, if the truth of things were fairly represented, the relative duties might be safely trusted to themselves, and moral philosophy lose the name of a science."

Of *The Duchess of Malfy,* by John Webster: "To move a horror skilfully, to touch a soul to the quick, to lay upon fear as much as it can bear, to wean and weary a life till it is ready to drop, and then step in with mortal instruments to take its last forfeit—this only a Webster can do. Writers of an inferior genius may 'upon horror's head horrors accumulate,' but they cannot do this. They mistake quantity for quality, they 'terrify babes with painted devils,' but they know not how a soul is capable of being moved; their terrors want dignity, their affrightments are without decorum."

Of *The White Devil,* by John Webster: "This White Devil of Italy sets off a bad cause so speciously, and pleads with such an

innocence-resembling boldness, that we seem to see that match-
less beauty of her face which inspires such gay confidence into
her; and are ready to expect, when she has done her pleadings,
that her very judges, her accusers, the grave ambassadors who sit
as spectators, and all the court, will rise and make proffer to
defend her in spite of the utmost conviction of her guilt."

Of *The Broken Heart,* by John Ford: "What a noble thing is
the soul in its strengths and in its weaknesses! who would be
less weak than Calantha? who can be so strong? the expression
of this transcendent scene almost bears me in imagination to
Calvary and the Cross; and I seem to perceive some analogy between the scenical sufferings which I am here contemplating,
and the real agonies of that final completion to which I dare no
more than hint a reference.

"Ford was of the first order of Poets. He sought for sublimity,
not by parcels in metaphors or visible images, but directly where
she has her full residence in the heart of man; in the actions and
sufferings of the greatest minds. There is a grandeur of the soul
above mountains, seas, and the elements."

"The passion for wealth has worn out much of its grossness
by tract of time. Our ancestors certainly conceived of money as
able to confer a distinct gratification in itself, not alone considered simply as a symbol of wealth. The old poets, when
they introduce a miser, constantly make him address his gold as
his mistress; as something to be seen, felt, and hugged; as
capable of satisfying two of the senses at least. The substitution
of a thin unsatisfying medium for the good old tangible gold,
has made avarice quite a Platonic affection in comparison with
the seeing, touching, and handling pleasures of the old Chrys-
ophilites. A bank-note can no more satisfy the touch of a true
sensualist in this passion, than Creusa could reurn her husband's
embrace in the shades."

Of *The Two Angry Women of Abingdon:* "Why do we go
on with ever-new editions of Ford, and Massinger, and the
thrice-reprinted Selections of Dodsley? what we want is as
many volumes more, as these latter consist of, filled with plays
(such as this), of which we know comparatively nothing. Not
a third part of the Treasures of old English Dramatic literature
has been exhausted. Are we afraid that the genius of Shakspeare would suffer in our estimate by the disclosure? He would
indeed be somewhat lessened as a miracle and a prodigy. But he
would lose no height by the confession. When a Giant is shown
to us, does it detract from the curiosity to be told that he has at
home a gigantic brood of brethren, less only than himself?
Along *with* him, not *from* him, sprang up the race of mighty
Dramatists, who, compared with the Otways and Rowes that
followed, were as Miltons to a Young or an Akenside. That he
was their elder brother, not their parent, is evident from the fact
of the very few direct imitations of him to be found in their
writings. Webster, Decker, Heywood and the rest of his great
contemporaries went on their own ways, and followed their
individual impulses, not blindly prescribing to themselves his
track. Marlowe, the true (though imperfect) father of our
tragedy, preceded him. The *comedy* of Fletcher is essentially
unlike to that of his. 'T is out of no detracting spirit that I speak
thus, for the plays of Shakspeare have been the strongest and
sweetest food of my mind from infancy; but I resent the comparative obscurity in which some of his most valuable co-
operators remain, who were his dear intimates, his stage and
chamber-fellows while he lived, and to whom his gentle spirit
doubtlessly then awarded the full portion of their genius, as
from them toward himself appears to have been no grudging of
his acknowledged excellence."

"If I were to be consulted as to a Reprint of our old English
Dramatists, I should advise to begin with the collected plays of

Heywood. He was a fellow Actor, and fellow Dramatist, with Shakspeare. He possessed not the imagination of the latter; but in all those qualities which gained for Shakspeare the attribute of *gentle,* he was not inferior to him;—generosity, courtesy, temperance in the depths of passion; sweetness, in a word, and gentleness; Christianism, and true hearty Anglicism of feelings, shaping that Christianism, shine throughout his beautiful writings in a manner more conspicuous than in those of Shakspeare, but only more conspicuous, inasmuch as in Heywood these qualities are primary, in the other subordinate to poetry. I love them both equally, but Shakspeare has most of my wonder. Heywood should be known to his countrymen, as he deserves. His plots are almost invariably English. I am sometimes jealous, that Shakspeare laid so few of his scenes at home. I laud Ben Jonson, for that in one instance having framed the first draught of his *Every Man in His Humour* in Italy, he changed the scene, and Anglicised his characters."

Where such riches abound the difficulty of making selection is obvious. These may be sufficient to show the range and originality of observations as well as to give an indication of the quality of the young critic just turned thirty, for these quoted passages are practically all from the original *Specimens.* It was the good fortune of readers of drama of that day that they could approach the subject under the tutelage of such enthusiasm and good taste.

According to the excellent Anthony Dykes Campbell, "the great quarterlies allowed this book, the publication of which constituted an epoch in the study of one of the most important sections of our national literature; to pass unnoticed—an omission all the more remarkable seeing that, with the exception of Lamb himself, no men, perhaps, were so much interested in its subject as the respective editors of the 'Edinburgh' (Francis Jeffrey) and the 'Quarterly' (William Gifford)."

On this side of the Atlantic, James Russell Lowell expressed an appreciation which was properly reserved for his time and might safely be made even more generous in our time. "Charles Lamb, for example, came to the old English Dramatists with the feeling of a discoverer. He brought with him an alert curiosity, and everything was delightful simply because it was strange. Like other early adventurers, he sometimes mistook shining sand for gold; but he had the great advantage of not feeling himself responsible for the manners of the inhabitants he found there, and not thinking it needful to make them square with any Westminster Catechism of aesthetics. Best of all, he did not feel compelled to compare them with the Greeks, about whom he knew little, and cared less. He took them as he found them, described them in a few pregnant sentances, and displayed his specimens of their growth and manufacture."

The *Specimens* must have had an influence upon Lamb's contemporaries greater than can actually be proved. Coleridge's lectures on Shakespeare, Hazlitt's lectures and critical essays on the more important Elizabethan dramatists owed much to Lamb's personal devotion to the old folios, his continued practice of making selections, and finally the published *Specimens*. Into that particular field he led; others followed. The evidence is in favour of Lamb's being the first among his contemporaries to interest himself in the Sixteenth and Seventeenth-Century writers. Characteristic of him is the persistence with which he kept up his work in spite of long hours at the office and the various illnesses of Mary, and after almost twenty years turned again to the Garrick collection and out of almost two thousand plays made the weekly selection for Hone.

Lamb's ambition to write a successful play never left him but was never realised. He had the proper appreciation of technique, no one was a better judge of the human qualities and literary excellences of a play, but when it came to creating situations in-

volving plot, or giving life to the characters, then he failed. He
came to realise his shortcomings but made at least two more
attempts—perhaps others—one a tragicomedy, a blank verse
version of Crabbe's poem "The Confidant," under the title *The
Wife's Trial, or The Including Widow,* and finally *The Pawn-
broker's Daughter* which was accepted by the actor-manager
Liston but was never given. Both were published in *Blackwood's,* the first in 1828, the other in 1830.

The frequency with which Charles and Mary went to the
theatre was in part explained by the free tickets which were
often available, due to the kindness of "godfather Fielde, the
most gentlemanly of oilmen." As their circle of friends was
enlarged, there were others who were equally fond of the stage,
Coleridge, Hazlitt and Crabb Robinson without whose faithful
diary we should be deprived of the record of many evenings
when together they saw their favourite actors at Covent Garden
or Drury Lane—Mrs. Siddons, Kemble, Kean, Mathews, Miss
O'Neil, Elliston, Liston, Macready, and for Lamb best of all,
Fanny Kelly. There were red-letter evenings when Lamb and
Hazlitt went together to see a play, one of which has been brilliantly described by Hazlitt. Perhaps the happiest times were
the picnics when the Lambs, Hunts and Novellos entertained
each other in rotation, to quote from Lucas, "the only refreshment, by mutual agreement, being bread and cheese, celery and
beer ... meetings at the theatre, when Munden, Dowton, Liston,
Bannister, Elliston and Fanny Kelly were on the stage; and pic-
nic repasts were enjoyed together by appointment in the fields
that then lay spread in green breadth and luxuriance between
the West-end of Oxford Street and the western slope of Hampstead Hill."

Seeing plays, reading plays, translating Shakespeare for the
young, writing reviews of particular actors or seriously discussing dramatic principles, trying repeatedly to write a successful

play—all bore testimony to Lamb's continued devotion to the theatre, but this would not have been complete without the close association of the men and women who made the stage their profession. Lamb liked people above everything else. In his Elia essay, "On Some of the Old Actors," he wrote of the enchantment which came to him at fifteen soon after his seven years at Christ's Hospital when the rules of the school did not permit him to go to the theatre.

"The casual sight of an old Play Bill, which I picked up the other day—I know not by what chance it was preserved so long—tempts me to call to mind a few of the Players, who make the principal figure in it. It represents the cast of parts in the Twelfth Night, at the old Drury-lane Theatre two-and-thirty years ago. There is something very touching in these old remembrances. They make us think how we *once* used to read a Play Bill—not, as now peradventure, singling out a favourite performer, and casting a negligent eye over the rest; but spelling out every name, down to the very mutes and servants of the scene."

Among his friends Lamb numbered some of the most distinguished actors and actresses of the day and it was indeed an exceptional evening at the Lambs' quarters when one did not drop in after the evening performance. With some he had close association. He has written sympathetically and longingly of them, and for one, Fanny Kelly, he had an affection which continued through life. There were Mrs. Jordan, the Irish actress whose naturalness in the parts of Ophelia, Helena, and Viola, Lamb especially praised; Mrs. Powel, as Olivia; Bensley, whose "swell of soul" and "true poetical enthusiasm" gave most intelligent interpretation of the parts of Iago and Malvolio; Dicky Suett, "the Robin Good-fellow of the stage"; Macready, introduced by Charles Lloyd, greatly admired by Lamb because of his interpretation of *Virginius,* James Sheridan Knowles's play; Dodd, famous for his Sir Andrew Aguecheek; Jack Bannister, be-loved for his "good natured moral persuasion," and Jack Pal-mer—both fine actors; Kemble and Kean, of course, and Ellis-ton, whom Lamb first met at the Leamington Spa Library, who was "a spirited performance always going on before your eyes, with nothing to pay.... Wherever Elliston walked, sate, or stood still, there was the theatre." What a splendid tribute and appar-ently well deserved!

Lamb liked especially the comedy of Liston, who often came as a guest to his house and of whom he wrote, as a joke, a pre-tended *Life,* which Crabb Robinson did not think in good taste. Robinson also liked Liston, whom he considered "our first comedian"; many entries in his diary record his enjoyment of his well-known parts, Malvolio, Dominic Sampson, Tony Lumpkin and Bob Acres.

The actor Munden, whose distinction consisted in "throwing a preternatural interest over the commonest daily life objects," had a particular influence over Lamb. Of Munden the story is told that Lamb, Elliston and he drove one day from Leaming-ton to Warwick Castle. On the return journey, as they were entering Leamington, Munden called out, "Stay, stay, my dear boys, I'll just slip out here. Here lives my dear old friend, Mis-tress Winifred Watson, so I'll look in on the old lady. In her eighty-sixth year, her eighty-sixth year, Mr. Lamb." As Munden disappeared, Elliston burst out laughing, exclaiming that the story was a trick of Munden's to escape paying his bill at the livery stable. This was Lamb's first meeting with Munden, whom he afterwards came to admire heartily and of whom he wrote generously in his Elia essay.

Talfourd has left a delightful account of Munden's last per-formance, on which occasion Mary made the pun which is justly famous, "Sic transit gloria Munden."

"On the last night of his appearance, Lamb was very desirous to attend, but every place in the boxes had long been secured; and Lamb was not strong enough to stand the tremendous rush, by enduring which, alone, he could hope to obtain a place in the pit; when Munden's gratitude for his exquisite praise anticipated his wish, by providing for him and Miss Lamb places in a corner of the orchestra, close to the stage.

"The play of the 'Poor Gentleman,' in which Munden played 'Sir Robert Bramble,' had concluded, and the audience was impatiently waiting for the farce, in which the great comedian was to delight them for the last time, when my attention was suddenly called to Lamb by Miss Kelly, who sat with my party far withdrawn into the obscurity of one of the Upper Boxes, but overlooking the radiant hollow which waved below us, to our friend. In his hand, directly beneath the line of stage-lights, glistened a huge porter pot, which he was draining; while the broad face of old Munden was seen thrust out from the door by which the musicians enter, watching the close of the draught, when he might receive and hide the portentous beaker from the gaze of the admiring neighbours. Some unknown benefactor had sent four pots of stout to keep up the veteran's heart during his last trial; and, not able to drink them all, he bethought him of Lamb, and without considering the wonder which would be excited in the brilliant crowd who surrounded him, conveyed himself the cordial chalice to Lamb's parched lips. At the end of the same farce, Munden found himself unable to deliver from memory a short and elegant address which one of his sons had written for him; but, provided against accidents, took it from his pocket, wiped his eyes, put on his spectacles, read it, and made his last bow. This was, perhaps, the last night when Lamb took a hearty interest in the present business scene; for though he went now and then to the theatre to gratify Miss Isola, or to please an author who was his friend, his real stage henceforth only spread itself out in the selectest chambers of his memory."

Lamb etches a character* by selecting a single incident, and
there you have Dodd for all time: "I am ill at dates, but I think
it is now better than five and twenty years ago that walking in
the gardens of Gray's Inn—they were then far finer than they
are now—the accursed Verulam Buildings had not encroached
upon all the east side of them, cutting out delicate green
crankles, and shouldering away one of two of the stately alcoves
of the terrace—the survivor stands gaping and relationless as if
it remembered its brother—they are still the best gardens of any
of the Inns of Court, my beloved Temple not forgotten—have
the gravest character, their aspect being altogether reverend
and law breathing—Bacon has left the impress of his foot upon
their gravel walks——taking my afternoon solace on a summer
day upon the aforesaid terrace, a comely sad personage came towards me, whom, from his grave air and deportment, I judged
to be one of the old Benchers of the Inn. He had a serious
thoughtful forehead, and seemed to be in meditations of mortality. As I have an instinctive awe of old Benchers, I was passing him with that sort of subindicative token of respect which
one is apt to demonstrate towards a venerable stranger, and
which rather denotes an inclination to greet him, than any positive motion of the body to that effect—a species of humility and
will-worship which I observe, nine times out of ten, rather
puzzles than pleases the person it is offered to—when the face
turning full upon me, strangely identified itself with that of
Dodd. Upon close inspection I was not mistaken. But could
this sad thoughtful countenance be the same vacant face of
folly which I had hailed so often under circumstances of gaiety;
which I had never seen without a smile, or recognised but as
the usher of mirth; that looked out so formally flat in Fopping-
ton, so frothily pert in Tattle, so impotently busy in Backbite;
so blankly divested of all meaning, or resolutely expressive of

---

* "On Some of the Old Actors."

none, in Acres, in Fribble, and a thousand agreeable imperti-
nences? Was this the face—full of thought and carefulness—
that had so often divested itself at will of every trace of either to
give me diversion, to clear my cloudy face for two or three hours
at least of its furrows? Was this the face—manly, sober, intelligent,—which I had so often despised, made mocks at, made
merry with? The remembrance of the freedoms which I had
taken with it came upon me with a reproach of insult. I could
have asked it pardon. I thought it looked upon me with a sense
of injury. There is something strange as well as sad in seeing
actors—your pleasant fellows particularly—subjected to and
suffering the common lot—their fortunes, their casualties, their
deaths, seem to belong to the scene, their actions to be amen-
able to poetic justice only. We can hardly connect them with
more awful responsibilities. The death of this fine actor took
place shortly after this meeting. He had quitted the stage some
months; and, as I learned afterwards, had been in the habit of
resorting daily to these gardens almost to the day of his decease.
In these serious walks probably he was divesting himself of
many scenic and some real vanities—weaning himself from the
frivolities of the lesser and the greater theatre—doing gentle
penance for a life of no very reprehensible fooleries,—taking off
by degrees the buffoon mask, which he might feel he had worn
too long—and rehearsing for a more solemn cast of part. Dying
he 'put on the weeds of Dominic.'

[Footnote] "Dodd was a man of reading, and left at his death
a choice collection of old English literature. I should judge him
to have been a man of wit. I know one instance of an impromptu
which no length of study could have bettered. My merry friend,
Jem White, had seen him one evening in Aguecheek, and rec-
ognising Dodd the next day in Fleet Street, was irresistibly im-
pelled to take off his hat and salute him as the identical Knight
of the preceding evening with a 'Save you, *Sir Andrew.*' Dodd,

not at all disconcerted at this unusual address from a stranger, with a courteous half-rebuking wave of the hand, put him off with an 'Away, *Fool*.'

" 'What a lass that were,' said a stranger who sate beside us, speaking of Miss KELLY in *Rachel,* 'to go a-gypseying through the world with!' " So Lamb reported a remark made to him at the theatre. We strongly suspect that he who paid such an original compliment was no other than Charles himself.

Frances Maria Kelly was born in 1790; that is, she was fifteen years younger than Lamb. She had a hard life as a young actress, making her début in *Bluebeard* at the age of seven. She distinguished herself in opera and on her appearance in London Lamb was the first to write words of high praise in the *Examiner,* reviewing her acting as Rachel in Richard Brome's *The Jovial Crew,* or *The Merry Beggars.*

"Her gabbling lachrymose petitions; her tones, such as we have heard by the side of old woods, when an irresistible face has come peeping on one on a sudden; with her full black locks, and a *voice*—how shall we describe it?—a voice that was by nature meant to convey nothing but truth and goodness, but warped by circumstance into an assurance that she is telling us a lie—that catching twitch of the thievish irreproveable finger—those ballad-singers' notes, so vulgar, yet so unvulgar—that assurance, so like impudence, and yet so many countless leagues removed from it—her jeers, which we had rather stand, than be caressed with other ladies' compliments, a summer's day long—her face, with a wild out-of-doors grace upon it——"

Crabb Robinson wrote of her as "an unaffected, sensible, clear-headed, warm-hearted woman. She has none of the vanities or arrogance of the actress. No one would suspect her profession from her conversation or manners." Both Robinson and

Miss Frances Maria Kelly

FRANCES MARIA KELLY AT TWENTY-NINE
From a drawing by Partridge. Engraved by Thompson in 1819

SAMUEL TAYLOR COLERIDGE AT TWENTY-SIX

From a drawing by Robert Hancock in 1798, National Portrait Gallery

Lamb, ardent theatre-lovers as they were, were not enthusiastic over women in the profession of acting. Other critics, including Hazlitt, described her with enthusiasm. She was a frequent visitor in the Lamb household, admired and loved by both Charles and Mary. Among the entries favourably describing her, Crabb Robinson mentions her coming in one evening after the theatre—Wordsworth was there and "politics were hardly touched on, for Miss Kelly stepped in." It was a rare occasion when politics were touched on at Lambs', even without the charm of Fanny's presence.

In June 1816, an attempt was made on Fanny's life by her frenzied lover, George Barrett. The play at Covent Garden was *The Merry Mourners,* and Mary Lamb was sitting in the pit; some of the shot fell into her lap. Fanny Kelly fainted but was soon revived and a panic was averted. Immediately after the performance Fanny was at the Lambs' in perfect composure. There is no mention of the incident in any of the letters which we have.

The affection of both Charles and Mary for Fanny Kelly, Charles's hearty appreciation of her acting and her good sense (a characteristic which impressed other observers as well), frequent visits at dinner, after the theatre and at the houses of friends, all were leading to an inevitable conclusion. Charles was in love. That he had previously renounced any thought of matrimony for Mary's sake was well known, but here was something different. Fanny was almost as much a member of the family as she could be. Well, it is all told in three wonderful letters whose existence has been known for only a few years. They were discovered most unexpectedly in 1903 by the former manager of the Gaiety Theatre. No tribute could add to the words which came from full hearts and which left both to go on as true friends as before and to give the world an example of frank and honest friendship.

"*20 July, 1819*

"Dear Miss Kelly,

"We had the pleasure, *pain* I might better call it, of seeing you last night in the new Play. It was a most consummate piece of Acting, but what a task for you to undergo! At a time when your heart is sore from real sorrow! it has given rise to a train of thinking, which I cannot suppress.

"Would to God you were released from this way of life: that you could bring your mind to consent to take your lot with us, and throw off for ever the whole burden of your Profession. I neither expect or wish you to take notice of this which I am writing, in your present over occupied & hurried state.—But to think of it at your leisure. I have quite income enough, if that were all, to justify for me making such a proposal with what I may call even a handsome provision for my survivor. What you possess of your own would naturally be appropriated to those, for whose sakes chiefly you have made so many hard sacrifices. I am not so foolish as not to know that I am a most unworthy match for such a one as you, but you have for years been a principal object in my mind. In many a sweet assumed character I have learned to love you, but simply as F. M. Kelly I love you better than them all. Can you quit these shadows of existence, & come & be a reality to us? can you leave off harassing yourself to please a thankless multitude, who know nothing of you, & begin at last to live to yourself & your friends?

"As plainly & frankly as I have seen you give or refuse assent in some feigned scene, so frankly do me the justice to answer me. It is impossible I should feel injured or aggrieved by your telling me at once, that the proposal does not suit you. It is impossible that I should ever think of molesting you with idle importunity and persecution after your mind [was] once firmly spoken—but happier, far happier, could I have leave to hope a time might come, when our friends might be your friends; our interest yours; our book-knowledge, if in that inconsiderable particular we have any little advantage, might impart something to you, which you would every day have it in your power ten thousand fold to repay by the added cheerfulness and joy which you could not fail to bring as a dowry into whatever family should have the honor and happiness of receiving *you,* the most welcome accession that could be made to it.

"In haste, but with entire respect & deepest affection, I subscribe myself,

"C. LAMB."

It is the most serious letter he ever wrote. The letter is folded and sealed and sent by a maid to the lady who lives in Henrietta Street, just the other side of Covent Garden.

Later in the afternoon there is a knock on the door, a maid enters and gives Lamb a letter as nicely folded as the one he had sent only a few hours before. He breaks the seal and reads:

"An early & deeply rooted attachment has fixed my heart on one from whom no worldly prospect can well induce me to withdraw it, but while I thus *frankly* & decidedly decline your proposal, believe me, I am not insensible to the high honour which the preference of such a mind as yours confers upon me—let me, however, hope that all thought upon this subject will end with this letter, & that you will henceforth encourage no other sentiment towards me than esteem in my private character and a continuance of that approbation of my humble talents which you have already expressed so much & so often to my advantage and gratification.

"Believe me I feel proud to acknowledge myself

"Your obliged friend
"F. M. KELLY."

It is not difficult to imagine the scene that July afternoon in his lodgings in Great Russell Street, the spot he liked best in all London. He will not put off the answer. We can now read what he wrote in a hand less steady than that in which he wrote his proposal. He had often urged others to play the part of men, good losers—now it is his turn.

"DEAR MISS KELLY,

"*Your injunctions shall be obeyed to a tittle.* I feel myself in a lackadaisacal no-how-ish kind of a humour. I believe it is the rain or something. I had thought to have written seriously, but I fancy I succeed best in epistles of mere fun: puns & *that* nonsense. You will be good friends with us, will you not? let what has past 'break no bones'* between us. You will not refuse us them next time we send for them?

"Yours very truly,
"C. L."

"Do you observe the delicacy of not signing my full name? N. B. Do not paste that last letter of mine into your Book."

A few days later Fanny Kelly wrote to her sister, regretting that her letter might cause Lamb great despondency but expressing again her decision as the only one she could make. "I could not give my assent to a proposal which would bring me into that atmosphere of sad mental uncertainty which surrounds his domestic life. Marriage might well bring to us both added causes for misery and regrets in later years."

This was Lamb's last attempt at romance. Fanny Kelly never married although she later became the mother of a daughter. She lived to be a very old woman, and when she died at the age of ninety-two, was forgotten by the theatre and few followed her to her grave on a cold December day in 1882.

An American friend, Mrs. Mary Balmanno, friend of the Cowden Clarkes, has described in *Pen and Pencil,* 1858, an evening at Tom Hood's with Lamb as guest. "Miss Kelly (charming, natural Miss Kelly, who has drawn from her audiences

---

* Bones were small ivory discs, about the size of a two-shilling piece, for the actors to give to their friends as tickets of admission. On one side was the name of the theatre, on the other the name of the actor or actress.

more heart-felt tears and smiles than perhaps any other English actress), with quiet good humour listened and laughed at the witty sallies of her host and his gifted friend, seeming as little an actress as it is possible to conceive. Once however, when some allusion was made to a comic scene in a new play then just brought out, wherein she had performed to the life the character of a low-bred lady's maid passing herself off as her mistress, Miss Kelly arose, and with [a] kind of resistless ardour repeated a few sentences so inimitably, that everybody laughed as much as if the real lady's maid, and not the actress, had been before them; while she who had so well personated the part, quietly resumed her seat without the least sign of merriment, as grave as possible."

A fitting close to the story of Charles's friendship with one of the most distinguished representatives of the theatre may be conveyed in the somewhat florid style of Mary Clarke, long an intimate friend of both Charles and Mary. One evening after a long walk through the green Enfield meadows she found Charles Lamb and his sister seated with Fanny Kelly on a rustic bench in the shade, "outside a small road-side inn, quaffing porter, supremely indifferent to the strangeness of the situation, nay heartily enjoying it. The umbrageous elm, the water trough, the dip in the road where there was a ford and a foot-bridge, the rough wooden table at which the little party was seated, the pleasant voices of Charles and Mary Lamb and Fanny Kelly—all are vividly present to the imagination of her who now writes these memorial lines."

9

The Poet

AT FIRST and for a long time, Lamb conceived his destiny to be that of poet. At Christ's Hospital he and Coleridge often talked of poetic subjects and later as young men in their long evenings at the Salutation and Cat they argued many poetic questions, such as metre, vocabulary and the treatment of nature in verse. His first poetry included sonnets to Mrs. Siddons, to Anna, and his sister Mary, and also poems expressing a fondness for scenes of childhood. When Coleridge published his first poems in 1796, he included four sonnets by Lamb with these complimentary words, "The effusions signed 'C. L.' were written by Mr. Charles Lamb of the India House; independently of their signature, their superior merit would have sufficiently distinguished them." Very good for the young clerk of twenty-one, who had been only four years with the India Company. But neither was Coleridge so well known in 1796.

After the tragedy in September of that year, it will be remembered, Lamb destroyed everything he had written. We do not know whether later he recalled some of these poems, but he never entirely gave up the writing of verse.

During the rest of his life he wrote sonnets, many occasional poems, epigrams, epitaphs, acrostics and album verses, besides prologues and epilogues and plays in blank verse. At the beginning his verse showed the influence of Bowles, that plaintive sonneteer whose poetry appeared while Lamb and Coleridge were at Christ's Hospital. As Lamb's interests extended and his knowledge of English poetry increased, he came under the special influence of the Elizabethan and Seventeenth-Century poets.

In 1808 and 1809, both Charles and Mary were occupied with books for children, *Tales from Shakspear, Mrs. Leicester's School* and poems. The poems were published in two volumes in 1809 by the Godwins, with the title *Poetry for Children*. By 1812, the books were out of print and an assistant schoolmaster at Christ's Hospital included more than twenty by Lamb in a collection of poems, published by Godwin. The original little volumes disappeared and until 1877 no copies were to be found. In 1876, some one who had bought them in Plymouth ten years before and later taken them to Australia, sent them back to England to be reprinted with other unpublished poems.

In the two-volume edition of his works published in 1818 is a dedication to Coleridge. As usual, his own statement is the best observation upon his poetic career and accomplishment. "You will smile to see the slender labours of your friend designated by the title of *Works;* but such was the wish of the gentlemen who have kindly undertaken the trouble of collecting them, and from their judgment could be no appeal.

"It would be a kind of disloyalty to offer to any one but yourself a volume containing the *early pieces,* which were first published among your poems, and were fairly derivatives from you and them. My friend Lloyd and myself came into our first battle (authorship is a sort of warfare) under cover of the greater Ajax. How this association, which shall always be a dear and proud recollection to me, came to be broken,—who snapped the three-fold cord,—whether yourself (but I know that was not the case) grew ashamed of your former companions,—or whether (which is by much the more probable) some ungracious bookseller was the author of the separation,—I cannot tell;—but wanting the support of your friendly elm, (I speak for myself,) my vine has, since that time, put forth few or no fruits; the sap (if ever it had any) has become, in a manner, dried up and extinct; and you will find your old associate, in his second volume, dwindled into prose and *criticism*.

"Am I right in assuming this as the cause? or is it that, as years come upon us, (except with some more health-happy spirits,) Life itself loses much of its Poetry for us? we transcribe but what we read in the great volume of Nature; and, as the characters grow dim, we turn off, and look another way. You yourself write no Christabels, nor Ancient Mariners, now.

"Some of the Sonnets, which shall be carelessly turned over by the general reader, may happily awaken in your remembrances, which I should be sorry should be ever totally extinct— the memory

Of summer days and of delightful years—

even so far back as to those old suppers at our old *********** Inn,—when life was fresh, and topics exhaustless,—and you first kindled in me, if not the power, yet the love of poetry, and beauty, and kindliness.—

What words have I heard
Spoke at the Mermaid!"

Lamb knew himself better than any one else did and was ever frank in speaking or writing of his limitations. Whether he was too generous in attributing to Coleridge the "kindling" of his love of poetry, it is unquestioned that he possessed to a superior degree "the love of poetry, and beauty, and kindliness." Although he wrote but few memorable lines, Lamb was a true poet in feeling and appreciation. And without his verse, we should be deprived of many pleasing lines describing his boyhood and the fond memories of a happy youth. If he seldom rose above mediocrity, he never wrote a line which was not simple and kindly and sympathetic. His most famous essays of Elia could not have been written by any one who lacked the qualities of a true poet.

The lines to the dear old "grandame," recalling the manner of Goldsmith, are a loving tribute to his grandmother Field about whose memory clings all the romance of his Hertfordshire childhood.

THE GRANDAME

                              On the green hill top,
Hard by the house of prayer, a modest roof,
And not distinguish'd from its neighbour-barn,
Save by a slender-tapering length of spire,
The Grandame sleeps. A plain stone barely tells
The name and date to the chance passenger.
For lowly born was she, and long had eat,
Well-earn'd, the bread of service:—hers was else
A mounting spirit, one that entertain'd
Scorn of base action, deed dishonourable,
Or aught unseemly. I remember well
Her reverend image: I remember, too,
With what a zeal she served her master's house;
And how the prattling tongue of garrulous age
Delighted to recount the oft-told tale
Or anecdote domestic. Wise she was,
And wondrous skill'd in genealogies,
And could in apt and voluble terms discourse
Of births, of titles, and alliances;
Of marriages, and intermarriages;
Relationship remote, or near of kin;
Of friends offended, family disgraced—
Maiden high-born, but wayward, disobeying
Parental strict injunction, and regardless
Of unmixed blood, and ancestry remote,
Stooping to wed with one of low degree.
But these are not thy praises; and I wrong
Thy honour'd memory, recording chiefly
Things light or trivial. Better 'twere to tell,
How with a nobler zeal, and warmer love,
She served her *heavenly Master*. I have seen
That reverend form bent down with age and pain,

And rankling malady. Yet not for this
Ceased she to praise her maker, or withdrew
Her trust in him, her faith, and humble hope—
So meekly had she learn'd to bear her cross—
For she had studied patience in the school
Of Christ, much comfort she had thence derived,
And was a follower of the NAZARENE.

The recollection of the sound of church bells is charmingly suggested by these simple lines of the young English poet who had grown up with a love for it in the country as well as in the city. Perhaps no incident of the present war days was more touching than the proclamation that the bells should ring again throughout the countryside in England.

THE SABBATH BELLS

The cheerful Sabbath bells, wherever heard,
Strike pleasant on the sense, most like the voice
Of one, who from the far-off hills proclaims
Tidings of good to Zion: chiefly when
Their piercing tones fall *sudden* on the ear
Of the contemplant, solitary man,
Whom thoughts abstruse or high have chanced to lure
Forth from the walks of men, revolving oft,
And oft again, hard matter, which eludes
And baffles his pursuit: thought-sick and tired
Of controversy, where no end appears,
No clue to his research, the lonely man
Half wishes for the society again.
Him, thus engaged, the Sabbath bells salute
Sudden! his heart awakes, his ears drink in
The cheering music; his relenting soul
Yearns after all the joys of social life,
And softens with the love of human kind.

Charles Lamb had an affection for the poet Cowper and an

early admiration for his poetry. With him too were poignant memories of the malady which Cowper himself had to bear.

TO THE POET COWPER

Cowper, I thank my God that thou art heal'd.
Thine was the sorest malady of all;
And I am sad to think that it should light
Upon the worthy head: but thou art heal'd,
And thou art yet, we trust, the destin'd man,
Born to re-animate the lyre, whose chords
Have slumber'd, and have idle lain so long;
To th' immortal sounding of whose strings
Did Milton frame the stately-pacèd verse;
Among whose wires with lighter finger playing
Our elder bard, Spenser, a gentler name,
The lady Muses' dearest darling child,
Enticed forth the deftest tunes yet heard
In hall or bower; taking the delicate ear
Of the brave Sidney and the Maiden Queen.
Thou, then, take up the mighty epic strain,
Cowper, of England's bards, the wisest and the best!

In the midst of great depression on account of his personal grief over the death of his mother and some unfriendly actions of his associates, he wrote the lines which are deservedly the most famous of his verses.

THE OLD FAMILIAR FACES

I have had playmates, I have had companions,
In my days of childhood, in my joyful school-days,
All, all are gone, the old familiar faces.

I have been laughing, I have been carousing,
Drinking late, sitting late, with my bosom cronies,
All, all are gone, the old familiar faces.

I loved a love once, fairest among women;
Closed are her doors on me, I must not see her—
All, all are gone, the old familiar faces.

I have a friend, a kinder friend has no man;
Like an ingrate, I left my friend abruptly;
Left him, to muse on the old familiar faces.

Ghost-like I paced round the haunts of my childhood.
Earth seem'd a desart I was bound to traverse,
Seeking to find the old familiar faces.

Friend of my bosom, thou more than a brother,
Why wert not thou born in my father's dwelling?
So might we talk of the old familiar faces—

How some they have died, and some they have left me,
And some are taken from me; all are departed;
All, all are gone, the old familiar faces.

After one of his holidays, Lamb penned the verses in memory of the pretty young Quakeress, Hester Savory, who used to pass his window when he lived in Pentonville. In writing to his friend Manning,* he said, "I send you some verses I have made on the death of a young Quaker you may have heard me speak of as being in love with for some years while I lived at Pentonville, though I had never spoken to her in my life. She died about a month since."

HESTER

When maidens such as Hester die,
Their place ye may not well supply,
Though ye among a thousand try,
    With vain endeavour.

---

* March 1803.

A month or more hath she been dead,
Yet cannot I by force be led
To think upon the wormy bed,
    And her together.

A springy motion in her gait,
A rising step, did indicate
Of pride and joy no common rate,
    That flush'd her spirit.

I know not by what name beside
I shall it call:—if 'twas not pride,
It was a joy to that allied,
    She did inherit.

Her parents held the Quaker rule,
Which doth the human feeling cool,
But she was train'd in Nature's school,
    Nature had blest her.

A waking eye, a prying mind,
A heart that stirs, is hard to bind,
A hawk's keen sight ye cannot blind,
    Ye could not Hester.

My sprightly neighbour, gone before
To that unknown and silent shore,
Shall we not meet, as heretofore,
    Some summer morning,

When from thy cheerful eyes a ray
Hath struck a bliss upon the day,
A bliss that would not go away,
    A sweet forewarning?

For his volume, *Select British Poets,* Hazlitt wrote: "Mr. C.
Lamb has produced no poems equal to his prose writings: but
I could not resist the temptation of transferring into this collec-

tion his *Farewell to Tobacco* and some of the sketches in *John Woodvil,* the first is rarely surpassed in *quaint wit*—and the last in pure feeling." Here is

A FAREWELL TO TOBACCO

May the Babylonish curse
Strait confound my stammering verse,
If I can a passage see
In this word-perplexity,
Or a fit expression find,
Or a language to my mind,
(Still the phrase is wide or scant)
To take leave of thee, GREAT PLANT!
  Or in any terms relate
Half my love, or half my hate:
For I hate, yet love, thee so,
That, whichever thing I shew,
The plain truth will seem to be
A constrain'd hyperbole,
And the passion to proceed
More from a mistress than a weed.

    Sooty retainer to the vine,
Bacchus' black servant, negro fine;
Sorcerer, that mak'st us dote upon
Thy begrimed complexion,
And, for thy pernicious sake,
More and greater oaths to break
Than reclaimèd lovers take
'Gainst women: thou thy siege dost lay
Much too in the female way,
While thou suck'st the lab'ring breath
Faster than kisses or than death.

    Thou in such a cloud dost bind us,
That our worst foes cannot find us,
And ill fortune, that would thwart us,

Shoots at rovers, shooting at us;
While each man, thro' thy height'ning steam,
Does like a smoking Etna seem,
And all about us does express
(Fancy and wit in richest dress)
A Sicilian fruitfulness.

Thou through such a mist dost shew us,
That our best friends do not know us,
And for those allowèd features,
Due to reasonable creatures,
Liken'st us to fell Chimeras,
Monsters that, who see us, fear us;
Worse than Cerberus or Geryon,
Or, who first lov'd a cloud, Ixion.

Bacchus we know, and we allow
His typsy rites. But what art thou,
That but by reflex can'st shew
What his deity can do,
As the false Egyptian spell
Aped the true Hebrew miracle?
Some few vapours thou may'st raise.
The weak brain may serve to amaze,
But to the reins and nobler heart
Can'st nor life nor heat impart.

Brother of Bacchus, later born,
The old world was sure forlorn
Wanting thee, that aidest more
The god's victories than before
All his panthers, and the brawls
Of his piping Bacchanals.
These, as stale, we disallow,
Or judge of *thee* meant: only thou
His true Indian conquest art;
And, for ivy round his dart,
The reformèd god now weaves
A finer thyrsus of thy leaves.

Scent to match thy rich perfume
Chemic art did ne'er presume
Through her quaint alembic strain,
None so sov'reign to the brain.
Nature, that did in thee excel,
Fram'd again no second smell.
Roses, violets, but toys
For the smaller sort of boys,
Or for greener damsels meant;
Thou art the only manly scent.

Stinking'st of the stinking kind,
Filth of the mouth and fog of the mind,
Africa, that brags her foyson,
Breeds no such prodigious poison,
Henbane, nightshade, both together,
Hemlock, aconite——

Nay, rather,
Plant divine, of rarest virtue;
Blisters on the tongue would hurt you.
'Twas but in a sort I blam'd thee;
None e'er prosper'd who defam'd thee;
Irony all, and feign'd abuse,
Such as perplext lovers use,
At a need, when, in despair
To point forth their farest fair,
Or in part but to express
That exceeding comeliness
Which their fancies doth so strike,
They borrow language of dislike;
And, instead of Dearest Miss,
Jewel, Honey, Sweetheart, Bliss,
And those forms of old admiring,
Call her Cockatrice and Siren,
Basilisk, and all that's evil,
Witch, Hyena, Mermaid, Devil,
Ethiop, Wench, and Blackamoor,

Monkey, Ape, and twenty more;
Friendly Trait'ress, loving Foe,—
Not that she is truly so,
But no other way they know
A contentment to express,
Borders so upon excess,
That they do not rightly wot
Whether it be pain or not.

　　Or, as men, constrain'd to part
With what's nearest to their heart,
While their sorrow's at the height,
Lose discrimination quite,
And their hasty wrath let fall,
To appease their frantic gall,
On the darling thing whatever
Whence they feel it death to sever,
Though it be, as they, perforce,
Guiltless of the sad divorce.

　　For I must (nor let it grieve thee,
Friendliest of plants, that I must) leave thee.
For thy sake, TOBACCO, I
Would do anything but die,
And but seek to extend my days
Long enough to sing thy praise.
But, as she, who once hath been
A king's consort, is a queen
Ever after, nor will bate
Any tittle of her state,
Though a widow, or divorced,
So I, from thy converse forced,
The old name and style retain,
A right Katherine of Spain;
And a seat, too, 'mongst the joys
Of the blest Tobacco Boys;
Where, though I, by sour physician,
Am debarr'd the full fruition

Of thy favours, I may catch
Some collateral sweets, and snatch
Sidelong odours, that give life
Like glances from a neighbour's wife;
And still live in the by-places
And the suburbs of thy graces;
And in thy borders take delight,
An unconquer'd Canaanite.

A kind of book very popular in the drawing-rooms of Lamb's day was the album, so called because of the white pages. "What is an Album?" asked Lamb.

'Tis a Book kept by modern Young Ladies for show,
Of which their plain grandmothers nothing did know.
'Tis a medley of scraps, fine verse, & fine prose,
And some things not very like either, God knows.
The soft First Effusions of Beaux and of Belles,
Of future Lord Byrons and Sweet L. E. L.'s.*

Albums flourished in the reign of George IV and were usually owned and displayed on the drawing-room table. The famous Beau Brummel had one which was almost as famous as he was. Lamb wrote many "advertisement verses," as he called them, for the albums of his friends and their children, and they were all published, after his death, in two small volumes.

That the vogue of the album became a bore to Lamb is evident in his letters. "What nonsense seems verse, when one is seriously out of hope and spirits! I mean that at this time I have some nonsense to write, pain of incivility. Would to the fifth heaven no coxcombess had invented Albums!"

But how quickly he surrendered, when Emma Isola came to

---

* Letitia Elizabeth Landon, L. E. L., was a famous contributor to albums of the day.

him, produced an album, and begged him to get verses from Barry Cornwall!* "I had another favour to beg, which is the beggarliest of beggings. A few lines of verse for a young friend's Album (six will be enough). M. Burney will tell you who she is I want 'em for. A girl of gold. Six lines—make 'em eight— signed Barry C——. They need not be very good, as I chiefly want 'em as a foil to mine. But I shall be seriously obliged by any refuse scrap. We are in the last ages of the world, when St. Paul prophesied that women should be 'headstrong, lovers of their own wills, having Albums.' I fled hither to escape the Albumean persecution, and had not been in my new house twenty-four hours, when the daughter of the next house came in with a friend's Album to beg a contribution, and the following day intimated she had one of her own. Two more have sprung up since. If I take the wings of the morning and fly unto the uttermost parts of the earth, there will Albums be. New Holland has Albums. But the age is to be complied with. M. B. will tell you the sort of girl I request the ten lines for."

Even the heroes of novels had similar troubles. It is related in *Granby* by Thomas Henry Lister that Lord Chesterfield "retired to a bow window, paper in hand, and began casting up his eyes, knitting his brows and drumming upon his chin with a golden pencil in all the agonies of inspiration"—but nothing came. Walter Scott, in 1825, suggested a Society for the Suppression of Albums. Before many years the fashion had passed in England, to continue in America for many years with as great popularity.

From the many verses of this sort, two may be selected as typical. Lamb's *Album Verses* contains a number of sonnets and simple lyrics whose charm springs from reminiscences and realisation of the mingled pleasure and pain of mortal joys.

* Letter, January 1829.

IN THE ALBUM OF LUCY BARTON

Little Book, surnamed of *white,*
Clean as yet, and fair to sight,
Keep thy attribution right.

Never disproportion'd scrawl;
Ugly blot, that's worse than all;
On thy maiden clearness fall!

In each letter, here design'd,
Let the reader emblem'd find
Neatness of the owner's mind.

Gilded margins count a sin,
Let thy leaves attraction win
By the golden rules within;

Sayings fetch'd from sages old;
Laws which Holy Writ unfold,
Worthy to be graved in gold:

Lighter fancies not excluding;
Blameless wit, with nothing rude in,
Sometimes mildly interluding

Amid strains of graver measure:
Virtue's self hath oft her pleasure
In sweet Muses' groves of leisure.

Riddles dark, perplexing sense;
Darker meanings of offence;
What but *shades*—be banish'd hence.

Whitest thoughts in whitest dress,
Candid meanings, best express
Mind of quiet Quakeress.

IN MY OWN ALBUM

Fresh clad from heaven in robes of white,
A young probationer of light,
Thou wert, my soul, an Album bright,

A spotless leaf; but thought, and care,
And friend and foe, in foul or fair,
Have "written strange defeatures" there;

And Time with heaviest hand of all,
Like that fierce writing on the wall,
Hath stamp'd sad dates—he can't recall;

And error gliding worst designs—
Like speckled snake that strays and shines···
Betrays his path by crooked lines;

And vice hath left his ugly blot;
And good resolves, a moment hot,
Fairly began—but finish'd not;

And fruitless, late remorse doth trace—
Like Hebrew lore, a backward pace —
Her irrecoverable race.

Disjointed numbers; sense unknit;
Huge reams of folly, shreds of wit;
Compose the mingled mass of it.

My scalded eyes no longer brook
Upon this ink-blurr'd thing to look—
Go, shut the leaves, and clasp the book.

Much of Lamb's verse was for children and although it cannot be called first rate, it does have the qualities of simplicity and tenderness. It deals with the simple sights and incidents with which children are familiar, rainbows, birds and animals, bees and wasps, the clock striking, the broken doll, the journey from school, birthdays, the fun of fables and fairy stories and the *King and Queen of Hearts.*

If the verse was not as popular for children as the poems of Robert Louis Stevenson's *A Child's Garden of Verses,* there was something of Puck in him, as Mrs. Stevenson once said of her son. He had a playful manner which to friends who knew him well passed for what it was intended to be. To strangers it was sometimes forbidding, making them judge him unfairly. There were occasions when his pranks, though innocently conceived, came near getting him into serious trouble, as they do for many an innocent prankster. It was something of the child that made him see his London as a fairyland, a city from an Arabian tale, inspiring mystery. It was that imagination, directed by the artist's hand, which transmuted mud and stone and people into a city of gold and romance.

One turns for a comparison in Lamb's knowledge of and affection for children to another and later English writer, also beloved, who was also part of London, Charles Dickens, whose name calls up hosts of children, Paul Dombey, Oliver Twist, Little Nell, Pip, Little Dorrit, Emily, the Marchioness and Tiny Tim. Some of these might have come from the imagination of Charles Lamb and he would have liked them in Dickens.

There was probably no place outside of London which attracted Lamb more when he could find a free day, than Oxford or Cambridge. Probably the latter was preferred, as Cambridge and the University had brought to him many delightful experiences and good friends. These simple lines certainly reveal the thoughts which must have often come to him as he dreamed of what might have been.

WRITTEN AT CAMBRIDGE

I was not train'd in Academic bowers,
And to those learned streams I nothing owe
Which copious from those twin fair founts do flow;
Mine have been anything but studious hours.
Yet can I fancy, wandering 'mid thy towers,
Myself a nursling, Granta, of thy lap;
My brow seems tightening with the Doctor's cap,
And I walk *gowned;* feel unusual powers.
Strange forms of logic clothe my admiring speech,
Old Ramus' ghost is busy at my brain;
And my scull teems with notions infinite.
Be still, ye reeds of Camus, while I teach
Truths, which transcend the searching Schoolmen's vein,
And half had stagger'd that stout Stagirite!

The lines of his famous *Going or Gone* are suggestive of the modern *Spoon River Anthology.* They are an excellent illustration of the simple pathos and sense of the irrevocable so commonly appearing in the Elia essays, the union of laughter and tears.

GOING OR GONE*

I.

Fine merry franions,
Wanton companions,
My days are ev'n banyans
     With thinking upon ye;
How Death, that last stinger,
Finis-writer, end-bringer,
Has laid his chill finger,
     Or is laying on ye.

---

* Known also as "Epicedium."

II.

There's rich Kitty Wheatley,
With footing it featly
That took me completely,
    She sleeps in the Kirk House;
And poor Polly Perkin,
Whose Dad was still firking
The jolly ale firkin,
    She's gone to the Work-house;

III.

Fine Gard'ner, Ben Carter
(In ten counties no smarter)
Has ta'en his departure
    For Proserpine's orchards:
And Lily, postilion,
With cheeks of vermilion,
Is one of a million
    That fill up the church-yards;

IV.

And, lusty as Dido,
Fat Clemitson's widow
Flits now a small shadow
    By Stygian hid ford;
And good Master Clapton
Has thirty years nap't on,
The ground he last hap't on,
    Intomb'd by fair Widford;

V.

And gallant Tom Dockwra,
Of Nature's finest crockery,
Now but thin air and mockery,
    Lurks by Avernus,

Whose honest grasp of hand
Still, while his life did stand,
At friend's or foe's command,
    Almost did burn us.

VI.

Roger de Coverley
Not more good man than he;
Yet has he equally
    Push'd for Cocytus,
With drivelling Worral,
And wicked old Dorrell,
'Gainst whom I've a quarrel,
    Whose end might affright us!—

VII.

Kindly hearts have I known;
Kindly hearts, they are flown;
Here and there if but one
    Linger yet uneffaced,
Imbecile tottering elves,
Soon to be wreck'd on shelves,
These scarce are half themselves,
    With age and care crazed.

VIII.

But this day Fanny Hutton
Her last dress has put on;
Her fine lessons forgotten,
    She died, as the dunce died:
And prim Betsy Chambers,
Decay'd in her members,
No longer remembers
    Things as she once did:

IX.

And prudent Miss Wither
Not in jest now doth *wither,*
And soon must go—whither
        Nor I well, nor you know;
And flaunting Miss Waller,
That soon must befall her,
Whence none can recal her,
        Though proud once as Juno!

The editor of the *Gem* refused Lamb's "Gipsy's Malison," on the ground that it would "shock all mothers," but it was accepted by *Blackwood's Magazine* and appeared in January 1829. Lamb's sense of poetic style reaches a climax in the chiming and haunting lines of this sonnet.

THE GIPSY'S MALISON

"Suck, baby, suck! mother's love grows by giving,
Drain the sweet founts that only thrive by wasting;
Black manhood comes, when riotous guilty living
Hands thee the cup that shall be death in tasting.

"Kiss, baby, kiss! mother's lips shine by kisses;
Choke the warm breath that else would fall in blessings;
Black manhood comes, when turbulent guilty blisses
Tend thee the kiss that poisons 'mid caressings.

"Hang, baby, hang! mother's love loves such forces,
Strain the fond neck that bends still to thy clinging;
Black manhood comes, when violent lawless courses
Leave thee a spectacle in rude air swinging."

So sang a wither'd Beldam energetical,
And bann'd the ungiving door with lips prophetical.

10

Essays of Elia

WE ARE accustomed to regard the *Tatler* and *Spectator* in the days of Queen Anne as marking the only literary renaissance since Shakespeare, the awakening of a general interest in reading and an enlargement of the intellectual horizon. However, the first quarter of the Nineteenth Century was as important and equally exciting. This difference is made clear by a comparison of the *Tatler* and *Spectator* of the earlier period with the *Edinburgh* and *Quarterly Reviews* of the later: the former more calm, reasonable, almost stately; the latter passionate, personal, nervous, abusive, no polite respecter of feelings—fitting reflection of the political and social confusion then existing in England and Europe. Between the two periods the magazine and review underwent great change. The language of periodical literature showed a deterioration in smoothness and in dignity; the popularity and respect for such writing gave way to the more immediate appeal of the novel. Part of this change was made possible by conditions which were imposed by such slave-drivers as Ralph Griffiths, a bookseller and publisher, whose dealings with his hirelings can be read in any life of Oliver Goldsmith. The articles were "puffs" or "slatings," to sell a book or to injure some other bookseller's offering; the pay was nominal, never more than two guineas per sheet of sixteen printed pages; hence the magazine became a hotbed for the hackwriter.

The story of the founding of the *Edinburgh Review* in 1802, by Smith, Jeffrey, Horner and Brougham, though often repeated, has not lost in interest as the importance of the event in social and literary history has not diminished. The statement by Lord Cockburne is probably not an exaggeration: "It is impossible for those who did not live at the time, and in the heart of the scene, to feel, or almost to understand, the impression made by the new luminary, or the anxieties with which its motions were observed." The success of the venture exceeded all expectations. From seven hundred and fifty subscribers, its circulation increased to nine thousand in six years and twelve thousand in ten years, with the daily *Times* concurrently drawing only eight thousand. The "new luminary" took its tone from the need which was everywhere. The "Blue and Yellow," as the *Edinburgh Review* was often called, appeared four times a year, allowing more time for reflection on topics of lasting interest than had been possible with a monthly. The editor and contributors were dissociated from bookselling or publishing, and of equal standing with the best authors. Every article was to be paid for; the *Review* began at ten guineas, later went to sixteen, and many of the contributors received as much as twenty to twenty-four. And the editor was to be paid. Sydney Smith said to the publisher Constable, "If you will give £200 per annum to your editor and ten guineas a sheet, you will soon have the best *Review* in Europe."

Most important was the change in nature of the article. By the best minds of the day, the article covered the subjects of literary, political and social nature about which people were thinking. The subject might be a poem or book, but this was only a peg to hang something on—illustrated by the remark of Horner to Jeffrey, "Have you any good subjects in view for your nineteenth? There are two I wish you, *yourself,* would undertake, if you can pick up books which would admit them." In a word, then, the aim was not primarily to write about a book but about an idea or subject which had current and potential interest.

The reason for the success of the *Edinburgh* is clear: it led writers to express their convictions on subjects of which men were thinking. The French Revolution had stirred men's imaginations and, as in 1944, there were great questions as to the sort of world which would come afterwards—after the Revolution, after Napoleon could be got rid of. Political institutions were being examined, religion was being assailed, and a new breeze was blowing in men's hearts and passions which stirred expression in verse and prose. There were the spread of education, the growth of the middle class, along with an increasing demand among professional and industrial leaders for information, for the views of important thinkers on pressing questions and for guidance in criticism of literature, science and art.

After the success of the *Edinburgh,* it was to be expected that there would be successors. Many persons less Whiggish in principles as well as many broad-minded persons of the Tory persuasion felt the need of a new journal; so the *Quarterly* was started in 1809, to defend the Church and State. Gifford was editor, and Walter Scott, Southey and Croker lent support. Croker's immortality derives from his essay on Keats as the "poet's poet," long considered to have contributed to Keats' early death. Then came *Blackwood's Magazine*—"Maga," as its supporters liked to call it—a monthly founded in 1817, with John Wilson ("Christopher North") and Lockhart, son-in-law and biographer of Walter Scott, as editors. The *London Magazine* followed in 1820, with John Scott at the desk, formerly editor of the newspaper called *The Champion*.

These two great reviews and these two brilliant magazines, though borrowing characteristics from one another, retained the original distinction of type. The difference has been admirably stated by Arthur Elliot, a subsequent editor of the *Edinburgh Review*.

"The review made it its business to discuss works of literature, art, and science, to consider national policy and public events, to enlighten its readers upon these subjects and to award praise or censure to authors and statesmen. It did not publish original matter but confined itself to commenting upon or criticising the works and doings of others. Its articles professed to be the serious consideration of specified books, or of parliamentary or other speeches of public men. They were not, at least in form, independent and original studies.

"The magazine, on the other hand, was a miscellany. Though it contained reviews and criticisms of books, it did not confine itself to reviewing. To its pages, authors and poets sent original contributions. It admitted correspondence from the outside world; and it aimed at the entertainment of its readers rather than at the advocacy of views. Through the instrumentality of the magazine, much valuable and permanent literary matter first came before the public."

At the present moment our concern is with the *London*. Possibly no magazine ever appeared under more promising auspices. Its aim was to supply a larger amount of serious prose and poetry than was to be found in other periodicals. Although *Blackwood's* was in a prosperous condition, it was thought that a new magazine under proper editorship, with these aims and with the list of distinguished contributors whom John Scott had secured, would certainly be assured of a great future. It was little short of a tragedy that, only a few months later, the enterprise so brilliantly inaugurated should receive a staggering blow in the death of its editor. The story of his duel with Lockhart's second, Christie, in February 1821 has many times been told. Today we can scarcely understand how such a tragic result could have followed from incidents which would be a setting almost for an extravaganza. John Scott, it would seem, had all the characteristics of a great editor—sympathy, patience, discrimination, generosity and curiosity, and with these traits he combined a confidence and authority which brought respect to the magazine. After the death of Scott in 1821, Taylor and Hessey, the publishers—Keats always called Hessey "Mistessey" —took over the editorial supervision in an arrangement that made Thomas Hood what we would call today managing editor.

References in Lamb's letters, in Robinson's diary and other contemporary sources permit us to see the wide-spread curiosity and interest in the reviews and magazines and the attempts of such writers as Coleridge, Hazlitt, Hunt and Lamb to find the proper outlets for expression. Lamb's contributions included brilliant criticism, such as the papers on Hogarth and the tragedies of Shakespeare, and the essay on Wordsworth's *Excursion*. They appeared in Leigh Hunt's *Indicator* and *Reflector* and *Examiner,* and in the *Champion,* the *Gentleman's Magazine,* the *New Monthly,* Hone's *Every-Day Book,* the *Englishman's Magazine,* and the *Edinburgh Review*. Although some of these articles are first rate and at the time were much appreciated, they either were not of a quality to elicit wide approval or did not reach the public through the proper channel.

Just when Lamb was introduced to John Scott we cannot be sure, but in the early part of 1820 it became known that he had promised to do something for the *London* as one of a group of contributors which for brilliancy and literary distinction has not been surpassed. Fortunately the management of the *London* left to Lamb unrestricted choice of subject matter and manner. This freedom was never used to better purpose than by the contributor who soon became widely known by his *nom de plume*.

Wishing to remain anonymous, Lamb chose for his signature the name of a former Italian friend who had worked with him years before at the South Sea House. The name appealed to Lamb and he adopted it. He intended to tell the owner at once but almost a year went by and when he went to find the man he learned that his friend had died a few months before. "So the name has fairly devolved to me, I think; and 'tis all he has left me." Lamb insisted that the name should be pronounced E-l-l-i-a, but that usage never became common and it has always been pronounced with the long E.

The delightful way in which a fellow clerk, John Bates Dibdin, guessed the secret is described by his sister. After mentioning that she had visited Lamb at Islington, she wrote: "My brother had become very intimate with him [Lamb], after a previously somewhat long acquaintance. He was engaged in the city, and had constant occasion to conduct the giving or taking of cheques, as it might be, at the India House. There he always selected the 'little clever man' in preference to the other clerks. At that time the *Elia* essays were appearing in print. No one had the slightest conception who 'Elia' was. He was talked of everywhere, and everybody was trying to find him out, but without success. At last, from the style and manner of conveying his ideas and opinions on different subjects, my brother began to suspect that Lamb was the individual so widely sought for, and wrote some lines to him, anonymously, sending them by post to his residence, with the hope of sifting him on the subject. Although Lamb could not *know* who sent him the lines, yet he looked very hard at the writer of them the next time they met, when he walked up, as usual, to Lamb's desk in the most unconcerned manner, to transact the necessary business. Shortly after, when they were again in conversation, something dropped from Lamb's lips which convinced his hearer, beyond a doubt, that his suspicions were correct. He therefore wrote some more lines (anonymously, as before), beginning—

" 'I've found thee out, O Elia!' "

and sent them to Colebrook Row. The consequence was that at their next meeting Lamb produced the lines, and after much laughing, confessed himself to be *Elia*. This led to a warm friendship between them."

The essays appeared more or less regularly for more than a year and a half and were then collected in a volume with the title *The Essays of Elia,* published in 1823. The second and last series, continuing through 1825, was first published in England by Moxon in 1833. In the first there were twenty-nine essays; in the last, twenty-five. An American reprint of each series was published separately in Philadelphia in 1828.

If, as has been said, the writing of verse is the best requisite for a good prose style, Lamb had fulfilled this condition. He had really never given up writing poetry and had always found it an easy way to express himself. But the real preparation had come from his association with books and authors, especially of the Sixteenth and Seventeenth Centuries—the plays of Shakespeare, Beaumont and Fletcher, Massinger, Ford and Webster, the poetry of Spenser, Milton, Wither, Quarles and Marvell, and the prose of Bunyan, Burton, Fuller and above all Sir Thomas Browne—straight from good old English stock. Montaigne had influence, but it was not any foreign model—as has so often happened in English literature—that gave us the *Essays of Elia.*

When Thomas Browne wrote his *Religio Medici,* he did not intend it to be an exposition of any creed or narrow dogmatism. It was an exaltation of his own thinking and hoping—in a word, his own self. What could be more interesting than his own religion, not somebody else's religion? And so the Montaigne conception of the essay developed and took on more and more individuality and sometimes transcendental vagueness. The qualities which Addison hoped to establish would effect a more urbane style with a disregard of the mystical as mere subjective whim. The influence of Samuel Johnson's essays, as for example, the *Rambler* and the *Idler,* far removed from the clarity and simplicity of Addison, became an incubus on the essay during the last quarter of the Eighteenth Century. To rescue that literary form from its sterility, its pompousness and its impersonality, was the more or less conscious purpose of the Romantic essayists, especially Hazlitt and Lamb.

It is not possible to classify the *Essays of Elia.* There is no order in the present arrangement. They might appear in any other order. Therefore they may be arranged to suit one's liking at the particular moment. For the present purpose it seems best to notice first the essays of autobiographical content.

The Elia series begin with "The South-Sea House," where Lamb worked for a few months almost thirty years before. With his good memory he could recall much, and he had his brother John who had been there most of the time and could help with names and incidents. The effect of the opening paragraph upon the contemporary reader may be imagined. Here was a fresh mingling of realism and romance, people who could really be identified, in a setting which had the mystery of a Gothic romance: Evans the cashier, with his care in counting up the cash, his well-known rap at the door announcing six o'clock, and his interest in the old sites of London; Thomas Tame, whose "mind was in its original state of white paper"; "the fine rattling, rattle-headed Plumer"; and John Tipp, whose description has not been surpassed by Elia himself.

"Of quite another stamp was the then accountant, John Tipp. He neither pretended to high blood, nor in good truth cared one fig about the matter. He 'thought an accountant the greatest character in the world, and himself the greatest accountant in it.' Yet John was not without his hobby. The fiddle relieved his vacant hours. He sang, certainly, with other notes than to the Orphean lyre. He did, indeed, scream and scrape most abominably. His fine suite of official rooms in Threadneedle-street, which, without anything very substantial appended to them, were enough to enlarge a man's notions of himself that lived in them (I know not who is the occupier of them now), re-

sounded fortnightly to the notes of a concert of 'sweet breasts,'
as our ancestors would have called them, culled from club-
rooms and orchestras—chorus singers—first and second violon-
cellos—double basses—and clarionets—who ate his cold mutton,
and drank his punch, and praised his ear. He sate like Lord
Midas among them. But at the desk Tipp was quite another sort
of creature. Thence all ideas, that were purely ornamental,
were banished. You could not speak of anything romantic without rebuke. Politics were excluded. A newspaper was thought
too refined and abstracted. The whole duty of man consisted in
writing off dividend warrants. The striking of the annual
balance in the company's books (which, perhaps, differed from
the balance of last year in the sum of 25 £. 1s. 6d.) occupied his
days and nights for a month previous. Not that Tipp was blind
to the deadness of *things* (as they call them in the city) in his
beloved house, or did not sigh for a return of the old stirring
days when South Sea hopes were young—(he was indeed equal
to the wielding of any of the most intricate accounts of the most
flourishing company in these or those days):—but to a genuine
accountant the difference of proceeds is as nothing. The frac-
tional farthing is as dear to his heart as the thousands which
stand before it. He is the true actor, who, whether his part be
a prince or a peasant, must act it with like intensity. With Tipp
form was everything. His life was formal. His actions seemed
ruled with a ruler. His pen was not less erring than his heart.
He made the best executor in the world: he was plagued with
incessant executorships accordingly, which excited his spleen
and soothed his vanity in equal ratios. He would swear (for
Tipp swore) at the little orphans, whose rights he would guard
with a tenacity like the grasp of the dying hand, that commended their interests to his protection. With all this there was
about him a sort of timidity—(his few enemies used to give it
a worse name)—a something which, in reverence to the dead,

we will place, if you please, a little on this side of the heroic.
Nature certainly had been pleased to endow John Tipp with a
sufficient measure of the principle of self-preservation. There is
a cowardice which we do not despise, because it has nothing
base or treacherous in its elements; it betrays itself, not you:
it is mere temperament; the absence of the romantic and the
enterprising; it sees a lion in the way, and will not, with
Fortinbras, 'greatly find quarrel in a straw,' when some supposed honour is at stake. Tipp never mounted the box of a
stage-coach in his life; or leaned against the rails of a balcony;
or walked upon the ridge of a parapet; or looked down a precipice; or let off a gun; or went upon a water-party; or would
willingly let you go if he could have helped it: neither was it
recorded of him, that for lucre, or for intimidation, he ever for-
sook friend or principle."

Probably if it had been possible for Lamb to choose a place
in which to live, anywhere except London, Cambridge would
have been the place. His first knowledge of Cambridge was at
Christ's Hospital when the "Grecians" began their training for
the University and Lamb was deeply disappointed because his
stammering and family circumstances would prevent his following his desire for university training. By aptitude he was inclined to the scholar's life, and the walks about Cambridge and
the Bodleian in Oxford were as a magnet when he was near
either university. His whimsical concealment of persons and
places by a change of name accounts for his use of Oxford in the
title of his famous essay, when it was really Cambridge that was
most in his mind. In all the descriptions of university or college
is there any one that catches so well the particular essence, that
something which makes the walks and greens and "backs"
different from those of the common town?

"I can here play the gentleman, enact the student. To such a one as myself, who has been defrauded in his young years of the sweet food of academic institution, nowhere is so pleasant, to while away a few idle weeks at, as one or other of the Universities. Their vacation, too, at this time of the year, falls in so pat with *ours*. Here I can take my walks unmolested, and fancy myself of what degree or standing I please. I seem admitted *ad eundem*. I fetch up past opportunities. I can rise at the chapel-bell, and dream that it rings for *me*. In moods of humility I can be a Sizar, or a Servitor. When the peacock vein rises, I strut a Gentleman Commoner. In graver moments, I proceed Master of Arts. Indeed I do not think I am much unlike that respectable character. I have seen your dim-eyed vergers, and bed-makers in spectacles, drop a bow or curtsy, as I pass, wisely mistaking me for something of the sort. I go about in black, which favours the notion. Only in Christ Church reverend quadrangle, I can be content to pass for nothing short of a Seraphic Doctor.

"The walks at these times are so much one's own,—the tall trees of Christ's, the groves of Magdalen! The halls deserted, and with open doors inviting one to slip in unperceived, and pay a devoir to some Founder, or noble or royal Benefactress (that should have been ours) whose portrait seems to smile upon their over-looked beadsman, and to adopt me for their own. Then, to take a peep in by the way at the butteries, and sculleries, redolent of antique hospitality: the immense caves of kitchens, kitchen fire-places, cordial recesses; ovens whose first pies were baked four centuries ago; and spits which have cooked for Chaucer! Not the meanest minister among the dishes but is hallowed to me through his imagination, and the Cook goes forth a Manciple."

In "Christ's Hospital" Lamb purposed to add to the essay which he had written and published in his *Works* and which had been a "magnificent eulogy of my old school." He touches the subject with the same affection and gives some details, probably exaggerated, of the character of the two teachers, Field and Boyer, and of the treatment which boys received in the form of punishment. The two essays should be read together. Can one recall a bit of writing which gives so much of the atmosphere of school and what it means to a sensitive boy? From this description there emerge some distinct never-to-be-forgotten pictures: the feeding of the little boy by the good old aunt "squatting down on some odd stone in a by-nook of the cloisters"; the bathing excursions in the New River where the boys stripped and "under the first warmth of the sun wantoned like young dace in the streams"; the suspected gag-eater—"the young stork, at the expense of his own good name, had all this while been only feeding the old birds"; finally the generous tributes to his friends the "Grecians," especially that "inspired charity boy," Samuel Taylor Coleridge.

The difference between the two brothers, John and Charles Lamb, is pointedly implied in a passage from "My Relations," an essay which describes chiefly Aunt Hetty and brother John, under the name of James.

"It does me good, as I walk towards the street of my daily avocation, on some fine May morning, to meet him marching in a quite opposite direction, with a jolly handsome presence, and shining sanguine face, that indicates some purchase in his eye— a Claude—or a Hobbima—for much of his enviable leisure is consumed at Christie's, and Phillips's—or where not, to pick up pictures, and such gauds. On these occasions he mostly stoppeth me, to read a short lecture on the advantage a person like me possesses above himself, in having his time occupied with business which he *must do*—assureth me that he often feels it hang heavy on his hands—wishes he had fewer holidays—and goes

off—Westward Ho!—chanting a tune, to Pall Mall—perfectly
convinced that he has convinced me—while I proceed in my
opposite direction tuneless."

John's shirking of responsibility as the eldest child in the
family under trying conditions certainly did not deserve generous expression from Charles, and yet he wrote, "I would not
have him in one jot or tittle other than he is," and felt his
brother's death very keenly only a few weeks after these lines
were written.

Lamb wrote of the Temple as one having a thorough knowledge few men have had. In one of the most beautiful pieces of
prose in the English language Lamb has caught the glamour of
this old institution in a description with all the suggestion of an
old painting. By selecting the word "Benchers" from the volumi-
nous title of the governing board, "The Worshipful Masters of
the Bench of the Honorable Society of the Inner Temple," he
gave himself the pleasure of writing of London and the Temple
as shrines of great antiquity. And what better frame could there
be for the picture of his father, a touching tribute which gives
us all we know and all we need to know of John Lamb, senior!

"I knew this Lovel. He was a man of an incorrigible and
losing honesty. A good fellow withal, and 'would strike.' In
the cause of the oppressed he never considered inequalities, or
calculated the number of his opponents. He once wrested a
sword out of the hand of a man of quality that had drawn upon
him; and pommelled him severely with the hilt of it. The
swordsman had offered insult to a female—an occasion upon
which no odds against him could have prevented the interference of Lovel. He would stand next day bare-headed to the
same person, modestly to excuse his interference—for L. never
forgot rank, where something better was not concerned. L. was
the liveliest little fellow breathing, had a face as gay as Gar-

rick's, whom he was said greatly to resemble (I have a portrait of him which confirms it), possessed a fine turn for humorous poetry—next to Swift and Prior—moulded heads in clay or plaster of Paris to admiration, by the dint of natural genius merely; turned cribbage boards, and such small cabinet toys, to perfection; took a hand at quadrille or bowls with equal facility; made punch better than any man of his degree in England; had the merriest quips and conceits; and was altogether as brimful of rogueries and inventions as you could desire. He was a brother of the angle, moreover, and just such a free, hearty, honest companion as Mr. Izaac Walton would have chosen to go a fishing with. I saw him in his old age and the decay of his faculties, palsy-smitten, in the last sad stage of human weakness—'a remnant most forlorn of what he was,'—yet even then his eye would light up upon the mention of his favourite Garrick. He was greatest, he would say, in Bayes—'was upon the stage nearly throughout the whole performance, and as busy as a bee.' At intervals, too, he would speak of his former life, and how he came up a little boy from Lincoln to go to service, and how his mother cried at parting with him, and how he returned, after some years' absence, in his smart new livery to see her, and she blessed herself at the change, and could hardly be brought to believe that it was 'her own bairn.' And then, the excitement subsiding, he would weep, till I have wished that sad second-childhood might have a mother still to lay its head upon her lap. But the common mother of us all in no long time after received him gently into hers."

Best of all descriptions are those of Bridget Elia—Mary, slightly disguised as Lamb thought was necessary, so thin a veil that it is easy to recognise her character. Judging from his letters and hers, from the journal of Dorothy Wordsworth, the diary of Crabb Robinson and the letters of the Hazlitts, we can be sure that few details are missing from this affectionate portrait in "Mackery End in Hertfordshire."

"Bridget Elia has been my housekeeper for many a long year. I have obligations to Bridget, extending beyond the period of memory. We house together, old bachelor and maid, in a sort of double singleness; with such tolerable comfort, upon the whole, that I, for one, find in myself no sort of disposition to go out upon the mountains, with the rash king's offspring, to bewail my celibacy. We agree pretty well in our tastes and habits—yet so, as 'with a difference.' We are generally in harmony, with occasional bickerings—as it should be among near relations. Our sympathies are rather understood than expressed; and once, upon my dissembling a tone in my voice more kind than ordinary, my cousin burst into tears, and complained that I was altered. We are both great readers in different directions. While I am hanging over (for the thousandth time) some passage in old Burton, or one of his strange contemporaries, she is abstracted in some modern tale, or adventure, whereof our common reading-table is daily fed with assiduously fresh supplies. Narrative teases me. I have little concern in the progress of events. She must have a story—well, ill, or indifferently told— so there be life stirring in it, and plenty of good or evil accidents. The fluctuations of fortune in fiction—and almost in real life—have ceased to interest, or operate but dully upon me. Out-of-the-way humours and opinions—heads with some diverting twist in them—the oddities of authorship please me most. My cousin has a native disrelish of any thing that sounds odd or bizarre. Nothing goes down with her, that is quaint, irregular, or out of the road of common sympathy. She 'holds Nature more clever.' I can pardon her blindness to the beautiful obliquities of the Religio Medici; but she must apologise to me for certain disrespectful insinuations, which she has been pleased to throw out latterly, touching the intellectuals of a dear favourite of mine, of the last century but one—the thrice noble, chaste, and virtuous,—but again somewhat fantastical, and original-brained, generous Margaret Newcastle.

"It has been the lot of my cousin, oftener perhaps than I could have wished, to have had for her associates and mine, free-thinkers—leaders, and disciples, of novel philosophies and systems; but she neither wrangles with, nor accepts, their opinions. That which was good and venerable to her, when a child, retains its authority over her mind still. She never juggles or plays tricks with her understanding.

"We are both of us inclined to be a little too positive; and I have observed the result of our disputes to be almost uniformly this—that in matters of fact, dates, and circumstances, it turns out, that I was in the right, and my cousin in the wrong. But where we have differed upon moral points; upon something proper to be done, or let alone; whatever heat of opposition, or steadiness of conviction, I set out with, I am sure always, in the long run, to be brought over to her way of thinking.

"I must touch upon the foibles of my kinswoman with a gentle hand, for Bridget does not like to be told of her faults. She hath an awkward trick (to say no worse of it) of reading in company: at which times she will answer *yes* or *no* to a question without fully understanding its purport—which is very provoking, and derogatory in the highest degree to the dignity of the putter of the said question. Her presence of mind is equal to the most pressing trials of life, but will sometimes desert her upon trifling occasions. When the purpose requires it, and is a thing of moment, she can speak to it greatly; but in matters which are not stuff of the conscience, she hath been known sometimes to let slip a word less seasonably.

"Her education in youth was not much attended to; and she happily missed all that train of female garniture, which passeth by the name of accomplishments. She was tumbled early, by accident or design, into a spacious closet of good old English reading, without much selection or prohibition, and browsed at will upon that fair and wholesome pasturage. Had I twenty girls, they should be brought up exactly in this fashion. I know not whether their chance in wedlock might not be diminished by it; but I can answer for it, that it makes (if the worst comes to the worst) most incomparable old maids.

"In a season of distress, she is the truest comforter; but in the teazing accidents, and minor perplexities, which do not call out the *will* to meet them, she sometimes maketh matters worse by an excess of participation. If she does not always divide your trouble, upon the pleasanter occasions of life she is sure always to treble your satisfaction. She is excellent to be at a play with, or upon a visit; but best, when she goes a journey with you.

"We made an excursion together a few summers since, into Hertfordshire, to beat up the quarters of some of our less-known relations in that fine corn country."

In "Blakesmoor in H——shire" Lamb employs his fashion of concealment by transcribing Blakesware into Blakesmoor. Blakesware, it will be recalled, was the seat of the Plumers, where his mother's mother, Mrs. Field, had for more than fifty years been the housekeeper. Since the family had spent most of the later years in another house, Mrs. Field was commonly considered the real occupant of the Blakesware house. The story of Lamb's early life is enriched by the descriptions in this essay: his liking for the old house, its high walls and old pictures, the grounds about, and the memories which had come down from many years. Nothing was more sincere than his exhortation inspired by visits to Blakesware: "But wouldst thou know the beauty of holiness?—go alone on some week-day, borrowing the keys of good Master Sexton, traverse the cool aisles of some country church: think of the piety that has kneeled there—the congregations, old and young, that have found consolation there—the meek pastor—the docile parishioner. With no disturbing emotions, no cross conflicting comparisons, drink in the tranquillity of the place, till thou thyself become as fixed and motionless as the marble effigies that kneel and weep around thee."

In "Poor Relations" Elia presents us with two portraits, one the male, and "a worse evil under the sun," the female variety. These two characters are lifelike, glowing with sympathy without sentimentality. The first might be another Ancient Mariner, described with thoughtful regard for the psychological effect of an old word or verb-ending. "He entereth smiling and—embarrassed. He holdeth out his hand to you to shake, and—draweth it back again. He casually looketh in about dinner-time—when the table is full. He offereth to go away, seeing you have company, but is induced to stay."

Anniversaries, birthdays and holidays meant much to Charles Lamb. They were happy occasions which helped him recall something he had liked in former years. Remembering other times made him more ready to enjoy the present and the friends with whom he was living. It made the experiences the richer. Life was here to be lived. A congenial setting for such a mood was New Year's Eve, and naturally that season appealed to Lamb.

"The elders, with whom I was brought up, were of a character not likely to let slip the sacred observance of any old institution; and the ringing out of the Old Year was kept by them with circumstances of peculiar ceremony.—In those days the sound of those midnight chimes, though it seemed to raise hilarity in all around me, never failed to bring a train of pensive imagery into my fancy. Yet I then scarce conceived what it meant, or thought of it as a reckoning that concerned me. Not childhood alone, but the young man till thirty, never feels practically that he is mortal. He knows it indeed, and, if need were, he could preach a homily on the fragility of life; but he brings it not home to himself, any more than in a hot June we can appropri- ate to our imagination the freezing days of December. But now, shall I confess a truth?—I feel these audits but too pow- erfully. I begin to count the probabilities of my duration, and to grudge at the expenditure of moments and shortest periods, like miser's farthings. In proportion as the years both lessen and shorten, I set more count upon their periods, and would fain lay my ineffectual finger upon the spoke of the great wheel. I am not content to pass away 'like a weaver's shuttle.' Those metaphors solace me not, nor sweeten the unpalatable draught of mortality. I care not to be carried with the tide, that smoothly bears human life to eternity; and reluct at the inevitable course of destiny. I am in love with this green earth; the face of town and country; the unspeakable rural solitudes, and the sweet security of streets. I would set up my tabernacle here. I am content to stand still at the age to which I am arrived; I, and my friends: to be no younger, no richer, no handsomer. I do not want to be weaned by age; or drop, like mellow fruit, as they say, into the grave.—Any alteration, on this earth of mine, in diet or in lodging, puzzles and discomposes me. My house- hold-gods plant a terrible fixed foot, and are not rooted up without blood. They do not willingly seek Lavinian shores. A new state of being staggers me.

"Sun, and sky, and breeze, and solitary walks, and summer holidays, and the greenness of fields, and the delicious juices of meats and fishes, and society, and the cheerful glass, and candle- light, and fire-side conversations, and innocent vanities, and jests, and *irony itself*—do these things go out with life?

"Can a ghost laugh, or shake his gaunt sides, when you are pleasant with him?

"And you, my midnight darlings, my Folios! must I part with the intense delight of having you (huge armfuls) in my embraces? Must knowledge come to me, if it come at all, by some awkward experiment of intuition, and no longer by this familiar process of reading?

"Shall I enjoy friendships there, wanting the smiling indications which point me to them here,—the recognisable face—the 'sweet assurance of a look'—?"

Lamb's skill in remembering bits of old and curious information and folk-lore and carefully fitting them together in a kaleidoscopic pattern is illustrated in "Rejoicings upon the New Year's Coming of Age," describing the procession of the "Merry Days." "The *Old Year* being dead, and the *New Year* coming of age, which he does, by Calendar Law, as soon as the breath is out of the old gentleman's body, nothing would serve the young spark but he must give a dinner upon the occasion, to which all the *Days* in the year were invited. . . .

"All the *Days* came to their day. Covers were provided for three hundred and sixty-five guests at the principal table; with an occasional knife and fork at the side-board for the *Twenty-ninth of February*"—and what a jolly party it was! . . .

"*Longest Day* set off westward in beautiful crimson and gold —the rest, some in one fashion, some in another; but *Valentine* and pretty *May* took their departure together in one of the prettiest silvery twilights a Lover's Day could wish to set in."

It is difficult to think that Lamb could have written *Elia* if he had not loved old books and read widely in them. He liked to discover them by the wayside, the unfamiliar books, the biography or the history with something quaint and individual about it. This was characteristic of his turn of mind. He ever preferred by-ways to the main road, chose the side which was unpopular, and liked to express himself in the original and unconventional way. There is a good deal of autobiographical fact in this passage from "All Fools' Day":

"I had more yearnings towards that simple architect, that built his house upon the sand, than I entertained for his more cautious neighbour; I grudged at the hard censure pronounced upon the quiet soul that kept his talent; and—prizing their simplicity beyond the more provident, and, to my apprehension, somewhat *unfeminine* wariness of their competitors—I felt a kindliness, that almost amounted to a *tendre,* for those five thoughtless virgins.—I have never made an acquaintance since, that lasted; or a friendship, that answered; with any that had not some tincture of the absurd in their characters. I venerate an honest obliquity of understanding. The more laughable blunders a man shall commit in your company, the more tests he giveth you, that he will not betray or overreach you. I love the safety, which a palpable hallucination warrants; the security, which a word out of season ratifies. And take my word for this, reader, and say a fool told it you, if you please, that he who hath not a dram of folly in his mixture, hath pounds of much worse matter in his composition. It is observed, that 'the foolisher the fowl or fish—woodcocks,—dotterels,—cods'-heads, &c., the finer the flesh thereof, and what are commonly the world's received fools, but such whereof the world is not worthy? and what have been some of the kindliest patterns of our species, but so many darlings of absurdity, minions of the goddess, and her white boys?—Reader, if you wrest my words beyond their fair construction, it is you, and not I, that are the *April Fool.*"

Valentine's Day is another anniversary which Lamb liked to think about, to find its origin and the qualities which set it apart from other days. His essay contains the charming sketch of the young maiden, described with abounding good humour and reflecting generously on the kindliness of the artist.

"All Valentines are not foolish; and I shall not easily forget thine, my kind friend (if I may have leave to call you so) E. B.—E. B. lived opposite a young maiden whom he had often seen, unseen, from his parlour window in C—e-street. She was all joyousness and innocence, and just of an age to enjoy receiving a Valentine, and just of a temper to bear the disappointment of missing one with good humour. E. B. is an artist of no common powers; in the fancy parts of designing, perhaps inferior to none; his name is known at the bottom of many a well executed vignette in the way of his profession, but no further; for E. B. is modest, and the world meets nobody half-way. E. B. meditated how he could repay this young maiden for many a favour which she had done him unknown; for when a kindly face greets us, though but passing by, and never knows us again, nor we it, we should feel it as an obligation; and E. B. did. This good artist set himself at work to please the damsel. It was just before Valentine's day three years since. He wrought, unseen and unsuspected, a wondrous work. We need not say it was on the finest gilt paper with borders—full, not of common hearts and heartless allegory, but all the prettiest stories of love from Ovid, and older poets than Ovid (for E. B. is a scholar). There was Pyramus and Thisbe, and be sure Dido was not forgot, nor Hero and Leander, and swans more than sang in Cayster, with mottos and fanciful devices, such as beseemed,—a work in short of magic. Iris dipt the woof. This on Valentine's eve he commended to the all-swallowing indiscriminate orifice —(O ignoble trust!)—of the common post; but the humble medium did its duty, and from his watchful stand, the next morning, he saw the cheerful messenger knock, and by and by the precious charge delivered. He saw, unseen, the happy girl unfold the Valentine, dance about, clap her hands, as one after one the pretty emblems unfolded themselves. She danced about, not with light love, or foolish expectations, for she had no lover; or, if she had, none she knew that could have created those bright images which delighted her. It was more like some fairy present; a God-send, as our familiarly pious ancestors termed a benefit received, where the benefactor was unknown. It would do her no harm. It would do her good for ever after. It is good to love the unknown. I only give this as a specimen of E. B. and his modest way of doing a concealed kindness."

A distinguishing mark of the Elia essays is the portrayal of persons, not merely those whom Lamb knew and liked but also the nameless people whom he saw as he went about or talked with on a stage-coach, at the theatre, or wherever he happened to be—father, sister, brother; the old clerks at the South Sea House, Tipp, Man, Plumer, Evans; George Dyer as "Amicus Redivivus"; the teachers at Christ's Hospital, Boyer and Field; the inimitable Sarah Battle, Captain Jackson, Ralph Bigod, Esq.; himself as the "Superannuated Man"; the little girl who makes us remember Valentine's Day; the Quaker who was enduring the Foxian orgasm; the old pedagogue, "about the wrong side of thirty," who annoyed Lamb with his startling questions; the greatest liar that ever lived from "The Old Margate Hoy"; the actors, Dodd, Dicky Suett, Elliston, Munden and Fanny Kelly; old men in the "Benchers of the Inner Temple"—was ever old age made more attractive?—and Jem White, who gave the supper for the chimney sweeps. The steel of the etcher never made more truthful record of a face than the words which the magician summoned to do his bidding, and which leave for us real persons, not to be laughed at or made over in sentimental fashion, but rather bits of mortality like ourselves. Not to be forgotten are those incidents or place descriptions which remain in memory after a reading of the essays: the old place at "Mackery End"; the garden in "Dream-Children"; the doorway at the end of Cross Street leading into Drury Lane; the old sundial; the hair-raising picture of the witch raising up Samuel in Stackhouse's *History of the Bible;* the brush rising from the chimney in the "Chimney-Sweepers"; the joys of eating strawberries and of drinking tea from "the sweet wood yclept Sassafras"; the visits to the theatre, the bookstalls; and, perhaps most fun of all, just looking into the faces of people in the streets of London.

Lamb's fondness for the theatre has often been described and has not infrequently been mentioned here. We are not surprised, therefore, to find some of the Elia essays on actors and the stage. "My First Play," "On Some of the Old Actors," "On the Artificial Comedy of the Last Century," "On the Acting of Munden," "Stage Illusion," "To the Shade of Elliston," "Ellistoniana," and "Barbara S——"—all have to do with the theatre, either recalling plays and actors that Lamb liked or setting forth earnestly some principle or criticism of the drama. With a searching criticism of Congreve, Wycherley and Farquhar, Lamb maintained that the comedy of the Seventeenth Century must not be judged by the standards of the Nineteenth. "I am glad for a season to take an airing beyond the diocese of the strict conscience . . . to imagine a world with no meddling restrictions. . . . I come back to my cage and my restraint the fresher and more healthy for it. . . . They are a world of themselves almost as much as fairy-land." There is much here of pungent criticism and of imaginative insight into the vital forces of the dramatic art.

In "The Old and the New Schoolmaster" Lamb recurs to a theme which he often used. He was by nature a scholar; he liked the universities; the dearest days in his life had been spent at Christ's Hospital. He never concealed his lack of formal education, his ignorance of geography, science and history. There is the suspicion that he did not sympathise with some of the methods of the pedagogues, and he was equally conscious that some of the modern schoolteachers were superficial, but even when he saw a lack he did not fail to remember the imperfection of human nature and viewed it with humour and sympathy.

"Witches and Other Night Fears" gave Lamb the opportunity to sound a warning quite characteristic of his way of thinking. Witches, what of them? Most of us are too quick in condemning our ancestors and deploring their intolerance and bigotry. How much of witchcraft he was able to put into this short passage! Lamb wrote with feeling about witches, because of experiences in childhood which lingered through life and left him with convictions as to the treatment of children affected by fear. Most of us have a scene or an experience which recalls feelings similar to those which Lamb has expressed with understanding of the child mind.

"We are too hasty when we set down our ancestors in the gross for fools, for the monstrous inconsistencies (as they seem to us) involved in their creed of witchcraft. In the relations of this visible world we find them to have been as rational, and shrewd to detect an historic anomaly, as ourselves. But when once the invisible world was supposed to be opened, and the lawless agency of bad spirits assumed, what measures of probability, of decency, of fitness, or proportion—of that which distinguishes the likely from the palpable absurd—could they have to guide them in the rejection or admission of any particular testimony?—that maidens pined away, wasting inwardly as their waxen images consumed before a fire—that corn was lodged, and cattle lamed—that whirlwinds uptore in diabolic revelry the oaks of the forest—or that spits and kettles only danced a fearful-innocent vagary about some rustic's kitchen when no wind was stirring—were all equally probable where no law of agency was understood. That the prince of the powers of darkness, passing by the flower and pomp of the earth, should lay preposterous siege to the weak fantasy of indigent eld—has neither likelihood nor unlikelihood *à priori* to us, who have no measure to guess at his policy, or standard to estimate what rate those anile souls may fetch in the devil's market. Nor, when the wicked are expressly symbolized by a goat, was it to be wondered at so much, that *he* should come sometimes in that body, and assert his metaphor.—That the intercourse was opened at all between both worlds was perhaps the mistake—but that once assumed, I see no reason for disbelieving one attested story of this nature more than another on the score of absurdity. There is no law to judge of the lawless, or canon by which a dream may be criticised."

The title of the essay "The Two Races of Men" would lead us to expect something different from the "two distinct races, *the men who borrow,* and *the men who lend.*" And we are introduced to a characteristic Elian discussion of something to lend or borrow more important than money.

By this time we do not expect the ordinary conventional subject and certainly not the expected treatment of the subject. How could anybody write "A Complaint of the Decay of Beggars," "the oldest and honourablest form of pauperism"? But because beggars will always be with us, why not find something in them with which we can sympathise and which will arouse in us a greater appreciation of what they might do for us? "The Mendicants of this great city were so many of her sights, her lions. I can no more spare them than I could the Cries of London. No corner of a street is complete without them. They are as indispensable as the Ballad Singer; and in their picturesque attire as ornamental as the Signs of old London." And perhaps, reader, Lamb would say, the presence of the beggars made it possible for you by your pennies to show charity like the Bank clerk who for twenty years daily dropped his halfpenny into the beggar's hat and was rewarded by receiving the "amassings of his alms" for a half-century.

Quite consistent with Lamb's liking for the unusual and the unexpected is "Popular Fallacies," *résumé* of the qualities exhibited in all the Elia Essays, with "the same effect here at the close of the book," William Macdonald aptly notes, "as that mustering of all the characters upon the stage at the end of a drama, nobody having anything very important to say, but their totality of presence making for remembrance and for good-humour and good-night." Such axioms as "That handsome is that handsome does," "That we must not look a gift-horse in the mouth," "That home is home though it is never so homely," "That we should rise with the lark," are examined to show that they are not to be accepted without caution.

"Grace before Meat" brings the thought which may not have occurred to us: Why confine our grace to eating? "I own that I am disposed to say grace upon twenty other occasions in the course of the day besides my dinner. I want a form for setting out upon a pleasant walk, for a moonlight ramble, for a friendly meeting, or a solved problem."

We may imagine the particular enjoyment which Lamb had in writing this essay. Food was to him not merely something to keep him alive but something to be distinguished, to be selected, to be talked about. "I am no Quaker at my food. I confess I am not indifferent to the kinds of it." Numerous references in his letters are to what they are to have for dinner, thanks for presents of game and fish, and sometimes how to prepare a choice dish. "We have a sure hot joint on Sundays and when had we better?"

"Imperfect Sympathies" must be taken with a grain of salt. Although Lamb expressed an aversion to Scotchmen, produced in part by an impression of their supposed intolerance and matter-of-factness, he liked individual Scotchmen—Edward Irving, Robert Burns, Allan Cunningham—and he had a real affection for Thomas Hood. For Jews in general he had no great liking, but John Braham, the great tenor of his day, was one of his most admired singers and a special friend. As for Quakers, although he distrusted the fanatical members of the sect, he liked their simple ways and their mysticism, and he advised his friends to read of the early Quakers and especially Penn and Woolman.

Lamb's liking for the Quakers and sincere admiration for their worship of silence finds affectionate expression in "A Quaker's Meeting." "Reader, would'st thou know what true peace and quiet mean; would'st thou find a refuge from the noises and clamours of the multitude; would'st thou enjoy at once solitude and society; would'st thou possess the depth of thine own spirit in stillness, without being shut out from the consolatory faces of thy species; would'st thou be alone, and yet accompanied; solitary, yet not desolate; singular, yet not without some to keep thee in countenance; a unit in aggregate; a simple in composite:—come with me into a Quaker's meeting."

He closes with a benediction in words suggestive of the painter's art. "The very garments of a Quaker seem incapable of receiving a soil; and cleanliness in them to be something more than the absence of its contrary. Every Quakeress is a lily; and when they come up in bands to their Whitsun-conferences, whitening the easterly streets of the Metropolis, from all parts of the United Kingdom, they show like troops of the Shining Ones."

"Dream-Children," which Lamb calls a Reverie, is as nearly a perfect piece of prose as anything he ever wrote and merits Swinburne's praise: "There is in his work a sweetness like no other fragrance, a magic like no second spell in all the world of letters." John Lamb, his brother, had died only a few weeks before Charles wrote the essay. Although the two were so different, John's death brought to him poignant memories of their childhood together and of those days when he wandered in the glades of Blakesware with "Alice" by his side. With inexpressible tenderness he touches the persons and incidents of early childhood with genius, all in one paragraph, using, as in the language of the Bible, the connective *and* to continue the fluency of the story in words so simple that a child can understand.

By many readers of Elia, "Old China" is the essay most admired. Liking for old china strikes the note for recalling old friends, old books, old scenes, and naturally suggests the tenderest memories of Charles's association with Mary, their walks together, buying the folio of Beaumont and Fletcher, going to the theatre and eating strawberries. Nowhere is displayed with better effect his magic power to arouse the reader's sympathy in the enjoyment of pleasant memories.

"The idea of the discovery of roasting pigs, I also borrowed from my friend Manning." Whether this, like his reference to the Chinese manuscript, is a figment of fancy is of little significance. With the characteristic stroke of genius he makes the borrowed story a masterpiece. Selecting as a title the formal word a "dissertation" and assuming ignorance of all details, he tells the story with such attention to the sympathetic enjoyment of the reader in the taste of Bo-bo and of all who shared the new delicacy that this story has become a classic.

Because Lamb had a special liking for and understanding of children and because it displays the qualities as writer and humourist that have made him so widely known, "The Praise of Chimney-Sweepers" shows Lamb at his best. One who was writing on this subject at that time might be expected to allude to cruelties incident to the climbing boys' occupation, which for some while had been causing discussion in the press and in Parliament and resulted in notable changes in the laws. That was not Lamb's way. The essay has a much wider appeal than a humanitarian plea for a change in child-labour conditions.

"THE PRAISE OF CHIMNEY-SWEEPERS"

"I like to meet a sweep—understand me—not a grown sweeper—old chimney-sweepers are by no means attractive—but one of those tender novices, blooming through their first nigritude, the maternal washings not quite effaced from the cheek—such as come forth with the dawn, or somewhat earlier, with their little professional notes sounding like the *peep peep* of a young sparrow; or liker to the matin lark should I pronounce them, in their aerial ascents not seldom anticipating the sun-rise?

"I have a kindly yearning toward these dim specks—poor blots—innocent blacknesses—

"I reverence these young Africans of our own growth—these almost clergy imps, who sport their cloth without assumption;

and from their little pulpits (the tops of chimneys), in the nipping air of a December morning, preach a lesson of patience to mankind.

"When a child, what a mysterious pleasure it was to witness their operation! to see a chit no bigger than one's-self, enter, one knew not by what process, into what seemed the *fauces Averni*—to pursue him in imagination, as he went sounding on through so many dark stifling caverns, horrid shades!—to shudder with the idea that 'now, surely, he must be lost for ever!'—to revive at hearing his feeble shout of discovered day-light—and then (O fulness of delight) running out of doors, to come just in time to see the sable phenomenon emerge in safety, the brandished weapon of his art victorious like some flag waved over a conquered citadel! I seem to remember having been told, that a bad sweep was once left in a stack with his brush, to indicate which way the wind blew. It was an awful spectacle certainly; not much unlike the old stage direction in Macbeth, where the 'Apparition of a child crowned, with a tree in his hand, rises.'

"Reader, if thou meetest one of these small gentry in thy early rambles, it is good to give him a penny. It is better to give him two-pence. If it be starving weather, and to the proper troubles of his hard occupation, a pair of kibed heels (no unusual accompaniment) be superadded, the demand on thy humanity will surely rise to a tester.

"There is a composition, the ground-work of which I have understood to be the sweet wood 'yclept sassafras. This wood boiled down to a kind of tea, and tempered with an infusion of milk and sugar, hath to some tastes a delicacy beyond the China luxury. I know not how thy palate may relish it; for myself, with every deference to the judicious Mr. Read, who hath time out of mind kept open a shop (the only one he avers in London) for the vending of this 'wholesome and pleasant beverage,' on the south side of Fleet-street, as thou approachest Bridge-street—*the only Salopian house,*—I have never yet adventured to dip my own particular lip in a basin of his commended ingredients—a cautious premonition to the olfactories constantly whispering to me, that my stomach must infallibly, with all due courtesy, decline it. Yet I have seen palates, otherwise not uninstructed in dietetical elegances, sup it up with avidity.

"I know not by what particular conformation of the organ it happens, but I have always found that this composition is surprisingly gratifying to the palate of a young chimney-sweeper—whether the oily particles (sassafras is slightly oleaginous) do attenuate and soften the fuliginous concretions, which are sometimes found (in dissections) to adhere to the roof of the mouth in these unfledged practitioners; or whether Nature, sensible that she had mingled too much of bitter wood in the lot of these raw victims, caused to grow out of the earth her sassafras for a sweet lenitive—but so it is, that no possible taste or odour to the senses of a young chimney-sweeper can convey a delicate excitement comparable to this mixture. Being penniless, they will yet hang their black heads over the ascending steam, to gratify one sense if possible, seemingly no less pleased than those domestic animals—cats—when they purr over a new-found sprig of valerian. There is something more in these sympathies than philosophy can inculcate.

"Now albeit Mr. Read boasteth, not without reason, that his is the *only Salopian house;* yet be it known to thee, reader—if thou art one who keepest what are called good hours, thou art haply ignorant of the fact—he hath a race of industrious imitators, who from stalls, and under open sky, dispense the same savoury mess to humbler customers, at that dead time of the dawn, when (as extremes meet) the rake, reeling home from his midnight cups, and the hard-handed artisan leaving his bed to

resume the premature labours of the day, jostle, not unfre-
quently to the manifest disconcerting of the former, for the
honours of the pavement. It is the time when, in summer, between the expired and the not yet relumined kitchen-fires, the
kennels of our fair metropolis give forth their least satisfactory
odours. The rake, who wisheth to dissipate his o'ernight vapours in more grateful coffee, curses the ungenial fume, as he
passeth; but the artisan stops to taste, and blesses the fragrant
breakfast.

"This is *Saloop*—the precocious herb-woman's darling—the
delight of the early gardener, who transports his smoking cab-
bages by break of day from Hammersmith to Covent Garden's
famed piazzas—the delight, and oh I fear, too often the envy, of
the unpennied sweep. Him shouldest thou haply encounter,
with his dim visage pendent over the grateful steam, regale him
with a sumptuous basin (it will cost thee but three half-pennies)
and a slice of delicate bread and butter (an added half-penny)—
so may thy culinary fires, eased of the o'er-charged secretions
from thy worse-placed hospitalities, curl up a lighter volume to
the welkin—so may the descending soot never taint thy costly
well-ingredienced soups—nor the odious cry, quick-reaching
from street to street, of the *fired chimney,* invite the rattling
engines from ten adjacent parishes, to disturb for a casual scintil-
lation thy peace and pocket!

"I am by nature extremely susceptible of street affronts; the
jeers and taunts of the populace; the low-bred triumph they
display over the casual trip, or splashed stocking, of a gentleman. Yet can I endure the jocularity of a young sweep with
something more than forgiveness.—In the last winter but one,
pacing along Cheapside with my accustomed precipitation when
I walk westward, a treacherous slide brought me upon my back
in an instant. I scrambled up with pain and shame enough—yet
outwardly trying to face it down, as if nothing had happened—

when the roguish grin of one of these young wits encountered me. There he stood, pointing me out with his dusky finger to the mob, and to a poor woman (I suppose his mother) in particular, till the tears for the exquisiteness of the fun (so he thought it) worked themselves out at the corners of his poor red eyes, red from many a previous weeping, and soot-inflamed, yet twinkling through all with such a joy, snatched out of desolation, that Hogarth——but Hogarth has got him already (how could he miss him?) in the March to Finchley, grinning at the pye-man——there he stood, as he stands in the picture, irremovable, as if the jest was to last for ever—with such a maximum of glee, and minimum of mischief, in his mirth—for the grin of a genuine sweep hath absolutely no malice in it—that I could have been content, if the honour of a gentleman might endure it, to have remained his butt and his mockery till midnight.

"I am by theory obdurate to the seductiveness of what are called a fine set of teeth. Every pair of rosy lips (the ladies must pardon me) is a casket, presumably holding such jewels; but, methinks, they should take leave to 'air' them as frugally as possible. The fine lady, or fine gentleman, who show me their teeth, show me bones. Yet must I confess, that from the mouth of a true sweep a display (even to ostentation) of those white and shining ossifications, strikes me as an agreeable anomaly in manners, and an allowable piece of foppery. It is, as when

> A sable cloud
> Turns forth her silver lining on the night.

It is like some remnant of gentry not quite extinct; a badge of better days; a hint of nobility:—and, doubtless, under the obscuring darkness and double night of their forlorn disguisement, oftentimes lurketh good blood, and gentle conditions, derived from lost ancestry, and a lapsed pedigree. The premature apprenticements of these tender victims give but too much encouragement, I fear, to clandestine, and almost infantile abductions;

the seeds of civility and true courtesy, so often discernible in these young grafts (not otherwise to be accounted for) plainly hint at some forced adoptions; many noble Rachels mourning for their children, even in our days, countenance the fact; the tales of fairy-spiriting may shadow a lamentable verity, and the recovery of the young Montagu be but a solitary instance of good fortune, out of many irreparable and hopeless *defiliations*.

"In one of the state-beds at Arundel Castle, a few years since— under a ducal canopy—(that seat of the Howards is an object of curiosity to visitors, chiefly for its beds, in which the late duke was especially a connoisseur)—encircled with curtains of deli-catest crimson, with starry coronets inwoven—folded between a pair of sheets whiter and softer than the lap where Venus lulled Ascanius—was discovered by chance, after all methods of search had failed, at noon-day, fast asleep, a lost chimney-sweeper. The little creature, having somehow confounded his passage among the intricacies of those lordly chimneys, by some unknown aperture had alighted upon this magnificent chamber; and, tired with his tedious explorations, was unable to resist the delicious invitement to repose, which he there saw exhibited; so, creeping between the sheets very quietly, laid his black head upon the pillow, and slept like a young Howard.

"Such is the account given to the visitors at the Castle.—But I cannot help seeming to perceive a confirmation of what I had just hinted at in this story. A high instinct was at work in the case, or I am mistaken. Is it probable that a poor child of that description, with whatever weariness he might be visited, would have ventured, under such a penalty as he would be taught to expect, to uncover the sheets of a Duke's bed, and deliberately to lay himself down between them, when the rug, or the carpet, presented an obvious couch, still far above his pretensions—is this probable, I would ask, if the great power of nature, which I con-tend for, had not been manifested within him, prompting to the adventure? Doubtless this young nobleman (for such my mind misgives me that he must be) was allured by some memory, not amounting to full consciousness, of his condition in infancy, when he was used to be lapt by his mother, or his nurse, in just such sheets as he there found, into which he was now but creeping back as into his proper *incunabula,* and resting-place.— By no other theory, than by this sentiment of a pre-existent state (as I may call it), can I explain a deed so venturous, and, indeed, upon any other system, so indecorous, in this tender, but unseasonable, sleeper.

"My pleasant friend JEM WHITE was so impressed with a belief of metamorphoses like this frequently taking place, that in some sort to reverse the wrongs of fortune in these poor changelings, he instituted an annual feast of chimney-sweepers, at which it was his pleasure to officiate as host and waiter. It was a solemn supper held in Smithfield, upon the yearly return of the fair of St. Bartholomew. Cards were issued a week before to the master-sweeps in and about the metropolis, confining the invitation to their younger fry. Now and then an elderly stripling would get in among us, and be good-naturedly winked at; but our main body were infantry. One unfortunate wight, indeed, who, relying on his dusky suit, had intruded himself into our party, but by tokens was providentially discovered in time to be no chimney-sweeper (all is not soot which look so), was quoited out of the presence with universal indignation, as not having on the wedding garment; but in general the greatest harmony prevailed. The place chosen was a convenient spot among the pens, at the north side of the fair, not so far distant as to be impervious to the agreeable hubbub of that vanity; but remote enough not to be obvious to the interruption of every gaping spectator in it. The guests assembled about seven. In those little temporary parlours three tables were spread with napery, not so fine as substantial, and at every board a comely

hostess presided with her pan of hissing sausages. The nostrils
of the young rogues dilated at the savour. JAMES WHITE, as head
waiter, had charge of the first table; and myself, with our trusty
companion BIGOD, ordinarily ministered to the other two. There
was clambering and jostling, you may be sure, who should get
at the first table—for Rochester in his maddest days could not
have done the humours of the scene with more spirit than my
friend. After some general expression of thanks for the honour
the company had done him, his inaugural ceremony was to
clasp the greasy waist of old dame Ursula (the fattest of the
three), that stood frying and fretting, half-blessing, half-cursing
'the gentleman,' and imprint upon her chaste lips a tender
salute, whereat the universal host would set up a shout that
tore the concave, while hundreds of grinning teeth startled the
night with their brightness. O it was a pleasure to see the sable
younkers lick in the unctuous meat, with *his* more unctuous sayings—how he would fit the tit bits to the puny mouths, reserv-
ing the lengthier links for the seniors—how he would intercept
a morsel even in the jaws of some young desperado, declaring
it 'must to the pan again to be browned, for it was not fit for
a gentleman's eating'—how he would recommend this slice of
white bread, or that piece of kissing-crust, to a tender juvenile,
advising them all to have a care of cracking their teeth, which
were their best patrimony,—how genteelly he would deal about
the small ale, as if it were wine, naming the brewer, and protesting, if it were not good, he should lose their custom; with a
special recommendation to wipe the lip before drinking. Then
we had our toasts—'The King,'—the 'Cloth,'—which, whether
they understood or not, was equally diverting and flattering;—
and for a crowning sentiment, which never failed, 'May the
Brush supersede the Laurel!' All these, and fifty other fancies,
which were rather felt than comprehended by his guests, would
he utter, standing upon tables, and prefacing every sentiment

with a 'Gentlemen, give me leave to propose so and so,' which
was a prodigious comfort to those young orphans; every now
and then stuffing into his mouth (for it did not do to be squeam-
ish on these occasions) indiscriminate pieces of those reeking
sausages, which pleased them mightily, and was the savouriest
part, you may believe, of the entertainment.

> Golden lads and lasses must,
> As chimney-sweepers, come to dust—

"James White is extinct, and with him these suppers have
long ceased. He carried away with him half the fun of the
world when he died—of my world at least. His old clients look
for him among the pens; and, missing him, reproach the altered
feast of St. Bartholomew, and the glory of Smithfield departed
for ever."

There could be no better conclusion to our reading of the
essays than the preface to the second series, in which Elia
himself, posing as a friend of the late Elia, in his own whimsical
way looks back over his achievement and bids adieu.

"This poor gentleman, who for some months past had been in
a declining way, hath at length paid his final tribute to nature.

"To say truth, it is time he were gone. The humour of the
thing, if ever there was much in it, was pretty well exhausted;
and a two years' and a half existence has been a tolerable duration for a phantom.

"I am now at liberty to confess, that much which I have heard
objected to my late friend's writings was well-founded. Crude
they are, I grant you—a sort of unlicked, incondite things—vil-
lainously pranked in an affected array of antique modes and
phrases. They had not been *his,* if they had been other than
such; and better it is, that a writer should be natural in a self-
pleasing quaintness, than to affect a naturalness (so called) that
should be strange to him. Egotistical they have been pronounced

by some who did not know, that what he tells us, as of himself, was often true only (historically) of another; as in a former Essay (to save many instances)—where under the *first person* (his favourite figure) he shadows forth the forlorn estate of a country-boy placed at a London school, far from his friends and connections—in direct opposition to his own early history. If it be egotism to imply and twine with his own identity the griefs and affections of another—making himself many, or reducing many unto himself—then is the skilful novelist, who all along brings in his hero or heroine, speaking of themselves, the greatest egotist of all; who yet has never, therefore, been accused of that narrowness. And how shall the intenser dramatist escape being faulty, who, doubtless, under cover of passion uttered by another, oftentimes gives blameless vent to his most inward feelings, and expresses his own story modestly?

"My late friend was in many respects a singular character. Those who did not like him, hated him; and some, who once liked him, afterwards became his bitterest haters. The truth is, he gave himself too little concern what he uttered, and in whose presence. He observed neither time nor place, and would e'en out with what came uppermost. With the severe religionist he would pass for a free-thinker; while the other faction set him down for a bigot, or persuaded themselves that he belied his sentiments. Few understood him; and I am not certain that at all times he quite understood himself. He too much affected that dangerous figure—irony. He sowed doubtful speeches, and reaped plain, unequivocal hatred.—He would interrupt the gravest discussion with some light jest; and yet, perhaps, not quite irrelevant in ears that could understand it. Your long and much talkers hated him. The informal habit of his mind, joined to an inveterate impediment of speech, forbade him to be an orator; and he seemed determined that no one else should play that part when he was present. He was *petit* and ordinary in his person and appearance. I have seen him sometimes in what is called good company, but where he has been a stranger, sit silent, and be suspected for an odd fellow; till some unlucky occasion provoking it, he would stutter out some senseless pun (not altogether senseless perhaps, if rightly taken), which has stamped his character for the evening. It was hit or miss with him; but nine times out of ten, he contrived by this device to send away a whole company his enemies. His conceptions rose kindlier than his utterance, and his happiest *impromptus* had the appearance of effort. He has been accused of trying to be witty, when in truth he was but struggling to give his poor thoughts articulation. He chose his companions for some individuality of character which they manifested.—Hence, not many persons of science, and few professed *literati,* were of his councils. They were, for the most part, persons of an uncertain fortune; and, as to such people commonly nothing is more obnoxious than a gentleman of settled (though moderate) income, he passed with most of them for a great miser. To my knowledge this was a mistake. His *intimados,* to confess a truth, were in the world's eye a ragged regiment. He found them floating on the surface of society; and the colour, or something else, in the weed pleased him. The burrs stuck to him—but they were good and loving burrs for all that. He never greatly cared for the society of what are called good people. If any of these were scandalised (and offences were sure to arise), he could not help it. When he has been remonstrated with for not making more concessions to the feelings of good people, he would retort by asking, what one point did these good people ever concede to him? He was temperate in his meals and diversions, but always kept a little on this side of abstemiousness. Only in the use of the Indian weed he might be thought a little excessive. He took it, he would say, as a solvent of speech. Marry—as the friendly vapour ascended, how his prattle would curl up sometimes with it! the ligaments which tongue-tied him, were loosened, and the stammerer proceeded a statist!

"I do not know whether I ought to bemoan or rejoice that my old friend is departed. His jests were beginning to grow obsolete, and his stories to be found out. He felt the approaches of age; and while he pretended to cling to life, you saw how slender were the ties left to bind him. Discoursing with him latterly on this subject, he expressed himself with a pettishness, which I thought unworthy of him. In our walks about his suburban retreat (as he called it) at Shacklewell, some children belonging to a school of industry had met us, and bowed and curtseyed, as he thought, in an especial manner to *him*. 'They take me for a visiting governor,' he muttered earnestly. He had a horror, which he carried to a foible, of looking like anything important and parochial. He thought that he approached nearer to that stamp daily. He had a general aversion from being treated like a grave or respectable character, and kept a wary eye upon the advances of age that should so entitle him. He herded always, while it was possible, with people younger than himself. He did not conform to the march of time, but was dragged along in the procession. His manners lagged behind his years. He was too much of the boy-man. The *toga virilis* never sate gracefully on his shoulders. The impressions of infancy had burnt into him, and he resented the impertinence of manhood. These were weaknesses; but such as they were, they are a key to explicate some of his writings."

I I

Critic and Writer

IN A sense Charles Lamb was always a critic. He did not found, or belong to, any special school. He had no philosophy which aimed to analyse subjectively or æsthetically literary work or authors. He was not talking abstractions. He was under no special influence of German philosophy and criticism as was Coleridge. Criticism for Lamb meant the ceaseless exercise of a keen and discerning judgement upon what he read or saw or experienced. He was reading Bowles and Cowper and Burns and Wordsworth and Coleridge, and finding passages that he liked or passages which he thought might be improved. How do the poems answer such questions as, What does the poet want to say? Does he say it well? Is it worth saying? Do people like it?

He was not awed by Coleridge, the "inspired Charity boy" now grown up, because he was as honest as he was keen, and increasing in power and sureness. This possession came to Lamb as real critical ability should come, not from other critics but from a devotion to that which was good and proved to be good and which he himself liked. He had not gone to the authors because some teacher had sent him. Browsing in the Salt Library, in the old mansion in Hertfordshire, in the British Museum after office hours at the India House, had nourished his appetite and developed his taste and judgement so that they rarely failed him.

It is the common practice to minimise his influence upon

English literature. But it is apparent from his letters to Coleridge and to Wordsworth and in his essays that Charles Lamb fitted into the Romantic temper, even the same as they. That he had much influence upon them is certain. Lamb had nothing to give in the way of patronage or influence, so if men such as they continued to hold fast to him and value his criticism there must have been a keenness and quality to it which was of merit. We might expect him to be sentimental, romantic, carried away by the melancholy awe of Werther or Byron. Not so. Rather, he was a young man *not* from the university, merely an office clerk who was giving simple common-sense criticism of literary questions, based on an observation of human experience and a wide reading of English literature, to imaginative and very sensitive poets.

Lamb had great respect for Coleridge always, and Coleridge, ever discovering and trying new ways, must have led him into new paths. There was nothing beneath the heavens about which Coleridge did not have curiosity or some theory, and this pressing curiosity was a driving force in the thought of the two men.

Coleridge was greatly moved by the French Revolution and for a time was absolutely lost to all its implications and promises. He went to Germany to prove the depths of transcendentalism. He wanted to know Kant at first hand. He wanted to be able to read the language. He became on fire with the yearning to have a part in the intellectual revolution. He developed schemes but followed no one of them to accomplishment. He wrote fine poetry. Then decline set in. When we think of the magnificent mind and spirit of Coleridge, it seems tragic that he did his work of lasting quality in only the years 1797 and 1798, but there was more than his accomplishment in poetry and criticism. There was the stimulus which he communicated to his immediate associates. They felt his power and that infinite capacity to be interested in the intangible and the mysterious. Coleridge more than any other person of that period gave to the English literary world a fresh expression of the sense of mystery and the supernatural. It is present in his own poems and left an imprint on the poems of Wordsworth. It had a part in turning Southey to the writing of romances. It was a factor in the development of Charles Lamb in nourishing his interest in old books and his devotion to old writers.

If Coleridge was the most vitalising power in the Romantic movement in England, it was Wordsworth who profited by that spiritual impulse and gave it a lasting form which was to accord him the leadership in poetry for a long period of the Nineteenth Century. By temperament they were two different men: Coleridge dreamy, philosophical, unstable and thoroughly imaginative; Wordsworth more practical and devoted to the common duties of human life, responsible, a man who could be stamp distributor of his country community and could be a friend and companion of the common man.

It is significant that each of these three men tried to write drama. It is equally significant that in each case there was comparative failure. The failure is often attributed to the fact that it was not an age of drama. But we may enjoy the speculation that if there had appeared a figure with the tolerance, the sympathy for humanity, the sense of reality, the realisation of the value of passion and emotion, and the all-pervading humour of Shakespeare, there might have been another golden age. The one of the Romantic poetic figures who seemed to recognise this possibility was the one whom we least suspect as a possible author of drama, Keats. That poet, feeling his life had been a failure, expressed the hope that he might write a play because he felt that what should be said could best be expressed in drama.

Tangible evidence of Lamb's critical ability appears in the friendly letters which went to Coleridge in 1796 from the desk in the East India House when Lamb was twenty-one.

What were Coleridge and Lamb talking about during those December evenings in 1794 at the Salutation and Cat tavern? Coleridge had left Cambridge and, for a time, gave up thought of taking his degree. He was twenty-two, in love with Mary Evans and engaged to Sara Fricker. But, postponing his duty to go on to Bristol to make matters straight with Sara, he was lingering most engagingly in London, spending long hours of talk with Lamb, after Charles had left his desk at the East India House. Lamb was nineteen. Now they were snugly ensconced in the old tavern on Newgate Street almost opposite the school which they had left not so long before.

Just outside the tavern were the slums of London at their worst. In the immediate surroundings there was little to give hope to these two young dreamers and planners of Pantisocracy. It seemed so different from that other day when men met in the Mermaid, only a few steps from this very spot, and talked of new lands across the sea, of gold, of new vision and, even more to the liking of the two at the Salutation, of new plays, new poetry, the new world of books.

Beyond the immediate surroundings of the tavern were things which Coleridge and Lamb must have talked about, tendencies and fashions and plans and schemes and authors and books, and, most of all, their own futures. And we are equally confident that each had verses which he wanted to read and to have the other comment upon. What was there outside? We can answer better than the young poets on Newgate Street.

There was a great surge of humanitarianism, resulting in many social reforms and in important changes in the criminal code which would later affect the stark conditions of prison life in London. There was a revival of evangelical organization and religious thinking which had followed in the wake of preachers of Methodism, especially Whitefield and the Wesleys. Mere reason in philosophy and formalism in literary expression, it was apparent, were not enough. This reaction found concrete

expression in a return to faith, a new interest in the Middle
Ages, a turning away from the conventionalised pattern of
nature to nature as it is, an interest in mystery in all its phases,
a new emphasis on romance and imagination; in short, a discovery of the soul, the individual, the infinite possibilities of the
human mind and human emotion.

Of these things Coleridge and Lamb must have talked, but we
are equally sure that poetry was much thought about and talked
about. What old or new writer had either discovered? What
new verses had been written since Christ's Hospital days?
Doubtless they together had already felt the new spirit of an
awakening.

There was arising a new interest in the common man, in
everyday life. Even though some poets were still using a formal
and conventional language, nevertheless Burns had written of
the field mouse and the daisy, Crabbe and Cowper of the
homely things in village life, and Blake was soon to bring a new
magic into simple verse.

The mountain, the sea, the storm and other great manifestations of nature had always been subjects of poetic description,
but would there be some one who would really look at the things
which we see from sunrise to sunset and give them the magic
touch so that they would never pass into nothingness? Who
would make this the substance of poetry? Not in the words of
everyday speech, certainly. But Wordsworth thought otherwise.
Or could it be that this language, these words which had become set and lifeless, held the power to move the spirit of man,
with new courage, new faith and new ideals? For a time it
seemed that the French Revolution would bring the answer,
make the world all over to suit the dreamers. It did bring a
change, but not the change the revolutionists desired.

First of the influences upon Lamb was Shakespeare. Few
commentators on Shakespeare's plays have more successfully

read, understood and appreciated their excellences in content and expression along with the splendour, colour, humour and all the connotations of Elizabethan language. Unlike most of his contemporaries, Lamb discovered the real Shakespeare, long buried among notes which discussed the use of words, questionable passages and altered texts. His essay "On the Tragedies of Shakspeare" remains today one of the sanest pieces of interpretation and an incentive for the reader to turn again to the plays themselves for a closer reading. Lamb had often been irritated by the Shakespeare as "amended" by Tate and Garrick, by the ranting of some actors and more recently by reading the inscription on Garrick's tomb in Westminster Abbey, which eulogised Garrick as the "twin-star" of Shakespeare. He had been annoyed by the practise of using passages from the plays for declamation in the schools. "But Hamlet himself—what does he suffer meanwhile by being dragged forth as a public schoolmaster, to give lectures to the crowd!" This irritation caused Lamb to go too far in his essay and state the untenable position that Shakespeare's plays were more suited for reading than for acting. The only explanation which can be imagined to account for such a statement by one so devoted to the theatre may be found in the strain of perverseness in Lamb which led him sometimes to unreasonable extremes. Lamb went farther perhaps than he intended in upholding a weak position, but so fine are his expositions of the qualities of Shakespeare and the human elements of such characters as Hamlet, Iago, Ophelia, Malvolio, the Macbeths, that he may be forgiven for some of his extravagant assertions. His scorn and indignation reach a climax in the splendid passage on Lear.

Talfourd has left a delightful paragraph describing an evening which found him at the Lambs' with Thomas Barnes, the distinguished editor of the *Times,* when the subject was mentioned.

"I think I see him now, leaning forward upon the little table on which the candles were just expiring in their sockets, his fists clenched, his eyes flashing, and his face bathed in perspiration, exclaiming to Lamb, 'And do I not know, my boy, that you have written about Shakspeare, and Shakspeare's own Lear, finer than any one ever did in the world, and won't I let the world know it?'" And Talfourd added, "He was right, there is no criticism in the world more worthy of the genius it estimates than that little passage referred to on Lear; few felt it like Barnes; thousands have read it since then, and tens of thousands in America, and have felt as he did, and will answer for the truth of that excited hour."

"So to see Lear acted,—to see an old man tottering about the stage with a walking-stick, turned out of doors by his daughters in a rainy night, has nothing in it but what is painful and disgusting. We want to take him into shelter and relieve him. That is all the feeling which the acting of Lear ever produced in me. But the Lear of Shakspeare cannot be acted. The contemptible machinery by which they mimic the storm which he goes out in, is not more inadequate to represent the horrors of the real elements, than any actor can be to represent Lear: they might more easily propose to personate the Satan of Milton upon a stage, or one of Michael Angelo's terrible figures. The greatness of Lear is not in corporal dimension, but in intellectual: the explosions of his passion are terrible as a volcano; they are storms turning up and disclosing to the bottom that sea, his mind, with all its vast riches. It is his mind which is laid bare. This case of flesh and blood seems too insignificant to be thought on; even as he himself neglects it. On the stage we see nothing but corporal infirmities and weakness, the impotence of rage: while we read it, we see not Lear, but we are Lear,—we are in his mind, we are sustained by a grandeur which baffles the malice of daughters and storms; in the aberrations of his reason, we discover a mighty irregular power of reasoning, immethodized from the ordinary purposes of life, but exerting its powers, as the wind bloweth where it listeth, at will upon the corruptions and abuses of mankind. What have looks, or tones, to do with that sublime identification of his age with that of the *heavens themselves,* when in his reproaches to them for conniving at the injustice of his children, he reminds them that 'they themselves are old'? What gesture shall we appropriate to this? What has the voice or the eye to do with such things? But the play is beyond all art, as the tamperings with it shew: it is too hard and stony; it must have love-scenes, and a happy ending. It is not enough that Cordelia is a daughter, she must shine as a lover too. Tate has put his hook in the nostrils of this Leviathan, for Garrick and his followers, the showmen of the scene, to draw the mighty beast about more easily. A happy ending!—as if the living martyrdom that Lear had gone through,—the flaying of his feelings alive, did not make a fair dismissal from the stage of life the only decorous thing for him. If he is to live and be happy after, if he could sustain this world's burden after, why all this pudder and preparation,—why torment us with all this unnecessary sympathy? As if the childish pleasure of getting his gilt robes and sceptre again could tempt him to act over again his misused station,—as if, at his years and with his experience, any thing was left but to die."

Perhaps the deepest of Lamb's literary affections was for Milton. With the minor poems as well as with the epics and the prose works, his acquaintance was thorough. He seems to have preferred *Paradise Regained* to *Paradise Lost.* Although his devotion to Milton continued throughout life, it did not prevent his appreciating poets whose work was entirely different. Next came Beaumont and Fletcher, "in which authors I can't help thinking there is a greater richness of poetical fancy than in any one, Shakspeare excepted." The flavour of the poetry resulting from the collaboration of those two writers greatly pleased Lamb and influenced his style. "I wish you would try and do something to bring our elder bards into more general fame," he wrote to Coleridge.* "I writhe with indignation when in books of criticism, where common place quotation is heaped upon quotation, I find no mention of such men as Massinger, or B[eaumont] and Fl[etcher], men with whom succeeding Dramatic Writers (Otway alone excepted) can bear no manner of comparison." The happy occasion on which Charles and Mary at last decided to buy the Beaumont and Fletcher folio is humorously described in the Elia essay "Old China." That copy, with many notes written by both Lamb and Coleridge, is now one of the treasures of the British Museum. When sold at auction years ago, it brought the sum of eight shillings and sixpence!

Lamb liked the dainty, sweet and soothing fantasies of "honey-tongued Spenser." He admired Marlowe for his mighty line and especially for the character of Barabas. In the famous scene of Barabas and the Turkish captive, Ithamore was "a mixture of the ludicrous and the terrible, brimful of genius and antique invention." He liked the humour of Ben Jonson, and Massinger for the fine effect of his double endings. The gallant poet, Sir Philip Sidney, occupied a particular niche in his affection. The book referred to in his last letter was Phillips's *Theatrum Poetarum,* and Lamb had turned down the leaf at the account of Sidney.

Webster, whom he admired, only could "move a horror skilfully" and "touch a soul to the quick." When he finished Chapman's *Homer,* he wrote Coleridge, "Did you ever read it?—it has most the continuous power of interesting you all along, like a rapid original, of any, and in the uncommon excellence of the more finished parts goes beyond Fairfax or any of 'em. The

---

* Letter, June 1796.

metre is fourteen syllables, and capable of all sweetness and grandeur." "Gentle" in its finest sense was the word which he liked to describe his favourite Heywood. Lamb's devotion led readers who recognised his sincerity and judgement to old and much neglected riches of Elizabethan poetry.

It was as if Lamb's reading and knowledge of English literature developed in the same manner as the Seventeenth Century followed the Sixteenth. He appreciated the changes in the language and liked its eccentricities, the meaning of words now obsolete, and how it would be to speak as once spoke Thomas Fuller, Jeremy Taylor, Robert Burton and Thomas Browne. He was devoted to the poetry of Marvell, Quarles and Wither. The more closely they expressed the decorativeness and mysticism of their century, the more Lamb liked them. The temper and spirit and form of expression which developed through the three centuries, Sixteenth, Seventeenth, and Eighteenth, found a modern dwelling-place in the personality and artistry of Charles Lamb.

Of the Eighteenth Century Lamb liked especially Defoe, Pope, Smollett, Sterne, Goldsmith, and later in life he came, rather too slowly it seems to us, to admit Fielding into his circle.

Pope was a famous topic in the drawing-rooms of Lamb's time,—whether or not he was a poet. Lamb liked especially "The Rape of the Lock" and the translation of Homer. "I can read him over and over for ever." Procter once sent Lamb a portrait of Pope which had been executed as a frontispiece for the "Essay on Man" and received the following* as his reward: "I have hung up Pope, and a gem it is, in my town room; I hope for your approval. Though it accompanies the 'Essay on Man,' I think that was not the poem he is here meditating. He would have looked up, somehow affectedly, if he were just conceiving 'Awake, My St. John.' Neither is he in the 'Rape of the Lock'

---

* Letter, April 1823.

mood exactly. I think he has just made out the last lines of the
'Epistle to Jervis,' between gay and tender,

And other beauties envy Worsley's eyes.

"I'll be damn'd if that isn't the line. He is brooding over it,
with a dreamy phantom of Lady Mary floating before him. He
is thinking which is the earliest possible day and hour that she
will first see it. 'What a miniature piece of gentility it is! Why
did you give it me? I do not like you enough to give you anything so good."

In a superlative degree Lamb was hospitable to the use of conventional rhymes of the Eighteenth Century. "To the measure
in which these lines ['Mistress of Philarete'] are written the
wits of Queen Anne's days contemptuously gave the name of
Namby-Pamby, in ridicule of Ambrose Philips, who used it in
some instances, as in the lines of Cuzzoni, to my feeling at least,
very deliciously; but Wither, whose darling measure it seems
to have been, may shew, that in skilful hands it is capable of
expressing the subtilest movements of passion. So true it is,
which Drayton seems to have felt, that it is the poet who modi-
fies the metre, not the metre the poet."

As a result of his varied reading and his curiosity, Lamb acquired a vocabulary which was probably unique. No one since
the Seventeenth Century has used with greater precision the
words current at that time. Here are some that Lamb employed,
whose meaning the modern reader may like to ponder: arride,
agnise, additament, aridities, auspicate, acquists, ante-queer-
Diluvians, anti-Noahite, Albo-phobia, convictive, coronative,
copresence, Christmasly, disfurnishment, discommendable, dis-
commended, deoculated, disacquaintance, de-vited, discompli-
ments, elegantise, endorsation, endenzined, enthronization, ex-
pectated, "flying words," "furniture wives," holidaysically,
innutritious, illcomes (not welcomes), letterising, mumping vis-
nomy, muncheon, manducation, mumchance, nigrifying, one-

Goddite, Orpheusized, pericranicks, pray-books, plebeian'd, reluct, sciential, snugify, stanza'd, specimenifie'd, sithence, Sybillise, take-downable book, unfrequentedest, untristorify'd, unclify, underish, unforgetter, un-Unitarian.

Seldom did he change the form of the word, but employed it in the sense which had become obsolete, and he revived it in a manner which is characteristic and consistent. It was as if he brought out from his cellar an old bottle of wine to add to the flavour of the meal. Lamb realised the possibilities of suggestion concealed in a word, and no once gleaned more successfully from the folios of the Sixteenth and Seventeenth Centuries words which would convey the particular connotation that he wished for. The effect was not due merely to his use of individual words but to the way in which he combined them by parallel construction, by achieving climax, and by varying the length of sentences, all so cleverly managed, the art so excellently concealed, that the reader thinks: How easy to write like Lamb! But let one try like Robert Louis Stevenson to "play the sedulous ape" and he will be overwhelmed with difficulty.

Lamb's limitations in appreciation were most conspicuous in his judgement of contemporary writers. He was not unique in this respect. He was not the only critic and writer of his time who was unfortunate in some of his choices and allowed personal prejudice to affect his judgement, but in the main his opinions were supported by intelligence and expressed with simplicity and sincerity.

He praised Burns and he loved Cowper, as we have seen. In a sense he discovered Blake, whom he called "one of the most extraordinary persons of the age." Of Wordsworth and Coleridge he was ever the illuminating interpreter. In most of his estimates of their poems his judgements are as valid today as when first expressed. Walter Scott he greatly admired as a man, but he did not care for the Waverley Novels. Novels never appealed to him. Of Byron he wrote, "He was to me offensive, and I never can make out his great *power,* which his admirers talk of. Why, a line of Wordsworth's is a lever to lift the immortal spirit! Byron can only move the Spleen. He was at best a Satyrist,—in any other way he was mean enough. I dare say I do him injustice; but I cannot love him, nor squeeze a tear to his memory."* Of Shelley: "For his theories and nostrums they are oracular enough; but I either comprehend 'em not, or there is miching malice and mischief in 'em. But for the most part ringing with their own emptiness. . . . His voice was the most obnoxious squeak I ever was tormented with, ten thousand times worse than the Laureat's [Southey's], whose voice is the worst part about him, except his Laureacy." This was not a generous return for Shelley's praise of *Rosamund Gray* and for Shelley's expression of the regret which he felt when he learned that "the calumny of an enemy" had deprived him of Lamb's society while he was in England. Keats he met at the dinners of the *London Magazine,* certainly at one of the musical evenings at the Novellos' and at Haydon's, and he wrote an enthusiastic review of "The Eve of Saint Agnes" and "Lamia."

Of the famous dinner at Monkhouse's in Gloucester Place he wrote to Bernard Barton, "It is a lie that Poets are envious. I have known the best of them, and can speak to it, that they give each other their merits, and are the kindest critics as well as best authors."

As a contemporary record of that dinner Crabb Robinson's entry for April 4, 1823, is interesting. "Our party consisted of Wordsworth, Coleridge, Lamb, Moore, and Rogers. Five poets of very unequal worth and most disproportionate popularity, whom the public probably would arrange in the very inverse order, except that it would place Moore above Rogers."

---

* Letter to Barton, May 1824.

I 2

Charles Lamb, the Man

"Methinks I see him before me now, as he appeared then, and as he continued, with scarcely any perceptible alteration to me, during the twenty years of intimacy which followed, and were closed by his death. A light frame, so fragile that it seemed as if a breath would overthrow it, clad in clerk-like black, was surmounted by a head of form and expression the most noble and sweet. His black hair curled crisply about an expanded forehead; his eyes, softly brown, twinkled with varying expressions, though the prevalent feeling was sad; and the nose slightly curved, and delicately carved at the nostril, with the lower outline of the face regularly oval, completed a head which was finely placed on the shoulders, and gave importance and even dignity to a diminutive and shadowy stem. Who shall describe his countenance—catch its quivering sweetness—and fix it for ever in words? There are none, alas! to answer the vain desire of friendship. Deep thought, striving with humour; the lines of suffering wreathed into cordial mirth; and a smile of painful sweetness, present an image to the mind it can as little describe as lose. His personal appearance and manner are not unfitly characterised by what he himself says in one of his letters to Manning of Braham,—'a compound of the Jew, the gentleman, and the angel.' "—These are the words of Thomas Talfourd, long-time associate and subsequent biographer of Lamb and first collector of his letters.

Almost as with a camera, B. W. Procter ("Barry Cornwall") pictured Lamb as he set out on his daily walk to the East India House.

"Persons who had been in the habit of traversing Covent Garden . . . might by extending their walk a few yards into Russell Street have noted a small spare man, clothed in black, who went out every morning and returned every afternoon, as regularly as the hands of the clock moved towards certain hours. You could not mistake him. He was somewhat stiff in his manner, and almost clerical in dress; which indicated much wear. He had a long, melancholy face, with keen penetrating eyes; and he walked with a short, resolute step, City-wards. He looked no one in the face for more than a moment, yet contrived to see everything as he went on. No one who ever studied the human features could pass by without recollecting his countenance; it was full of sensibility, and it came upon you like a new thought, which you could not help dwelling upon afterwards; it gave rise to meditation and did you good."

Here is the way Lamb appeared to Thomas Hood, then assistant editor of the *London Magazine,* on the occasion of their first meeting in 1821, when Lamb was forty-six.

"I was sitting one morning beside our Editor, busily correcting proofs, when a visitor was announced, whose name, grumbled by a low ventriloquial voice, like Tom Pipes calling from the hold through the hatchway, did not resound distinctly on my tympanum. However, the door opened, and in came a stranger,—a figure remarkable at a glance, with a fine head, on a small spare body, supported by two almost immaterial legs. He was clothed in sables, of a by-gone fashion, but there was something wanting, or something present about him, that certified he was neither a divine nor a physician, nor a schoolmaster: from a certain neatness and sobriety in his dress, coupled with

CHARLES LAMB AT TWENTY-THREE
From a drawing by Robert Hancock in 1798
National Portrait Gallery

LEIGH HUNT AT FORTY-FOUR
From the portrait by J. Hayter. Engraved by Henry Meyer

his sedate bearing, he might have been taken, but that such a costume would be anomalous, for a *Quaker* in black."

Beside this may be placed the sketch written with characteristic Gallic appreciation of the nuances of a sensitive subject, by the French critic Philarète Chasles, for the *Revue des Deux Mondes*.

"I was at James Valpy's one evening in June, 1818, in his office where the candle must be lit at mid-day, and the fire in June, when a little, dark, old fellow came in; one could only distinguish a head, then big shoulders, then a delicate body, and finally two artistically slender legs, which were almost imperceptible. Under his arm was a green umbrella, and over his eyes a very old hat. Wit, sweetness, melancholy, and gaiety gushed in torrents from this extraordinary physiognomy. After first seeing him, you did not think any more of his ridiculous body; it seemed as if something purely intellectual was before you, soaring above matter, burning through the material form like light, and overflowing everywhere. There was neither health, nor strength and scarcely sufficient anatomical reality on those poor little spindles, clothed in stockings of Chinese silk, ending in impossible feet, encased in large shoes, which placed flatly on the ground, advanced slowly in the manner of a web-footed creature. But one did not notice these singularities, one saw only the magnificently developed forehead, on which his lustrous black hair curled naturally, the great, sad eyes, the expression of the large brownish, clear pupil, the excessively fine nostrils, cut more delicately than had ever been seen in others, the curves of the nose very like that of Jean Jacques in his portraits. All this, the oval of the face, nobly long, the exquisite contour of the mouth, and the beautiful pose of the head, lent dignity, and that of the highest kind—intellectual dignity—to this weakly and disproportioned organisation."

Lamb wrote quaint and penetrating descriptions of other

persons. Fortunately he used equal skill in portraying himself in a sketch written in 1827.

"Charles Lamb, born in the Inner Temple, 10th February, 1775; educated in Christ's Hospital; afterwards a clerk in the Accountants' Office, East India House; pensioned off from that service, 1825, after thirty-three years' service; is now a gentleman at large, can remember few specialities in his life worth noting, except that he once caught a swallow flying (*teste suâ manu*). Below the middle stature; cast of face slightly Jewish, with no Judaic tinge in his complexional religion; stammers abominably, and is therefore more apt to discharge his occasional conversation in a quaint aphorism, or a poor quibble, than in set and edifying speeches; has consequently been libelled as a person always aiming at wit, which, as he told a dull fellow that charged him with it, is at least as good as aiming at dulness: a small eater, but not drinker; confesses a partiality for the production of the Juniper-Berry; was a fierce smoker of tobacco, but may be resembled to a volcano burnt out, emitting only now and then a casual puff. Has been guilty of obtruding upon the Public a Tale, in prose, called Rosamund Gray; a Dramatic sketch, named John Woodvil; a Farewell Ode to Tobacco, with sundry other Poems, and light prose matter, collected in Two slight crown octavos, and pompously christened his Works, tho' in fact they were his Recreations; and his true works may be found on the Shelves of Leadenhall Street, filling some hundred folios. He is also the true Elia, whose Essays are extant in a little volume, published a year or two since, and rather better known from that name without a meaning, than from anything he has done, or can hope to do, in his own. He was also the first to draw the Public attention to the old English Dramatists, in a work called 'Specimens of English Dramatic Writers who lived about the Time of Shakspeare,' published about fifteen years

since. In short, all his merits and demerits to set forth would
take to the end of Mr. Upcott's† book, and then not be told truly.
"He died   18   , much lamented.*
                    "Witness his hand,
                                        "CHARLES LAMB.
"* To anybody.—Please to fill
    up these dates."

With so many sympathetic descriptions, it may seem a dis-
cordant note to present the impression of one observer who
"wasted" an afternoon in travelling to Enfield and back. It may
be that Thomas Carlyle—and there is evidence in favour—
lived to regret that he wrote his splenetic impression of an
hour's interview for his *Diary* in November 1831. Lamb was
fifty-six and Carlyle twenty-six. It reflects far more seriously
on the man who wrote it than upon the subject of the interview.
"Charles Lamb I sincerely believe to be in some considerable
degree insane. A more pitiful, ricketty, gasping, staggering,
stammering Tomfool I do not know. He is witty by denying
truisms and abjuring good manners. His speech wriggles hither
and thither with an incessant painful fluctuation, not an opinion
in it, or a fact, or a phrase that you can thank him for——more
like a convulsion fit than a natural systole and diastole. Besides,
he is now a confirmed, shameless drunkard; *asks* vehemently
for gin and water in strangers' houses, tipples till he is utterly
mad, and is only not thrown out of doors because he is too much
despised for taking such trouble with him. Poor Lamb! Poor
England, when such a despicable abortion is named genius."

Portraits of Lamb are by William Hazlitt in 1804 and a water-

------

† According to E. V. Lucas, "William Upcott was an antiquary, autograph
collector, and Librarian of the London Institution. He amassed altogether thirty-
two thousand letters, of which this is one."

colour drawing by Robert Hancock in 1798, both in the National
Portrait Gallery in London; by G. J. Joseph in 1819, in the
British Museum; by Wageman in 1824 or 1825, in America; an
etching by James Brook Pulham in 1825; a portrait by Henry
Meyer in 1826, in the East India House; a sketch by Leigh
Hunt's son, Thornton Hunt; and two drawings by Daniel
Maclise. Of Charles and Mary together there is one by F. S.
Cary, painted from life in the summer of 1834, only a few weeks
before Charles's death. In this connection Leigh Hunt wrote in
his *Autobiography:* "Charles Lamb had a head worthy of Aris-
totle with as fine a heart as ever beat in a human bosom, and
limbs very fragile to sustain it. . . . There never was a true portrait of Lamb. His features were strongly yet delicately cut; he
had a fine eye as well as forehead and no face carried in it
greater marks of thought and feeling." The Meyer portrait is
usually considered the best.

We think of Lamb as one who liked to be at home. His
letters and essays have many descriptions of the view from their
windows and the contents of the rooms. He had never known
pretentious quarters. As a boy, he had wandered through the
big rooms and halls of the old mansion in Hertfordshire, but
home to him was close quarters in the Temple, or attic rooms in
Holborn, or rooms over the brazier's shop at Covent Garden.
There was a mahogany table in the centre and high-backed
chairs around the sides. On the walls were prints by Hogarth,
Titian and Leonardo da Vinci, but what made the place was
Lamb's one extravagance, the old books and folios whose disar-
ray greatly annoyed both Crabb Robinson and Leigh Hunt.

Both Charles and Mary were careful, economical housekeep-
ers. They had never known what it was to be rich, or to have a
superfluity of anything. Their eating was never excessive, although no one enjoyed eating more than Charles Lamb and no

one has written more delightfully about his favourite dishes. His letters have many acknowledgements of gifts from his friends for his table—a goose, partridge, turkey, salmon and an occasional Stilton cheese. He was never stingy in his hospitality. Almost the first time he met a person whom he thought he would like, there was an invitation to come to dinner or to spend the evening, when there would be a punch or brandy and a tankard of ale, and a veal pie or cold roast. An invitation to the Lambs' came to be regarded as something to be accepted and enjoyed and there is no record of anybody's regretting the acceptance of one.

Those who came in contact with Charles Lamb readily discovered a good mind. He was not a mouthpiece for other people's ideas; he had opinions of his own and did not hesitate to express them at what he considered the appropriate time. "No one ever stammered out such fine, piquant, deep, eloquent things in half a dozen half sentences as he does," wrote Hazlitt. We should hesitatingly accept such praise if similar observations were not made by others of their mutual friends. Lamb was sparing of words. Perhaps this habit had grown upon him not only from his impediment of speech, but also from his deep respect for the value of words. He liked people and he liked to talk with them. No one ever called him a snob, and he always found on his holidays, in the stage-coach, or on his walks about London, an opportunity to talk with all sorts of people.

One experience which he described in a letter to Louisa Badams in December 1832 at first disturbed him and might have proved very embarrassing, but afterwards greatly amused him, although he confessed, "It has almost sickened me of the Crown and Horseshoe, and I sha'n't hastily go into the taproom again." The account which follows relates to the murder of Danby by Johnson and Fare.

"On the night of our murder (an hour or two before it), the

maid being busy, I went out to order an additional pint of porter for Moxon who had surprised us with a late visit. Now I never go out quite disinterested upon such occasions. And I begged a half-pint of ale at the bar which our sweet-faced landlady good-humouredly complied with, asking me into the parlour, but a side door was just open that disclosed a more cheerful blaze, and I entered where four people were engaged over Dominoes. One of them, Fare, invited me to join in it, partly out of impudence, I believe; however, not to balk a Christmas frolic, I complied, and played with Danby, but soon gave over, having forgot the game. I was surprised with D. challenging me as having known me in the Temple. He must have been a child then. I did not recognise him, but perfectly remembered his father, who was a hairdresser in the Temple. This was all that passed, as I went away with my beer. Judge my surprise when the next morning I was summoned before Dr. Creswell to say what I knew of the transaction. My examination was conducted with all delicacy, and of course I was soon dismissed. I was afraid of getting into the papers, but I was pleased to find myself only noticed as a 'gentleman whose name we could not gather.' "—He had drunk with the murderers!

Next to his fondness for his own home and his friends one notes again his liking for old books. He gave a description of what must have been a typical adventure in his walks about London.

"Rummaging over the contents of an old stall, at a half-book, half-old-iron shop, in Ninety-four Alley, leading from Wardour St. to Soho yesterday, I lit upon a ragged duodecimo, which has been the strange delight of my infancy. The price demanded was sixpence, which the owner (a little squab duodecimo of himself) enforced with the assurance that his own mother should not have it for a farthing less. On my demurring to this extraordinary assertion, the dirty little vendor re-inforced his assertion with a sort of oath which seemed more than the occasion demanded, and now, said he, 'I put my soul to it.' Pressed by so solemn an asseveration I could no longer resist a demand which seemed to put me, however unworthy, upon a level with his nearest relations; and depositing a tester I bore away the tattered prize in triumph."

America has the good fortune to have in her keeping most of the books of Lamb's library. Their sale at an auction in New York in 1848 amid great excitement met with resentment by Thomas Westwood, who had learned to love literature from Lamb's shelves. "I have been told that his books were sold to the Yankees. Oh, pity! Oh, shame! They should have been held in honour and charge by some Londoner who was a London-lover—a haunter of the old streets and old bookstalls. . . . Must he not have shuddered at that cruel description?—he, a thin ghost, on the other side Styx, pacing with hungry heart, those Elysian fields, where there are *no* bookstalls."

Lamb was not the book-collector who buys to sell, or to have because few others possess the same edition, or merely to have the book on his shelves. He read his old books. Abundant notes attest to his careful reading, and besides there are frequent references in his letters and essays that furnish proof of the use which he made of the contents.

Then came his great fondness for the theatre, which has been discussed, and then his amateur liking of pictures. For the brief period when Hazlitt was practising the art and making portraits of him, Coleridge and Wordsworth, Lamb was going to the exhibitions. His brother John was a first-rate collector. Charles wrote with enthusiasm to Hazlitt a letter* which showed his preference for Claude, Leonardo da Vinci, and

---

* March 1806.

Titian. Along with Hogarth they were the artists who claimed his affection.

"What do you in Shropshire when so many fine pictures are a-going, a-going every day in London? Monday I visit the Marquis of Lansdowne's, in Berkeley Square. Catalogue 2s. 6d. Leonardos in plenty. Some other day this week I go to see Sir Wm. Young's, in Stratford Place. Hulse's, of Blackheath, are also to be sold this month; and in May, the first private collection in Europe, Wellbore Ellis Agar's. And there are you, perverting Nature in lying landscapes, filched from old rusty Titians, such as I can scrape up here to send you, with an additament from Shropshire Nature thrown in to make the whole look unnatural. I am afraid of your mouth watering when I tell you that Manning and I got into Angerstein's on Wednesday. *Mon Dieu!* Such Claudes! Four Claudes bought for more than £10,-000 (those who talk of Wilson being equal to Claude are either mainly ignorant or stupid); one of these was perfectly miraculous. What colors short of *bona fide* sunbeams it could be painted in, I am not earthly colourman enough to say; but I did not think it had been in the possibility of things. Then, a music-piece by Titian—a thousand-pound picture—five figures standing behind a piano, the sixth playing; none of the heads, as M. observed, indicating great men, or affecting it, but so sweetly disposed; all leaning separate ways, but so easy—like a flock of some divine shepherd; the colouring, like the economy of the picture, so sweet and harmonious—as good as Shakspeare's 'Twelfth Night,'—*almost,* that is. It will give you a love of order, and cure you of restless, fidgetty passions for a week after—more musical than the music which it would, but cannot, yet in a manner *does,* show."

Of painters and painting Lamb had no wide knowledge and so far as we know was not interested in the history or the technique of the art, but as an appreciative critic he tried to understand the picture and to praise it if he liked it.

He knew little about music and, though he pretended in "A Chapter on Ears" to have no ear for it, he was enthusiastic over the singing of Braham, the organ music of Novello and the voice of Emma Isola. Music never had a place at his Wednesday evenings and he was deeply indignant that music should be introduced in the theatres along with vaudeville and acrobatic performances!

Outside his own home, walking was Lamb's main diversion— as a little boy in the Temple Gardens, along the streets to school, and to the theatre, that regular walk every morning and evening to and from his work at Leadenhall, the trips that meant so much for him in Hertfordshire, Wiltshire and the Lake district, and finally in his years of retirement in the country about Enfield and Edmonton. His last walk, taken only a few days before the end, led to the fall which caused his death. For a number of years he walked as much as twenty or twenty-five miles a day. He did not talk much about it nor boast of it, but walking was his way to reach people and to see the things he wanted to see: the bookshops, art galleries, folios in the British Museum. He discovered, like Hunt, that there was not a street in London from which he could not see a tree, and in his rambles in the neighbouring country, he derived inexhaustible refreshment from the out-of-doors and the familiar objects about him.

From childhood he must have been a delightful companion. One day with Hood he remarked, "We have walked a pint," and proposed that they stop at the inn. Of a visit to his favourite Cambridge, Mary wrote to Sara Hutchinson: "In my life I never spent so many pleasant hours together as I did at Cambridge. We were walking the whole time—out of one College into another."

Quite exceptional were his knowledge of children and interest in their welfare. He understood them as few older persons know and appreciate them. Always present with him were his own childhood memories of the Temple, of school and of the country. His part in the work which he and Mary did together, the many poems which were written for children and for their albums were an expression of himself. His own creations of children, Alice in "Dream-Children," the Child Angel, Barbara S——, the little girl in "Valentine's Day," the chimney-sweepers, and little Bo-bo in "Roast Pig" revealed an ability equalled or surpassed only by Shakespeare and Dickens. His interest in the children of his friends, Wordsworth, Hazlitt, Coleridge and others, was genuine. His enjoyment of presents, of new purchases of books and pictures, his planning for holidays all indicated a nature as fresh and unspoiled as that of a child. His playfulness appealed to children and, on occasions in their company, he was accepted as one of them. He had the good fortune to discover in Emma Isola a child upon whom he could bestow an affection not exceeded by that of any parent. He liked to tell of an epitaph, discovered in the Islington churchyard, of an infant "*Aetatis* four months," with the inscription, "Honour thy father and mother that thy days may be long in the land."

A story recorded by Barry Cornwall* testifies to his kindness and consideration for children.

"One day Lamb encountered a small urchin, loaded with a too heavy package of grocery. It caused him to tremble and stop. Charles inquired where he was going, took (although weak) the load upon his own shoulder, and managed to carry it to Islington, the place of destination. Finding that the purchaser of the grocery was a female, he went with the urchin before her, and expressed a hope that she would intercede with the poor boy's master, in order to prevent his being overweighted in the future. 'Sir,' said the dame, frowning upon him, 'I buy my sugar, and have nothing to do with the man's manner of

---

* *Charles Lamb, A Memoir*, p. 238.

sending it.' Lamb at once perceived the character of the purchaser, and taking off his hat, said humbly, 'Then I hope, ma'am, you'll give me a drink of small beer.' This was of course refused. He afterwards called upon the grocer, on the boy's behalf—with what effect I do not know."

For dumb animals Lamb's sympathy is shown by many stories which were told by his close friends. Two of them saw him get up from the table while they were dining with him and Mary at Enfield, open the street door and give admittance to a stray donkey into the front strip of garden where there was a grass plot, which he said seemed to possess more attraction for the creature than the short turf of the Common on Chase-side, opposite to the house where the Lambs then dwelt.

His supposed excesses in drinking and smoking have been the subjects of much discussion and much writing. Perhaps a large part of this interest arose from his candour in admitting excesses of which he was not guilty and in describing his struggles to break the habits. Barry Cornwall, who knew him intimately for many years, was quite explicit: "During all my intimacy with him I never knew him to drink immoderately, except once." Friends who knew Lamb well recognised that he was very sensitive to drink, that a small quantity of liquor would cloud his mind and make him even more hesitating in his speech than in his usual conversation. Unfortunately he wrote an article, "Confessions of a Drunkard," which was accepted as autobiographical, greatly to the discomfiture of Mary Lamb. It would seem to us of today that contemporary readers might have discovered in this essay the whimsical blending of fact and fiction which was so characteristic of things he wrote. At a time when there was so much drinking, it was certainly unmanly not to drink, or to be occasionally in one's cups, as even Jane Austen could observe. At this distance, one can safely say that there was nothing disreputable in the drinking which Lamb was accustomed to indulge in. We are now aware, as some of his contemporaries were not, of his loneliness, and we sympathise more readily with the yearning which prompted him to try to escape from his ever-present sorrow. A great contrast is to be observed in his friend Coleridge, who became a victim to laudanum which, in time, made of that great genius a total physical and mental wreck. In Lamb's case, there was nothing really tragic in his weakness; it may be questioned whether his constitution was at all impaired by his drinking or smoking. It is possible that his convivial habits made him a better companion and helped to free a natural tendency to be silent. At any rate it would be difficult to imagine the situation without the various incidents—some more serious, others quite humorous—which developed.

One illustration of Lamb's playfulness in this connection is given in a letter of William Hone, printed in 1853. "One summer's evening I was walking on Hampstead Heath with Charles Lamb, and we had talked ourselves into a philosophic contempt of our slavery to the habit of snuff-taking, and with the firm resolution of never again taking a single pinch, we threw our snuff boxes away from the hill on which we stood, far among the furze and brambles below and went home in triumph; I began to be very miserable, was wretched all night; in the morning I was walking on the same hill, I saw Charles Lamb below, searching among the bushes; he looked up laughing, and saying, 'What! You are come to look for your snuff box, too!' 'O no,' said I taking a pinch out of a paper in my waistcoast pocket, 'I went for a halfpenny worth to the first shop that was open.'"

Resentment by his friends and later admirers made many apologists, among whom Augustine Birrell* may be quoted as one most annoyed—or shall we say more inspired?

---

* *Obiter Dicta.*

"One grows sick of the expressions, 'poor Charles Lamb,' 'gentle Charles Lamb,' as if he were one of those grown-up children of the Leigh Hunt type, who are perpetually begging and borrowing through the round of every man's acquaintance. Charles Lamb earned his own living, paid his own way, was the helper, not the helped; a man who was beholden to no one, who always came with gifts in his hand, a shrewd man capable of advice, strong in council. Poor Lamb, indeed! Poor Coleridge, robbed of his will; poor Wordsworth, devoured by his own *ego;* poor Southey, writing his tomes and deeming himself a classic; poor Carlyle, with his nine volumes of memoirs, where he

'Lies like a hedgehog rolled up the wrong way,
Tormenting himself with his prickles'—

call these men poor, if you feel it decent to do so, but not Lamb, who was rich in all that makes life valuable or memory sweet. But he used to get drunk. This explains all. Be untruthful, unfaithful, unkind; darken the lives of all who live under your shadow, rob youth of joy, take peace from age, live unsought for, die unmourned—and remaining sober you will escape the curse of men's pity and be spoken of as a worthy person. But if ever, amidst what Burns called 'social noise,' you so far forget yourself as to get drunk, think not to plead a spotless life spent with those for whom you have laboured and saved; talk not of the love of friends or of help given to the needy, least of all make reference to a noble self-sacrifice passing the love of women, for all will avail you nothing."

With Lamb's thoughtfulness for those whom he knew went a generosity which was widely recognised. He was always prompt in acknowledging gifts sent to him for his table—we have no record of other presents except the portrait of Pope sent to him by Barry Cornwall. He remembered the anniversaries of his

friends and the children of his friends, wrote letters of com
mendation, consolation, advice of various kinds, to Coleridge, to
Lloyd and in one notable case to Barton, and he never refused
appeals for financial aid from friends in trouble. We do not
recall that he made a single request for aid for himself.

Lamb's "pet aversions" are well known—tailors, bargainers,
bankrupts, bores of all kinds, Frenchmen and Scotchmen. Very
often what seems a grievance of long standing or a deep conviction was caused by some ill luck or injustice to a friend.

"It has long been my deliberate judgment," he wrote to
Bernard Barton, whom Hood liked to call the "busy B," "that
all Bankrupts of what denomination civil or religious whatever,
ought to be hang'd. The pity of mankind has for ages run in a
wrong channel, and has been diverted from poor Creditors
(how many have I known sufferers! Hazlitt has just been defrauded of £100 by his Bookseller-friend's breaking) to scoundrel debtors."

It would be as easy to make a complementary list of his
"likes"—Quakers, chimney-sweepers, beggars, the "underdog."
The poor fellow with one talent in the Bible, the five foolish virgins, the improvident architect who built his house on the sand,
even Guy Fawkes—these unfortunate persons commonly chosen
as texts for sermons called forth from Lamb extravagant words
of sympathy, largely because of his partiality for the unpopular side.

His humour was as much a part of him as his physical characteristics. His precious possession consisted of more than mere
superficial manifestations or the timely witty remark. It was
quaint, as Lamb was quaint, but the quaintness ran through the
grain, an everlasting quality of incongruity, not merely freakish
or fantastic. It had its origin in keen observation and in the
realisation of experience, in sympathy with the feelings of

others and the knowledge that real humour lies near to pathos and has little in common with the laughter to which the caricaturist appeals. His was the humour which is charged with poetry, with tenderness, kindliness and imagination combined with the sentiment of romance and sound common sense. It had its roots deep in English soil, was nourished by the lore of English tradition and flourished in association with his favourites among English authors and the varied personalities of many friends. He was attracted to great humourists like Robert Burton and Sterne, and became in turn the object of affection of later humourists such as Thackeray and Robert Louis Stevenson. In the expression of his humour, in his writing, Lamb kept to relative values, knew when to stop, what to leave out. In a word, he was an artist, choosing the effect to be produced and using every power to achieve the wished-for result. Without the savagery of Swift, the cynicism of Thackeray, or the caricature of Dickens, he became one of the most distinctive humourists of English literature.

So much may be said for Lamb's humour as expressed chiefly in what he wrote. There was the other side which appeared in his playfulness which pleased those who understood, in jokes, puns, good stories, and witty sayings and in pranks which sometimes had results quite different from what was intended. It is not always easy for us to understand or to sympathise with some of his contradictions in character. He was "terribly shy," said Barry Cornwall, so much so that one morning when they were going together to breakfast with the poet Rogers, Lamb confessed that it was difficult for him to undergo the scrutiny of servants. His difficulty of speech, the meanness of his family surrounding in his youth, the hereditary mental affliction, besides a personal oddness of manner and appearance, all contributed to make him conscious of this shyness. It would be profitable at this moment to turn back a few pages to the sketch

which he wrote of himself, doubtless as keen and penetrating
an analysis of himself as the accurate descriptions which he
wrote of other persons. That will help us to understand that
witty remarks which some persons attributed to ill-humor or
even cruelty were rather an expression of perverseness, or play
ful fooling or a rather awkward way of showing an aversion to
being "made over." Just as sometimes in his serious writing he
took a position which was not consistent with him or worthy of
him, so he seemed to err in sensing a situation and seemed to set
out intentionally to alienate his listeners. Something may be
laid to a too generous draught of wine or spirits which often
fixed the tone for the occasion, but it might as well be said that
the stimulant sometimes set free some of his best thoughts and
expressions. It seemed to clear his mind and free his tongue
to range at will. If the drink and smoking were not specially
effective in producing the good talk, they probably had little
evil effect. According to Patmore they were "the talisman that
not only unlocked the poor casket in which the rich thoughts
of Charles Lamb were shut up, but set in motion that machinery
in the absence of which they would have lain like gems in the
mountain or gold in the mine."

Besides Lamb's liking for joking, hoaxes and mystification
he had a marked preference for puns. In this he was not excep
tional as that habit in those days was much cultivated and
widely approved. Lamb came to this very naturally as he had a
profound interest in words, their history, sound, and possible
connotation. He indulged in all kinds of puns, some very
frivolous, some amusing, some which showed a sense of humour
mingled with real genius. Some lit up as with a flash a char
acter or play or situation which now are remembered by
Lamb's invective wit. Many examples of his puns and bons
mots have been preserved, but in the main they make melan
choly reading.

It is perhaps hazardous to make a selection of Lamb's witty

ayings or characteristic stories—they were apposite to the mo-
nent and the moment may not be recaptured, but some seem
till good to us and may help to represent the light and cheer-
ul side of his humour.

"A Pun is a thing of too much consequence to be thrown in as
a makeweight. You shall read one of the addresses over, and
miss the puns, and it shall be quite as good and better than
when you discover 'em. A Pun is a Noble Thing per se: O never
ug it in as an accessory. A Pun is a sole object for reflection
(vide *my* aids to that recessment from a savage state)—it is
entire, it fills the mind: it is perfect as a Sonnet, better. It
imps asham'd in the train and retinue of Humour: it knows it
hould have an establishment of its own. The one, for instance,
I made the other day, I forget what it was."

As an illustration of the prevalence of some of our sayings,
Barry Cornwall gives a story showing Lamb's acquaintance
with the qualities of the cucumber.

"The second son of George II, it was said, had a very cold and
ungenial manner. Lamb stammered out, 'This was very natural
n the Duke of Cu-Cum-ber-land.' "

Of a very eccentric person he wrote: "Why does not his guardian angel look to him? He deserves one—may be he has tired
him out."

In a Latin letter to Barton, "Solve me this enigma, and you
hall be an Œdipus.

"Why is a horse like a Quaker?

"Because all his communication is by Hay and Neigh, after the
Lord's counsel, 'Let all your communication be Yea and Nay.' "

"The following anecdote," wrote Leslie the painter, "is an illustration of Lamb's playfulness. I dined with him one day at
Mr. Gillman's. Returning to town in the stage-coach, which

was filled with Mr. Gillman's guests, we stopped for a minute or two at Kentish Town. A woman asked the coachman, 'Are you full inside?' Upon which Lamb put his head through the window and said, 'Quite full inside; that last piece of pudding at Mr. Gillman's did the business for me.'"

"Puns I have not made many (nor punch much), since the date of my last; one I cannot help relating. A constable in Salisbury Cathedral was telling me that eight people dined at the top of the spire of the cathedral; upon which I remarked that they must be very sharp-set. But in general I cultivate the reasoning part of my mind more than the imaginative."

Miss Mary Matilda Betham, a friend of the family for many years, had invited a party to go down to visit her brother's ship. Some one asked its name. "Antelope," was the reply. Upon which Lamb cried out, "Don't name it; I have such a respect for my aunt; I cannot bear to think of her doing such a foolish action."

Lamb suggested in a letter to Manning in China that the name of the Man-t-chou Tartars must have come from their cannibal habits.

One day Mrs. H—— was sitting on a sofa between Mr. Montagu and Mr. Lamb. The latter spoke to her, but all her attention was given to the other person. At last, turning to Mr. Lamb, she asked what he had said. "Ask Mr. Montagu, for it went in one ear and out another."

Barry Cornwall reports, "I once said something in his presence which I thought possessed smartness. He commended me with a stammer:

"Very well, my dear boy, very well. Ben (taking a pinch of snuff) Ben Jonson has said worse things than that—and b-b-better."

"The king never dies, which may be the reason that it always REIGNS here."

Lamb wrote to Manning:*
"I said that Holcroft said, being asked who were the best dramatic writers of the day, 'Hook AND I.' . . . You know what *hooks and eyes* are, don't you? They are what little boys do up their breeches with."

He called out to Martin Burney in a game at cards, "Martin, if dirt were trumps, what a hand you would hold!"

"There—a fuller plumper juiceier date never dropt from Idumean palm. Am I in the dateive case now? if not, a fig for dates, which is more than a date is worth."

Lamb said *à propos* of the water-cure, that it was neither new nor wonderful, for that it was at least as old as the Flood, when, "in *his* opinion, it killed more than it cured."

Wordsworth and Lamb were talking of Shakespeare and of his borrowing his plots from other sources, and Wordsworth was even suggesting that other poets with the *History of Hamb-et* before them, might have been equally successful in producing a great play. Lamb exclaimed,
"Oh! here's Wordsworth says he could have written *Hamlet, if he'd had the mind.*"

---

* February 1808.

A letter to P. G. Patmore,* who was in France, begins, "I am so poorly, I have been to a funeral, where I made a Pun." And then follow puns and much fooling, some of it difficult for us to enjoy today and all very characteristic of Lamb.

"Do try and get some frogs,—you must ask for 'grenouilles (green-eels). They don't understand whot phrogs is tho' it's a common phrase with us.

"If you go thro' Bulloign (Boulogne) enquire if old Godfrey is living, and how he got home from the Crusades: he must be a very old man now."

To show that Charles was not the only member of his household with a ready wit:

"Apropos—when I first opened upon the just mentioned poem, in a careless tone I said to Mary as if putting a riddle 'What is good for a bootless bean?' to which with infinite presence of mind (as the jest book has it) she answered, a 'shoeless pea.'"

His famous answer to Coleridge is recorded by Barry Cornwall. "Charles," said Coleridge to Lamb, "I think you have heard me preach?" "I n-n-never heard you do anything else," replied Lamb.

To Thomas Hood he wrote,† "And what dost thou at the Priory? *Cucullus non facit Monachum.* English me that, and challenge old Lignum Janua‡ to make a better." ("A 'Lamb pun.' The Hood does not make the monk.")

A characteristic story is recorded by Washington Allston in his *Life and Letters:*

---

* July, 1827.
† August 1824.
‡ Lignum Janua, pun on the name of the boatman at Hastings, Tom Woodgate

"Lamb was present when a naval officer was giving an account of an action which he had been in, and to illustrate the carelessness and disregard of life at such times, said a sailor had both his legs shot off, and as his shipmates were carrying him below, another shot came and took off both his arms; they, thinking he was pretty much used up, though life was still in him, threw him out of a port. 'Shame, d——d shame,' stuttered out Lamb. 'He m-m-might have l-lived to have been an a-a-ornament to Society.' "

When Crabb Robinson, just become a barrister, told how he felt on getting his first brief in the King's Bench, Charles said, "I suppose you said to it, 'Thou great First Cause, least understood.' "

Perhaps we all have our favourite Lamb bon mot. Here is ours. To the chiding of his fellow-clerks that he had recently been coming late to the office, Lamb replied: "I m-make up for it by going home early."

We come to the end of the story. Lamb himself—like Birrell—had deep resentment for the epithets coined by Coleridge, "poor Charles" and "gentle-hearted Charles." But William Archer in a well-known essay would accept the "gentle."

"We may call him 'gentle' in the sense in which we apply the term to Chaucer, to Izaak Walton, to Goldsmith, to Scott, and could not possibly apply it to Milton, or Johnson, or Byron, or Carlyle. So far is the epithet from conveying any suggestion of effeminacy that one is tempted to say with Antony:—

'His life was gentle; and the elements
So mix'd in him that Nature might stand up
And say to all the world, "This was a man." ' "

A realist in the experiences of life, not living in a world of dreams, he liked people, he liked to look into their faces. Fond of memories of old days, he did not shirk the duties that lay at hand. His courage never left him. He had a passion for life. "I am in love with this green earth; the face of town and country; the unspeakable rural solitude, and the sweet security of streets. I would set up my tabernacle here"—words of a dauntless spirit! He was human in every respect; he loathed cant and affectation, and, above all, he hated being "made over." Although, in his early days, he was associated with followers of the Unitarian creed, he was no adherent of any one sect. Thomas Allsop, who saw much of him in his later years, repeated Coleridge's estimate of his lifelong friend: "Believe me, who know him well, that Lamb, say what he will, has more of the *essentials* of Christianity than ninety-nine out of a hundred proposing Christians. He has all that would still have been Christian had Christ never lived or been made manifest upon earth."

If a man is to be judged by the way he meets discouragement or adversity, Lamb's life was successful. Not being able to continue to the university after Christ's Hospital, he faced a future which was to include a dreary home from which he could not or would not escape, the burden of a sister whose affliction was to be with him every hour of his life after he became twenty-one, his disappointments in love, and perhaps not least of all his concern about himself lest he go the way of his sister. How he met this future as it changed to conditions and duties daily confronting him is a fine page of human history—with no shirking of responsibility, and with as little complaint or regret as most of us express when annoyed by the petty ills of everyday living. He took it like a brave man.

The reward was great—periods of happiness, his beloved city with human faces, old buildings and old book-stalls to enjoy, regular work at the office, a home in the evening where there was one whom he could trust and love and who loved him as her own soul. And good friends! The steps which led up the four flights in the old building of the Temple were trod by some of the most worthy people of the day. There is no other English author so commonly known by his full name. Of his school days Charles Le Grice wrote to Talfourd: "I never heard his name mentioned without the addition of Charles, although, as there was no other boy of the name of Lamb, the addition was unnecessary, but there was an implied kindness in it, and it was a proof that his gentle manners excited that kindness."

"There are some reputations which will not keep, but Lamb's is not of that kind," wrote the Poet Laureate Southey who knew him long. "His memory will retain its fragrance as long as the best spice that ever was expended upon one of the Pharaohs."

THE END

BIBLIOGRAPHY

BIBLIOGRAPHY

The Letters of Charles Lamb, edited by Thomas Noon Talfourd, 2 vols., 1837, revised 1886.

The Works of Charles Lamb, edited by Thomas Noon Talfourd, 3 vols., 1838, new edition, 1840.

Final Memorials of Charles Lamb, edited by Thomas Noon Talfourd, 2 vols., 1848.

The Complete Correspondence and Works of Charles Lamb, Edward Moxon, 4 vols., 1870.

The Complete Works in Prose and Verse of Charles Lamb, edited by R. H. Shepherd, 1874.

The Life, Letters and Writings of Charles Lamb, edited by Percy FitzGerald, 6 vols., 1875.

The Life and Works of Charles Lamb, edited by Alfred Ainger, 12 vols., 1899-1900.

The Works of Charles Lamb, edited by William Macdonald, 12 vols., 1903.

The Works of Charles and Mary Lamb, edited by E. V. Lucas, 7 vols., 1903-1905.

The Letters of Charles Lamb, Boston, 1907. (Bibliophile Society)

The Works in Prose and Verse of Charles and Mary Lamb, edited by Thomas Hutchinson, 2 vols., 1908.

Bibliography of the First Editions in Book Form of the Writings of Charles and Mary Lamb, published prior to the death of Charles Lamb in 1834, Luther S. Livingston, 1903.

Bibliography of the Writings of Charles and Mary Lamb, Charles J. Thomson, 1908.

The Cambridge Bibliography of English Literature, F. W. Bateson, 1941.

Letters, Conversations and Recollections of S. T. Coleridge, Thomas Allsop, 2 vols., 1836.

Early Recollections of S. T. Coleridge, Joseph Cottle, 1837.

Memoirs of Charles Mathews, Mrs. Mathews, 4 vols., 1839.

Literary Reminiscences in Hood's Own, Thomas Hood, 1839.

Autobiography, Benjamin Haydon, 1846.

Autobiography, Leigh Hunt, 3 vols., 1850.

Pencillings by the Way, N. P. Willis, 1852.

My Friends and Acquaintances, P. G. Patmore, 3 vols., 1854.

Galleries of Literary Portraits, G. Gilfillan, 1856.

Autobiographical Recollections, C. R. Leslie, 1860.

Charles Lamb, His Friends, His Haunts and His Books, Percy Fitz-Gerald, 1866.

Charles Lamb, A Memoir, B. W. Procter ("Barry Cornwall"), 1866.

Diary, Reminiscences and Correspondence of Henry Crabb Robinson, edited by Thomas Sadler, 2 vols., 1870.

Mary and Charles Lamb, W. C. Hazlitt, 1874.

William Godwin, his Friends and Contemporaries, C. K. Paul, 2 vols., 1876.

George Boyle and Thomas Manning's Journey to Thibet and Llasa, C. R. Markham, 1876.

Recollections of Writers, Charles and Mary Cowden Clark, 1878.

Charles Lamb, a Biography, Alfred Ainger, 1882.

Literary Landmarks of London, Laurence Hutton, 1885.

Miscellanies, A. C. Swinburne, 1886.

Obiter Dicta, Second Series, Augustine Birrell, 1887.

Appreciations, Walter Pater, 1889.

Thomas De Quincey, *Works,* edited by David Masson, Vols. III and V, 1890.

In the Footprints of Lamb, B. E. Martin, 1891.

Bernard Barton and His Friends, E. V. Lucas, 1893.

The Lambs, Their Lives, Their Friends, and Their Correspondence, W. C. Hazlitt, 1897.

Charles Lamb and the Lloyds, E. V. Lucas, 1898.

Lamb and Hazlitt, W. C. Hazlitt, 1899.

Lamb and Keats, F. Harrison, 1899.

Makers of Literature, George E. Woodberry, 1900.

Personal Recollections, R. H. Stoddard, 1903.

Sidelights on Charles Lamb, Bertram Dobell, 1903.

Life of Charles Lamb, E. V. Lucas, 2 vols., 1905, revised 1921.

The Collected Works of William Hazlitt, edited by A. R. Waller and Arnold Glover, 13 vols., 1902-1906.

Stray Leaves, H. Paul, 1906.

Life and Letters of John Rickman, Orlo Williams, 1912.

Cambridge History of English Literature, Vol. XII, 1915.

The Amenities of Book-Collecting, A. Edward Newton, 1918.

Critical Essays of the Early Nineteenth Century, edited by R. M. Alden, 1921.

The Life of William Hazlitt, P. P. Howe, 1922.

The East India House, William Foster, 1924.

The Letters of Thomas Manning to Charles Lamb, edited by G. A. Anderson, 1925.

Bare Souls, Gamaliel Bradford, 1929.

Thomas Hood and Charles Lamb, W. Jerrold, 1930.

The Englishman and His Books, Amy Cruse, 1932.

Charles Lamb and his Contemporaries, Edmund Blunden, 1933.

Eighteenth Century London Life, Rosamond Bayne-Powell, 1938.

Justly Dear, E. Thornton Cook, 1939.

The Ordeal of Bridget Elia: A Chronicle of the Lambs, Ernest C. Ross, 1940.

Charles Lamb, Flora Masson (no date).

Letters of William and Dorothy Wordsworth, edited by Ernest de Sélincourt, 1935, 1937, 1939, 1941.

INDEX

INDEX

Addison, Joseph, 269

Adventures of Ulysses, The, 36, 101, 137, 219

Albion, the, 33

Album Verses and Other Poems, 41, 133, 255

Albums, poem about, 254

Alfoxden, 25

Alice W——n (Ann Simmons), 16-17, 19, 46, 157, 328

"All Fools' Day," 283

Allegra, daughter of Lord Byron, 99

Allen, Robert, 15

Allsop, Thomas, 38, 83, 95, 129-130, 340

Allston, Washington, 338-339

Alsager, Thomas Massa, 113, 118, 122, 139

Ambleside, Lake District, 170

Anatomy of Melancholy, The, Robert Burton, 32, 174

"Ancient Mariner, The," 27, 74

Anti-Jacobin Review and Magazine, 30-31

Antonio, William Godwin, 99-100

Ariosto, 80

Arnold, Samuel James, 119

Artaxerxes, 196

Aunt Hetty (Sara Lamb), 13, 21, 46, 155, 164, 274

Austen, Jane, 8, 329

Ayrton, William, 38, 119-120, 141-147

Badams, Louisa, 323

Balmanno, Mrs. Mary, 240

Bannister, Jack, 230, 232

"Barbara S——," 286, 328

Barbauld, Anna Letitia, 91

Barnes, Thomas, 37, 125, 139, 309

Barrett, George, 237

Barton, Bernard, 40, 55, 83, 126, 128-129, 185, 316, 332, 335

"Battle, Sarah," 138, 285

Beau Brummell, 254

Beaumont and Fletcher, 80, 218, 269, 291, 311

Becky, servant of the Lambs, 123, 135

Bell and Mouth, 28

Bensley, Robert, 231

Besant, Walter, 6, 7

Betham, Mary, 179, 336

Bigod, Ralph (John Fenwick), 285, 299

Bird, William, 13*f*.

Birds, The, Aristophanes, translated by H. F. Cary, 130

Birrell, Augustine, 330*f*.

Blackwood's Magazine, 83, 262, 265

Blake, William, 308, 315

"Blakesmoor in H——shire," 279

351

Bloomfield, Robert, 40

Bloxam, Sam, 177

"Blue and Yellow," see *Edinburgh Review*

Blue-coat School, see Christ's Hospital

Bodleian Library, Oxford, 272

Boldero, Merryweather, Bosanquet, and Lacy, the house of, 76

Bolt Court, London, 9

Bow Street runners, 4

Bowles, William, 16, 158, 242, 304

Boyer, James, 14

Braham, John, 120, 290, 317, 327

"Bridge of Sighs, The," Thomas Hood, 126

"Bridget Elia" (Mary Lamb), 276, 277-279; see Lamb, Mary

British Museum, 130, 304, 312, 322, 327

Brougham, Henry, 263

Browne, Sir Thomas, 114, 142, 158, 174, 269, 313

Bulwer-Lytton, 102

Bunyan, John, 146, 269

Burke, Thomas, 3

Burnet, Gilbert, *History of My Own Times,* 97

Burnett, George, 37, 53, 94

Burney, Admiral, 38

Burney, Dr. Charles, *History of Music,* 34

Burney, Fanny, 34

Burney, Captain James, 34, 137, 144

Burney, Martin, 34, 118, 137, 141, 144, 337

Burney, Sarah, 34, 137-138

Burns, Robert, 16, 158, 290, 304, 308, 315

Burton, Robert, *The Anatomy of Melancholy,* 32, 158, 174, 269, 313, 333

Bury St. Edmunds, 36

Bye, Tommy, 65*f.*

Byron, Lord, 40, 80, 99, 112, 129, 305, 316

Caleb Williams, William Godwin, 98, 103

Cambridge and the University, 37-39, 95, 272, 307, 327; lines on, 258-259

Carlyle, Jane Welsh, 153

Carlyle, Thomas, 321

Cary, F. S., 322

Cary, Henry Francis, 40, 42, 83, 130-131

Chambers, John, 67

Champion, John Scott, editor, 36, 265, 267

Channing, George, "The New Morality," 30

Chapel Street, Pentonville, 27

Chapman, George, *Homer,* 113, 312

"Chapter on Ears, A," 120, 327

Charles, Philarète, in *Revue des Deux Mondes,* 319

Chaucer, Geoffrey, 97, 114, 144

Cheshire Cheese, London, 9

Chessiad, The, Charles Dibdin, 127

"Child Angel, The," 328

Chitty, Joseph, 123

Christ's Hospital, 14, 78, 89, 109, 125, 159, 198, 272, 308, 340